LONDON THEATRE WALKS

Thirteen Dramatic Tours Through Four Centuries of History and Legend

JIM DE YOUNG

AND

JOHN MILLER

Photographs by
Nathan Silver

Supplementary photos by Jim De Young

APPLAUSE
THEATRE & CINEMA BOOKS

London Theatre Walks
Thirteen Dramatic Tours Through Four Centuries of History and Legend

Design and layout by Sue Knopf of Graffolio. Printed in Canada.

ISBN: 1-55783-516-0

Library of Congress Cataloging-in-Publication Data

De Young, Jim.
  London theatre walks : thirteen dramatic tours through four centuries of history and legend / Jim De Young and John Miller ; photographs by Nathan Silver ; supplementary photos by Jim De Young.— 2nd ed., rev. and expanded.
      p. cm.
  Includes bibliographical references and index.
    ISBN 1-55783-516-0
    1. London (England)—Guidebooks. 2. Literary landmarks —England—London—Guidebooks. 3. Historic buildings— England—London—Guidebooks. 4. Theaters—England— London—Guidebooks. 5. Walking—England—London—Guidebooks. I. Miller, John. II. Silver, Nathan. III. Title.

  DA679.D49 2003
  914.2104'86—dc21   2003003622

British Library Cataloging-in-Publication Data

A catalog record for this book is available from the British Library.

Applause Theatre & Cinema Books
151 West 46th Street, 8th Floor
New York, NY 10036
Phone: (212) 575-9265
Fax: (646) 562-5852
Email: info@applausepub.com
Internet: www.applausepub.com

SALES & DISTRIBUTION

North America:
HAL LEONARD CORP.
7777 West Bluemound Road
P. O. Box 13819
Milwaukee, WI 53213
Phone: (414) 774-3630
Fax: (414) 774-3259
Email: halinfo@halleonard.com
Internet: www.halleonard.com

UK:
ROUNDHOUSE PUBLISHING LTD.
Millstone, Limers Lane
Northam, North Devon Ex 39 2RG
Phone (0) 1237-474-474
Fax (0) 1237-474-774
Email roundhouse.group@ukgateway.net

CONTENTS

Foreword v

Walk 1: Shakespeare and the Globe: A Trip to Bankside 1

Walk 2: William Shakespeare and Then Some:
From Chancery Lane to Blackfriars 23

Walk 3: Lincoln's Inn Fields and Its Environs 39

Walk 4: Strolling the Strand:
From Trafalgar Square to Aldwych 51

Walk 5: A Fleet Ramble to St. Paul's:
From Temple Bar to the Cathedral 75

Walk 6: Pick a Daffy in Piccadilly and Beyond. 95

Walk 7: Clubland Is Also Playland:
From St. James to the Haymarket 107

Walk 8: Long Gone but Not Forgotten:
Tower Hill to St. Leonard Shoreditch 123

Walk 9: Doing Battle Around the Barbican

Part I—Visit the Barbican Center. 139

Part II—Visit the Museum of London 143

Part III—Go to the Bank and Find a Mermaid 146

Walk 10: The Not-So-Bright Lights of Soho. 155

Walk 11: Take a Stroll in Residential
Kensington and Holland Park. 177

Walk 12: Covent Garden Promenade

Part I—St. Martin's Lane and National Portrait Gallery. . 191

Part II—Check the Time in Seven Dials 203

Part III—Visit Drury Lane, the Royal Opera House,
and the Theatre Museum 208

Walk 13: The Old Vic to the New Eye and Beyond. 225

Unstrung Pearls 239

Bibliography 245

Index 248

FOREWORD

These walks have been developed on numerous forays to London over the past 25 years. Even though many of the historical places visited no longer exist, we feel that some sense of the past can be captured by knowing you are on the site and by physically coming to grips with the way in which the theatre districts, the theatres, and the theatre practitioners have moved about the city. If you do every walk and visit all the museums recommended, you'll have covered nearly every important theatre and theatrically associated site in central London. At the cost of a bit of shoe leather you should get a concrete sense of just how the various places fit together and how the centers of theatrical activity have moved across the face of the city. To explore Shoreditch, Bankside, Lincoln's Inn Fields, the Strand, Covent Garden, the West End, and, finally, the South Bank is to participate in the full sweep of one of the great professional theatre movements of the western world.

Even the casual tourist with an interest in theatre will find the walks a fascinating adjunct to the primary joy of seeing London's high quality live theatre. There is no need to fear you will sacrifice the city's major sights for out-of-the-way corners. Most of the walks follow established tourist routes and will take you by or near places like Trafalgar Square, Piccadilly Circus, the Tower of London, and Westminster Abbey.

All care has been taken to make the directions as clear and current as possible, but our warning to you is that landmarks, signs, and even buildings change or disappear rapidly. You should not set out on these walks without a good city map. We personally prefer the *A–Z London,* but there are many available and most will serve if you go astray or wish to truncate or deviate from a route.

Purposefully avoided have been pronouncements on how to pack, where to stay, where to eat, and how to deal with the city. The phone numbers and opening and closing hours of sites or attractions have also generally been omitted as they often change over time or by the season. Information of this nature is best gathered just before you leave for London or immediately upon your arrival.

Reasonable efforts have been made to check names, events, dates, and spellings for accuracy, but some anomalies and certainly some apocryphal stories have crept into the text. Secondary sources can sometimes be wrong or in disagreement. Needless to say we would be more than happy to receive factual corrections, notes on directions that were difficult to follow, and suggestions for new sites to include.

Our recommendation for approaching the walks is to review the titles, read the thumbnail descriptions, and look at the maps. Select those that most interest you and fit in with the other priorities of your trip. If major destinations are a part of any walk, make sure you check current tour times, opening hours, etc. the *Time Out* or *What's On In London* weekly magazines are excellent for that kind of information. For those with access to the Internet, there are several sources for up-to-date information on London and the London theatre. Most search engines will locate them with ease.

And finally a grateful thank you to my wife, Jan, who has walked every foot of these routes with me, to Glenn Young of Applause Books who never lost faith, and to my co-author, John Miller, who moved this project through to completion after a serious illness threatened to derail it.

Dr. Jim De Young
Director of Theatre, Monmouth College

NOTE BY THE BRITISH CO-AUTHOR

It has taken me more than 40 years of theatergoing in London to complete my tally of all the theatres covered by these walks, culminating in the long-awaited and triumphant opening of the reconstructed Globe Theatre in 1997. I also had the very great pleasure of being present when the other Globe, on Shaftesbury Avenue, was renamed in honour of our greatest living actor—John Gielgud—an occasion for which many of the names mentioned in this book gathered to do him honour. In my collaborations with Sir John on his memoirs for radio, television, and two subsequent books, I have learnt much from his encyclopaedic knowledge of the theatre, and I have endeavoured to add some of that history to these pages. I hope these walks will inspire in the reader the same deep love of the magic of the theatre that has motivated the authors.

John Miller
Author, broadcaster, and theatre historian

**Co-authors John
Miller (L) and
Jim De Young**

FOREWORD TO THE SECOND EDITION

With John Miller's blessing my wife and I have rewalked each of
the routes and made appropriate corrections, deletions, and additions.
We hope we have caught and corrected the minor errors of style, fact,
and clarity that crept into the first edition without creating too many
more new ones. We maintain that directions and descriptions are current as of publication, but recognize that a living city waits for no
book. Changes will continue to occur. **We reemphasize again the
importance of carrying a fully detailed city map with you. Our
maps are intended to give you only a general and schematic sense
of the routes and sites.**

*Jim De Young, Professor Emeritus
Monmouth College
Monmouth, Illinois 61462*

Break a blister!

WALK ONE

SHAKESPEARE
AND THE GLOBE:
A TRIP TO BANKSIDE

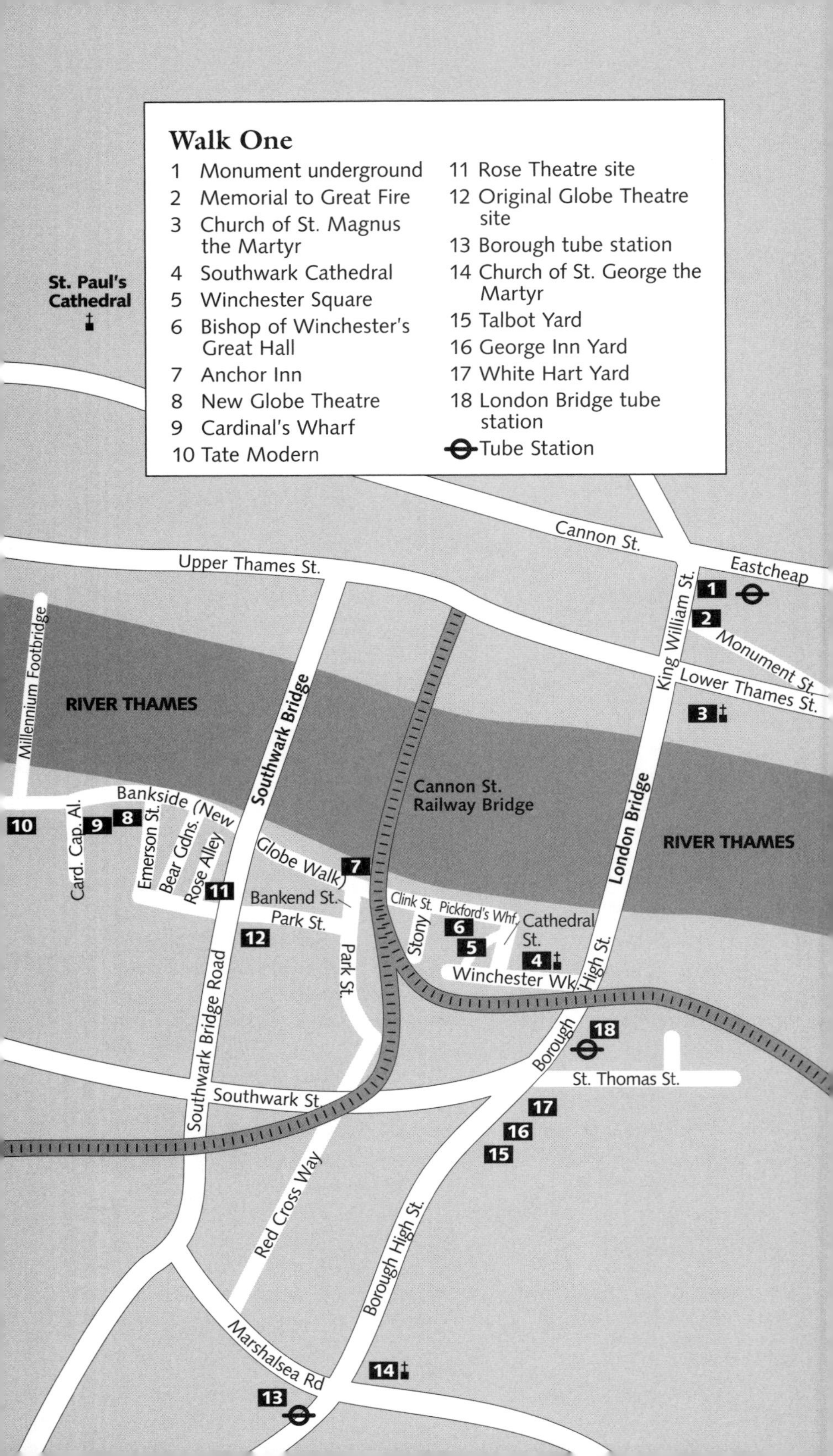

Walk One

1. Monument underground
2. Memorial to Great Fire
3. Church of St. Magnus the Martyr
4. Southwark Cathedral
5. Winchester Square
6. Bishop of Winchester's Great Hall
7. Anchor Inn
8. New Globe Theatre
9. Cardinal's Wharf
10. Tate Modern
11. Rose Theatre site
12. Original Globe Theatre site
13. Borough tube station
14. Church of St. George the Martyr
15. Talbot Yard
16. George Inn Yard
17. White Hart Yard
18. London Bridge tube station
⊖ Tube Station

St. Paul's
Cathedral
✝

Cannon St.

Eastcheap

Upper Thames St.

Millennium Footbridge

King William St.

1 ⊖

2

Monument St.

Lower Thames St.

3 ✝

RIVER THAMES

Southwark Bridge

Cannon St.
Railway Bridge

London Bridge

RIVER THAMES

Bankside (New

10

Card. Cap. Al.

9 **8**

Emerson St.

Bear Gdns.

Rose Alley

11

Globe Walk)

7

Bankend St.

Park St.

12

Park St.

Clink St.

Stony

Pickford's Whf.

6

5

Cathedral St.

4 ✝

Winchester Wk.

High St.

Southwark Bridge Road

Borough

18 ⊖

St. Thomas St.

Southwark St.

17

16

15

Red Cross Way

Borough High St.

Marshalsea Rd

14 ✝

13 ⊖

STARTING POINT: Monument underground station (District or Circle Line)

APPROXIMATE TIME: Two and one-half hours if you step along but up to four or five hours if you spend any time at Southwark Cathedral, the Anchor Inn, the Globe reconstruction, the site of the Rose, the George Inn, or the Tate Modern. We would personally recommend starting around 11:00 A.M. in order to take advantage of lunch on the river terrace at the Anchor Inn and a late afternoon refresher at the George.

his walk covers a number of Shakespeare sites and features visits to Southwark Cathedral, two theatre pubs—the Anchor and the George Inn—the newly reconstructed Shakespeare's Globe Theatre, the site of the Rose Theatre, and an optional excursion to the Tate Modern. *

O*ur starting point is the* **Monument underground station,** *which appropriately happens to be located on the site of the Old Boar's Head Tavern where Sir John Falstaff and Prince Hal gathered with their friends.* Leave the station by the **King William Street** south exit and turn left toward the newest London Bridge, dedicated by Queen Elizabeth II in 1973. There's also a sign at the top of the stairs pointing toward the bridge if you are in doubt. The first street on the left is **Monument Street** and it will give you a clear view of **Christopher Wren's memorial to the Great Fire of London.** There's no theatrical connection there, but if you have a driving desire to climb 311 stairs as a warm-up for a two-mile walk you are welcome to have a go. Otherwise continue down **King William Street** toward the Thames.

As the bridge approach gains height you cross Lower Thames Street. Look down and to your left for a view of Christopher Wren's church of **St. Magnus the Martyr.** Its rather pleasant little steeple is now nearly pasted up against an office block. Sometimes the juxtaposition of

Christopher Wren's memorial to the Great Fire of London

A special note: The Bankside area has been in the throes of major redevelopment for some years and walking in it can be somewhat of an adventure. Signs and landmarks are getting better but some things are still dodgy; entire streets, for instance, can and have disappeared. The demolition and gentrification of old buildings continues at a breakneck pace and clearly there will be many more changes in the years to come.

the old and new can create energetic new views, but this one is just a bit sad. *Continue walking out onto London Bridge, stopping about halfway across.*

You may still see its predecessor about 10,000 miles to the west. It was taken apart stone by stone and reassembled as a tourist attraction in Lake Havasu, Arizona. But the bridge of theatrical interest is neither of these. It is instead the great medieval bridge that was completed in 1209 and stood for over 600 years. That bridge stood a bit

London Bridge as Shakespeare knew it

downstream (towards Tower Bridge) from where you now stand. If you look at a current street map, think of it as more in line with Gracechurch Street. During Shakespeare's day both sides of the bridge were lined with shops and stores and at the Southwark end was a gate-tower on top of which was displayed, like so many martini olives on toothpicks, the severed heads of executed traitors and criminals.

In January of 1599 theatrical history moved across that bridge. When James Burbage and his brother-in-law built the first public playhouse in England in 1576, they called it The Theatre and put it up on leased ground in Shoreditch (see Walk Eight). When the lease expired in 1597 Richard and Cuthbert Burbage, who took over their father's affairs after his untimely death, could not renegotiate satisfactory terms and The Theatre was forced to close. The acting company apparently moved their main performance base to the nearby Curtain Theatre. In 1598 a decision was made to invest in a new theatre on the south bank of the Thames. A 31-year lease was conveyed to a group of so-called Housekeepers of the Chamberlain's Men. Half of the lease was in the names of the two young Burbage brothers; the other half was split five ways among a group of actors—John Heminge, Augustine Phillips, Thomas Pope, William Kempe, and William Shakespeare. Note that the Burbages were always the majority stockholders in this enterprise. It is unlikely that the acting company was ever thought of as Shakespeare's or that the Globe was ever thought of as Shakespeare's theatre during the Elizabethan era.

In December of 1598 or January of 1599, The Theatre was torn down and the timbers transported along Shoreditch High Street, through Bishopsgate, up Gracechurch Street, over the medieval London Bridge, and into the parish of St. Mary Overie, now known as Southwark. There the lumber was reused to erect a fine new playhouse called the Globe. The actual location was upstream of this bridge

1

and is now hidden from your view by other bridges and buildings.

But let's not get too far ahead in our story. If you are about in the middle of the bridge now and looking downstream, you should see the 1894 Tower Bridge, which visitors often assume is the London Bridge because it is so often pictured as a symbol of the city. The roadway between its twin towers is raised whenever a large ship needs access to the Pool of London. Visible on the left is a portion of the Tower of London and on the right, just in front of the bridge, the HMS Belfast, a World War II cruiser that is now a floating museum. Finish crossing the bridge, turn right, and cross the road at the first chance. There will be a large pointed modern sculpture piece at the corner. When you do get to the other side you will be approximately at the site of the infamous Thames river stairs where in Dickens' Oliver Twist, Nancy is overheard by Noah Claypole telling the secrets that will lead to her murder by Bill Sikes.

Walk now away from the river. Just before the railway bridge, new signage clearly points the way into the **Southwark Cathedral** *church-*

yard and toward the new **Shakespeare's Globe Theatre.** The churchyard is a space that William Shakespeare would have recognized and its age is advertised by the fact that you must literally go down to its level from the modern streets. *As you walk through it, you pass first the most ancient parts of the cathedral (the 13th-century retrochoir and choir), then the 15th-century transepts, then the 16th-century tower, and finally the Victorian nave, which was reconstructed to the original Gothic plan in 1897.*

Southwark Cathedral from just over London Bridge

The interior of Southwark Cathedral is usually open throughout the day. Access is of course limited during services. The church has a fine organ and is also the site of lovely lunchtime and evening concerts. Special programs in honor of Shakespeare are usually held on or around the Bard's birthday in April of each year.

After entering the cathedral, stand at the rear of the nave. There is no proof that Shakespeare was a regular visitor here, but we do know that he lived nearby for some time and that he did enter the church at least once. On December 31, 1607, the sexton's accounts include this entry, "Edmund Shakespeare, a player, buried in the church with

Medieval roof boss from Southwark Cathedral

1

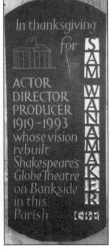

Scenes from Southwark Cathedral, clockwise from top left:

Detail of Shakespeare window

Entrance

Shakespeare statue

Sam Wanamaker plaque

Exterior tower

Monument to John Trehearne and his wife

a forenoone knell of the great bell, 20s." Of Edmund Shakespeare, William's younger brother, we know only that he was baptized in Stratford in 1580 and was buried in London in an unknown spot in this church. The critical thing about the sexton's note is the total of 20 shillings for the funeral. It cost only two shillings to be buried in the churchyard and only one shilling for a tolling of the small bell. Most sources agree that brother William must have been the purchaser of this far more costly obsequy.

Two other theatrical people, the Jacobean playwrights John Fletcher (1579–1625) and Philip Massinger (1583–1640) are also buried, reputedly in the same vault, somewhere in the church. Fletcher is perhaps best known for his collaborations with Francis Beaumont, e.g. *A Maid's Tragedy* (1611), but he also worked with Massinger. A good half of Massinger's 40 plays have been lost and he is chiefly remembered today for one satiric comedy *A New Way to Pay Old Debts*. One or both of these men are thought to have collaborated with Shakespeare on *Henry VIII* and *Two Noble Kinsmen*.

Philip Henslowe (?–1616), the theatre manager and builder whose diary is a source for much of our knowledge of Elizabethan theatre practice, is also buried here. Both he and his associate, the actor Edward Alleyn, lived within the parish and served as vestrymen in the church for a time. Alleyn is also closely associated with St. Giles Without Cripplegate (see Walk Nine).

If you now stroll down the south aisle of the nave (this is on your right if you are facing the altar) you will soon find the **Shakespeare Memorial Window and Monument***.* The rather romantic alabaster statue of the reclining bard dates from 1911, while the window was completed in 1954. It features a galaxy of Shakespearean characters, with Prospero the old magician, arms raised, holding court at the center. See how many of the rest you can identify. (The answers are listed at the end of the walk.) A recent addition just to the right of the monument is a new plaque in honor of Sam Wanamaker, the American actor who led the campaign to reconstruct the Globe Theatre. We had been told that this was the only memorial to a person of the Jewish faith in a Christian church in the United Kingdom, but a plaque in honor of Oscar Hammerstein in this same church's Harvard Chapel would seem to belie that assertion.

You can retrace your steps and leave the cathedral now, but if you continue on around the church to visit the retrochoir and transepts you will find several outstanding tombs, including that of John Gower—a good friend of the poet Geoffery Chaucer. Stop to look at the model of the old church and pay special attention to the model of the Bishop of Winchester's Palace. Keep it in mind when you leave. The Harvard Chapel is also worth a look, as is the marvelous collection of old medieval roof bosses at the very rear of the nave. On the floor in the southeast corner, just to the right of the entrance door, is a touching memorial to a

1

group of young people killed in a disastrous Thames boat accident that occurred in 1989.

Exit the church the way you entered, turn right out of the yard, and make your way to **Cathedral Street**. You are standing in what was a deserted Dickensian warehouse district in 1975, and a construction site throughout the '80s and '90s. It is now a thriving, gentrified business and commercial area. *Some few yards to your right and across Cathedral Street is* **Winchester Walk**. *Take it. Turn right at the first crossing, and you will be walking down the old entry to* **Winchester Square**. Nineteenth-century buildings, most of which are now gone, used to literally preserve the shape of the courtyard in front of the **palace of the Bishop of Winchester**. Remember that model back in the church or the relief of the Southwark skyline behind the reclining figure of Shakespeare in the Memorial.

Remember also that it was both convenient and politically prudent for bishops from provincial cities to have a dwelling available near the seats of power in Westminster and the City of London. It was common for them to take land near the City and literally annex it to their own diocese, thus making a real home away from home. The manor or park surrounding the Bishop's palace, some 70 acres in this case, was therefore a little piece of Winchester or what was known as a "liberty" area. A liberty was simply a parcel of land within a city that was exempt from the laws of the city because it was not legally a part of the city. In this case the city was the City of London and the City had definite proscriptions against certain types of public entertainment. Thus most professional Elizabethan theatre activity took place in liberty areas within and around the fringes of the City.

Move ahead now farther into the old Winchester Square. The street will bend around under some arches and deposit you on **Pickford's Wharf**. *Your gaze should immediately fall on a large colorful full-size replica of* **Sir Francis Drake's Golden Hinde**—*the ship in which he circumnavigated the globe between 1577 and 1580. It can be toured for a fee. Dead ahead is a pub and a paved court with a pleasant river overlook enhanced by signage that identifies most of the buildings visible on the far shore. Take a look; the view is excellent.*

When you are finished turn around and walk back away from the river next to the pub and look for the first narrow street on your right. It is labeled Pickford's Wharf but will shortly turn into **Clink Street**. *Walk on for a few yards keeping your eyes alert for a sunken rectangular excavation site on the left. At the far end of the site is a wall complete with a striking remnant of an old stone rose window.* The remains were first exposed in 1814 when a mustard factory on the site burned down, but they were covered up again by 19th-century warehouses. World War II bombing exposed them anew and later excavation has identified the foundation and wall fragments as parts of the **Bishop**

of Winchester's Great Hall from the 13th century. The openings low down on the west wall led to the kitchens, the domestic quarters, and the cellar. The rose window itself was apparently inserted into the existing wall in the 14th century.

We know that the Bishop gave a great banquet in this hall in 1604 to celebrate the accession of King James I to the throne of England and Scotland. We also know that a procession of great splendor preceded the affair. Might the procession have given Burbage's theatre company, the newly named King's Men (who formerly were the Chamberlain's Men), a chance to show off some of their freshly drawn livery from the Royal Wardrobe? (See Walk Two for more details on this event.) Might we even suppose that some of the talented neighbors from the Globe theatre just down the way entertained at that banquet?

Remains of Bishop of
Winchester's Great Hall

Continue walking now on Pickford's Wharf/Clink Street. This was a true Elizabethan theatrical enclave. Philip Henslowe, Philip Massinger, Francis Beaumont, and John Fletcher all had lodgings on or near this street. *You'll shortly arrive at the intersection of* **Stony Street** *coming in from the left.* What was a rubbish tip cum car park for over twenty years will soon be a new building, but excavations on the site in 1965 turned up vast quantities of oyster shells and other assorted debris from long-forgotten meals. This area once held the vast kitchens of Winchester Palace. Some old walls used to be visible at the far end of the lot and may have been from the kitchens or as now claimed from the Clink Prison. (An older sign used to designate the prison as about 200 yards further along Clink Street.)

Wherever the Clink Prison was, we are certainly close to it here. It was the Bishop of Winchester's personal jail and there he incarcerated heretics and ne'er-do-wells (including some of the Pilgrim fathers). The use of the term "clink" for jail probably originated here. Some say the name literally came from those outside who heard the clink of the chains from within. Other sources take it even further into the past citing middle English words such as "clinc" and "clenchen" for making fast with nails or rivets. Since this is what one would often do with prisoner's chains the derivation is probably on target.

Move on into the narrow unmarked opening that is all that remains of the Dickensian Clink Street. On your left shortly will be the entrance for a tourist attraction operating out of a basement called the **Clink**

1

*Prison Museum. Give it a pass unless you have ample time or an abiding interest in the macabre. There is a fee. Keep walking and you will shortly plunge under the forbidding arch of the **Cannon Street railway bridge**. As you emerge back into the light you should be able to see the river and the **Anchor Inn** on your right. On the left is a jazzy much-advertised tourist attraction called Vinopolis.*

Give your attention to the Anchor. A tavern has stood here since the 15th century and the site is not more than 200 yards or so from the original location of the Globe Theatre. The current tavern fabric, which dates from the 1750s, has seen several additions and renovations in this century and even though its charm may be a bit spurious, its clientele a bit touristy, and its upstairs restaurant prices a bit dear, it's still worth a wander around in its many tiny low-ceilinged rooms. Rather grab a pint and a snack from the bar and head for the riverfront terrace. On a  sunny day there may be no better place in town from which to enjoy London's greatest highway—the Thames. It takes no imagination at all to see Shakespeare and his fellow players as patrons of the origi-

View of the Thames from the Anchor Inn Terrace

nal inn on this site. We definitely know that Dr. Samuel Johnson, the great 18th-century author and lexicographer, was a regular patron of The Anchor. He had rooms on Park Street in the home of Mr. Thrale, a brewer.

*After a suitable rest and refreshment walk upstream along the river on what is now known formally as **Bankside**. You will shortly come up on and then pass below **Southwark Bridge**. You will find yourself still on Bankside and walking now in front of a building called Riverside House. At the first left turn possible (**Bear Gardens**), low on the wall of the building and just around the corner is a small piece of Elizabethan England that was there when Shakespeare walked this street.* It is an old Thames ferryman's seat, a resting spot for one of the many boatmen who took pleasure seekers across the river to taste the many delights of Bankside. **We regret to note that as of our last visit the waterman's seat was still present and intact but literally hidden behind a wooden grille.**

Continue walking along Bankside (now renamed New Globe Walk). Just past the next left, which used to be Emerson Street but now is a con-

1

tinuation of New Globe Walk, you will see Sam Wanamaker's Shakespeare's Globe Theatre reconstruction. The building is not actually on the site of the real Globe, but it's close enough for government work.

A preview season featuring a production of Shakespeare's *Two Gentleman of Verona* opened in late August of 1996; the formal grand opening took place in June, 1997. Two of the four plays in the first season were by Shakespeare: *Henry V* and *The Winter's Tale*; the others were Middleton's *A Chaste Maid in Cheapside*, and Beaumont and Fletcher's *The Maid's Tragedy*. The mythology of the New Globe is already beginning to form. The opening production was not "The Scottish Play," but apparently an actor fell and broke his leg during the first preview. How's that for taking the theatre's universal good luck wish literally?

The theatre entrance you can see leads to the box office, restaurant, and shop. If the theatre is in season, this is the time to book a performance if you have not already done so. The sheltered seats in the galleries are more expensive, just as they were in the original, but the standing-room in the open for the "groundlings" is a great deal more fun if you are up to it and will give you more of a sense of the experience the average citizen in the 16th century may have had. Even if you do get an expensive seat, at least try to go down and spend a few minutes in the pit.

Your next task while on site should be to locate the entrance to the Exhibition Centre and arrange for a theatre tour and/or admission to the exhibit area.

Sam Wanamaker, an indomitable American actor, director, producer, and entrepreneur, spent more than 25 years of his life trying to bring this dream to a reality. Please give it your full support and attention. A number of items in the shop can give you a history of the development of the theatre. One of the most thorough is Barry Day's 1996 *This Wooden "O": Shakespeare's Globe Reborn*.

After you have finished your theatre and exhibit tour make your way once again to the banks of the Thames. Find yourself a spot on the pleasant riverside wall, face the river, and try to picture this scene as it may have looked in 1600. On both sides, stretching out along the bank, would have been rows of decrepit houses of prostitution called stews— probably named after the fish ponds that lined the banks of the river. The women in these houses were sometimes called Winchester Geese. Birds of all feather would have frequented the ponds, and we are still in the Bishop of Winchester's liberty area. Of course there was also a liberal sprinkling of tawdry taverns and alehouses. Behind them would have been the high outlines of the theatres and bear baiting rings. Across the Thames, then as now a busy commercial waterway, could be seen the majestic bulk of Saint Paul's Cathedral. Shakespeare would have been looking at the old Saint Paul's, a Gothic church,

1

Scenes at the new Shakespeare's Globe Theatre

Top to bottom:

Looking down from the Tate Modern

Audience during the interval

Curtain call at the award-winning production of *Twelfth Night*, 2002

Top to bottom:
The Heavens
Stage as audience gathers
Galleries and pit

1

which was longer and higher than Sir Christopher Wren's. Before lightning struck it and burned the tower in 1561, Old Saint Paul's spire reached 489 feet into the air. The current Saint Paul's tops out at a paltry 365 feet.

Turn around now and look back at the Globe. Move your eyes to the right and look for a small group of older buildings. Walk toward them. A large gas lamp on one of them signals the entrance to tiny **Cardinal Cap Alley**—*one of London's narrowest streets.* The whitish 17th-century house, labeled **Cardinal's Wharf**, has been named by some sources as the home where Christopher Wren stayed while he was building Saint Paul's. If it wasn't it should have been, for the spot gives a picture postcard view of the great cathedral.

One used to be able to walk down Cardinal Cap Alley and get an even more splendid view of Saint Paul's, but the gate now appears to be permanently locked. From the outside of the alley you can still see how the pavement rises and then falls. That is an old Thames flood barrier. What you can no longer see is a small wooden door covered with vines almost at the end of the alley. There is a tiny, screened hole in that door and through it you could catch a glimpse of a wisp of a garden complete with singing birds and fishpond—a

Cream-colored house is Cardinal's Wharf. The little arch immediately to its right is Cardinal Cap Alley.

tiny little secret Eden tucked away in a most unlikely spot.

And now you must make a decision. Not more than 200 yards farther up the river stands the tall smoketower of the old Bankside Power Station now strikingly remodeled into the **Tate Modern** *Art Gallery.* This is one of London's great new attractions and needs to be scheduled one way or another if only for the highly theatrical view of the Globe and its Thamesian environs from the top floor.

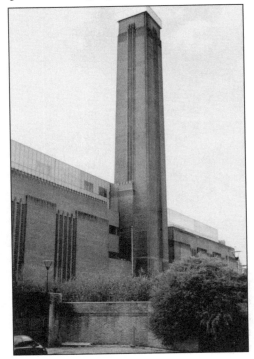

The new Tate Modern

Option one would truncate the walk here and move on to explore the Tate Modern thoroughly. This would involve returning to the city side of the river over the new Millennium footbridge and turning left to the Blackfriars tube station or right to the Cannon Street tube station. The bridge has a dubious claim to fame. It opened in 2000, was closed one day later because it swayed when people walked on it, and did not reopen for almost two years. It was given the soubriquet "Wibbly Wobbly Bridge" by the media and Londoners will probably refer to it by that name well into the next Millennium. *There is also a new underground link for the South Bank that can access the new Shakespeare's Globe and the Tate Modern. This is the Southwark station on the Jubilee Line. Directions are posted in the station.* If you have not been on the new Jubilee Line extension, it is worth experiencing and the Southwark station itself is worth seeing for its more modern approach to London Underground architecture.

Option two would involve a quick look at the Tate Modern (make sure you get up to one of the upper floors for a river view) and then return to this point to finish the walk.

Option three saves the Tate Modern for a later time and continues the Shakespeare walk now.

For those continuing (or returning to continue) the walk, your next step is to walk back past the Globe Theatre, turn right at New Globe Walk (old Emerson Street) and then left on Park Street. In Shakespeare's day it was called Maid Lane and this is the street on which the original Globe and Rose Theatres actually fronted. *A short stroll on Park Street will bring you to Bear Gardens.*

Walk down it a few paces. Along this street there may have been as many as five separate 16th- and 17th-century entertainment venues. According to information contained in a Museum of London report on excavations at Benbow House—a tract located near the river between New Globe Walk, Bear Gardens, and Park Street—there were probably two animal baiting rings located close to the river. Excavations seemed to support the Agas map of bankside between 1560–90. Philip Henslowe and Edward Alleyn ultimately held controlling interests in the buildings. One of them most probably was a 1563 rebuild of an arena that had collapsed. Under the building just ahead of you on the right is quite probably the remains of the Hope Theatre. It was built in 1613 and appears to have been used for both plays and animal sports. Ben Jonson's *Bartholomew Fair* was first performed there. Because of its dual usage this building soon reverted to being called the Bear Garden. It was demolished in 1656, but by 1662 there is some evidence that animal baiting continued on or near the site with a building called Davies Bear Garden or Amphitheatre. That structure lasted until 1682 and was once visited by Samuel Pepys and mentioned in his diary.

Ironically the current building housed the Bear Gardens Museum for many years and also contained the offices of Sam Wanamaker's Globe reconstruction movement—an operation that existed for years on hope while just underneath it was the Hope.

*Return to Park Street and turn left. The next crossing on your left is **Rose Alley** or what is left of it. In the basement of a new building for* The Financial Times, *on the right side of the alley and moving along Park Street toward Southwark bridge, encased in sand and sealed below a lid of cement and a pool of water, lies the remains of the **Rose Theatre**.* Access at this time can be arranged, for groups only, by inquiring at the Globe Exhibition Centre.

The Rose was the first public playhouse (animal baiting already being in place as early as the 1540s) on Bankside and was built by Phillip Henslowe around 1587. The Lord Admiral's Men played there until the Fortune Theatre was built in 1600 (see Walk Nine). It was demolished around 1605. If you wish to know more about the Rose, its discovery, and the valiant fight to preserve it, look for *The Rose Theatre* by Christine Eccles or a more recent publication by Julian Bowsher titled *The Rose Theatre: An Archaeological Discovery.*

Continue down Park Street passing under Southwark Bridge Road. As you come out from under the bridge, note the tower of Southwark Cathedral coming into view. It is once again a sight that William Shakespeare would have recognized. And indeed you are now almost on the doorstep of the actual site of the most famous theatre in the world. *Archaeologists have located pieces of the Globe in the courtyard and basement of Anchor Terrace just across the street to your right.* The Terrace has recently been redeveloped as a block of smart apartments. *A few steps farther and on the right side of the street is a small display that summarizes most of the pertinent archaeological information about the original Globe theatre.* Given the fact that Anchor Terrace itself is a listed building and that more of the theatre is also apparently underneath Southwark Bridge Road itself, there seems little chance of further archaeological research in the near future. You are about as close as you are ever going to get to the spot where the timbers dragged from The Theatre in Shoreditch were reassembled in 1599.

Take the image of the Globe reconstruction you have just seen and try to imagine yourself standing right here waiting for admission to the theatre on opening day in 1600. The tower of Southwark Cathedral would have been clearly visible in the distance. You should also remember that there were two Globes, not one. The first Globe burned in 1613 (ignited apparently by a piece of flaming wadding from a cannon fired during a production of *Henry VIII*) and was replaced by a similar structure on the same foundation in 1614. The second Globe lasted into the 1640s. Even though a large portion of the output of the world's preeminent dramatist was first performed here, we have never known very much about the theatre itself. The

Panel at site of original Globe Theatre. Anchor Terrace in the background.

surviving exterior views of the playhouse (mostly from maps of the period) are not the same and there is no extant interior view at all. Results from the most recent excavations (at the Globe and the Rose sites) as well as John Orrel's fascinating work on the contemporary maps have finally resolved some of the knotty problems surrounding the nature of Shakespeare's Globe, but there is still plenty of uncertainty left for the scholars of the 21st century to debate. The bookstalls at many London locations can provide more than enough material to occupy the person who wishes to address the whole of London's Elizabethan and Jacobean theatre in more depth than is possible here.

*We have now reached the culmination of our walk—the original site of the Globe theatre. If the flesh is weak or the hour is late, you can continue down Park Street to a "T" junction. A left turn will lead you quickly back to the Anchor Inn and from there you can retrace your steps back to Southwark Cathedral, through the Cathedral precincts, and up the stairs to the busy **Borough High Street**. You can then either turn left and walk back across the river to the Monument tube station where you started or turn right until you find the entrance to the London Bridge tube station on the Northern Line.*

If the spirit does remain willing and you wish to see the last remaining galleried coaching inn in London, take the right turn at the "T" intersection. Follow this as it makes a gentle curve to your right and then a curve to the left. Just before the railroad overpass, turn right on **Red Cross Way**. *Shortly you will reach a major road with more bridges crossing overhead (**Southwark Street**). Head directly across the street for an arch that is a continuation of Red Cross Way. Follow this narrow street all the way to* **Marshalsea Road**. *It will take you through a typical working class neighborhood, past a school, some cottages set back*

17

1

from the street, and some council flats. Turn left on Marshalsea Road for a block to reach Borough High Street.

As you reach the high street, the **Church of St. George the Martyr** *is almost directly across from you and the* **Borough station** *on the Northern Line is just to your right. Cross the street to reach the church.* In its grave-

yard is buried a true theatre curiosity in one Mr. Nahum Tate (1652–1715). His claim to fame rests on his 17th-century improvements of Shakespeare. Under his hand *Richard II* is reworked and titled *The Sicilian Adventurer.* Tate's version of *King Lear* omits the Fool and has Cordelia survive to marry Edgar. Lear also remains alive to give away the bride. What is even more unbelievable about all this is that Tate's adaptation of *King Lear* remained the standard acting edition until the early part of the 19th century when William Macready finally restored the original text. If all of the above seems faint praise, you might prefer to remember Tate as the composer of the lovely Christmas carol, "While Shepherds Watched Their Flocks by Night."

After a brief look at the church (if it is open), a right turn (assuming you are exiting from the front door) onto Borough High Street will set your course back toward London Bridge. If you are heading in the right direction **Tabard Street** *should be just*

Church of St. George the Martyr

ahead of you. The middle of the high street (they are high because the Romans actually raised them for better drainage and you are indeed walking on a Roman road) marks the site of the old Marshalsea Prison where Ben Jonson was incarcerated for sedition in 1597 and where Charles Dickens' father was imprisoned for debt. The young Dickens lived nearby with his family while his father was in the prison. *Shortly on your right you will come upon the John Harvard Public Library.* It appears to function as a socially active neighborhood center and often has nice exhibits of Borough history. It is well worth a look if you are interested in the ambience of real life as opposed to the servicing of the tourist industry. Read the bulletin boards. Fascinating!

As you continue down the high street you will come upon a string of tiny alleyways, some closed off and some open. Each of them used to lead to one of the many coaching inns that lined this main route into and out of London. *Just before the high street curves gently to the right is* **Queens Head Yard***, which was the site of an inn owned by the family of John Harvard and sold by them before they emigrated to America.*

George Inn

*After a bit of a walk, the road will curve slightly again and you'll be able to see the railway bridge next to Southwark Cathedral. **Talbot Yard** is just at that curve and is the site of the famous Tabard Inn where Chaucer's Canterbury Pilgrims launched their famous journey. The next opening is the **George Inn Yard** and it must be explored, for inside is the last remnant of a galleried coaching inn in London.* The facade dates from 1676–77 and its plain narrow rooms with crooked floors and low ceilings definitely recall an earlier day. Occasionally in the summer, Shakespearean plays are performed in the courtyard. New construction on two sides in the yard has removed some of the sense of age that used to be there but at least the balcony motif has been carried on.

With some more of that old imagination we have called upon so often, you should be able to see from this fragment how suitable the old inns would have been for drama. Some scholars believe that this is the main architectural model for the permanent Elizabethan theatre. It would have had controlled access, a place for a stage at one end, places for patrons to stand, galleries for the more affluent, convenient spaces for actors' dressing areas, and refreshments on the premises. It is easy to see how an enterprising professional with a bit of capital could find an advantage in an arrangement that would reproduce a similar physical space without the necessity of paying rent to an innkeeper for use of the yard. Other advantages are also quite obvious. The stage could be left in place and used for rehearsals, there would be permanent storage for costumes and props, the producing company could set its own admission prices, and most importantly,

1

the income from food and drink sales would swell the company coffers and not the innkeeper's.

Art aside, the reality check here is quite clear. The Elizabethan theatre of William Shakespeare and his colleagues was above all a competitive, professional, commercial enterprise. The times were hard, the margins narrow, and you had to use every edge you could find.

Enjoy some refreshment or just reflection at the George Inn, then return to the Borough High Street and turn right toward the river once again. The very next opening is **White Hart Yard** *and the site of the old* **White Hart Inn.** This was the rebel Jack Cade's headquarters in Shakespeare's *Henry VI, Part 2.* In act IV Cade's forces fight their way across London Bridge to Cannon Street (you walked under the Cannon St. railway bridge just before you got to the Anchor Inn a while ago) and then make plans to storm the Tower, the Savoy, and the Inns of Court. But by Scene Eight of the play, Cade has fallen back to Southwark again and in a parley with Buckingham and Clifford speaks to his own wavering forces, "Hath my sword therefore broke through London's gates, that you should leave me at the White Hart in Southwark?" Several centuries later the White Hart was still an inn and Mr. Pickwick first met Sam Weller there in Dickens' novel, *Pickwick Papers.*

You are now almost back to the river and you should shortly find an entrance to the London Bridge tube station (it's still in Zone 1 and on the Northern Line), or continue straight on back over London Bridge and return to the Monument station (Circle and District lines) where you started.

Wrought iron figure from front gate at the new Shakespeare's Globe

Quiz answers to help you identify the Shakespeare characters in the memorial window at Southwark Cathedral (see next page).
Left panel from top down—Puck and Bottom from *A Midsummer Night's Dream,* yellow cross-gartered Malvolio making his love appeal to Olivia while Maria evesdrops from the bushes in *Twelfth Night,* then Sir John Falstaff, then Portia in her law garb, "The quality of mercy is not strained" etc. from *The Merchant of Venice,* the contemplative Jaques sitting in the forest of Arden from *As You Like It,* and the Fool from *King Lear.*

Bouncing up to the top of the center panel you should see three characters from *The Tempest*—the sprite Ariel soaring over the figure of Prospero while Caliban crouches below.

At the top of the third panel you can see young Romeo and fair Juliet in the balcony scene, then Richard II holding in his hand the hollow crown, then Richard the III, King Lear, Othello, Lady Macbeth, and finally Hamlet with the skull of poor Yorick.

Across the bottom of all three panels from left to right is a visual representation of Jaques' famous "Ages of Man" speech from *As You Like It.*

> All the world's a stage,
> And all the men and women merely players.
> They have their exits and their entrances,
> And one man in his time plays many parts,
> His acts being seven ages. At first the infant,
> Mewling and puking in the nurse's arms.
> Then the whining schoolboy, with his satchel
> And shining morning face, creeping like snail
> Unwillingly to school. And then the lover,
> Sighing like a furnace, with a woeful ballad
> Made to his mistress' eyebrow. Then a soldier
> Full of strange oaths and bearded like the pard,
> Jealous in honor, sudden, and quick in quarrel,
> Seeking the bubble reputation
> Even in the cannon's mouth. And then the justice
> In fair round belly with good capon lined,
> With eyes severe and beard of formal cut,
> Full of wise saws and modern instances;
> And so he plays his part. The sixth age shifts
> Into the lean and slippered pantaloon
> With spectacles on nose and pouch on side,
> His youthful hose, well saved, a world too wide
> For his shrunk shank; and his big manly voice,
> Turning again toward childish treble, pipes
> And whistles in his sound. Last scene of all,
> That ends this strange eventful history,
> Is second childishness and mere oblivion,
> Sans teeth, sans eyes, sans taste, sans everything.

Shakespeare Memorial window at Southwark Cathedral

WALK TWO

✿

WILLIAM SHAKESPEARE

AND THEN SOME

FROM CHANCERY LANE TO BLACKFRIARS

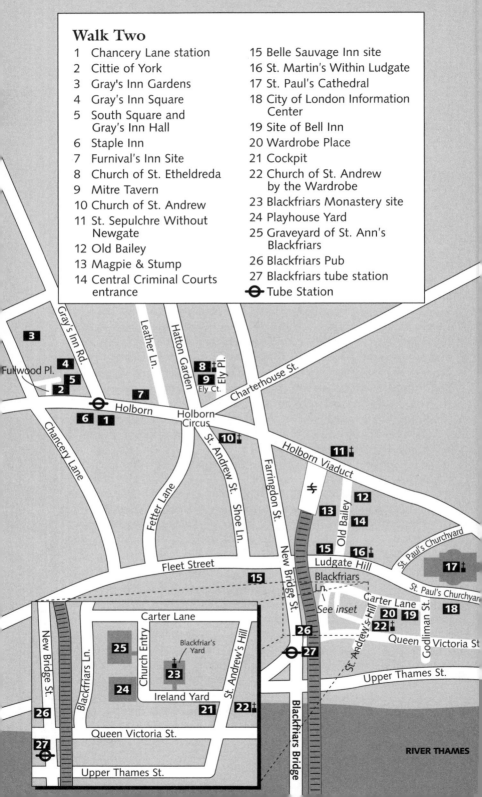

Walk Two

1 Chancery Lane station
2 Cittie of York
3 Gray's Inn Gardens
4 Gray's Inn Square
5 South Square and Gray's Inn Hall
6 Staple Inn
7 Furnival's Inn Site
8 Church of St. Etheldreda
9 Mitre Tavern
10 Church of St. Andrew
11 St. Sepulchre Without Newgate
12 Old Bailey
13 Magpie & Stump
14 Central Criminal Courts entrance
15 Belle Sauvage Inn site
16 St. Martin's Within Ludgate
17 St. Paul's Cathedral
18 City of London Information Center
19 Site of Bell Inn
20 Wardrobe Place
21 Cockpit
22 Church of St. Andrew by the Wardrobe
23 Blackfriars Monastery site
24 Playhouse Yard
25 Graveyard of St. Ann's Blackfriars
26 Blackfriars Pub
27 Blackfriars tube station
⊖ Tube Station

STARTING POINT: Chancery Lane station (Central Line). Note: This station is closed on Sundays and the Inns at Court are closed on weekends. We recommend doing this walk only on a weekday and especially a Wednesday if you wish to get into the Church of St. Sepulchre Without Newgate.

APPROXIMATE TIME: Two hours with minimal stops and three hours if you include the lunch hour and some breaks along the way.

2

his walk begins at an interesting pub, visits several locations associated with Shakespeare, two Inns of Court, a few fascinating churches, some historic theatre sites, and finishes at a marvelous Art Nouveau pub that was designed and decorated by a member of the Royal Academy.

Travel on the Central Line to the **Chancery Lane tube station** and once at the top of the escalator seek the exit labeled Number 1 (it is labeled Grays Inn Road but will bring you up onto the north side of Holborn). Once at street level keep walking straight ahead for about 100 paces past the Number 7 High Holborn building toward the large beckoning clock of the **Cittie of York pub.** Plan to arrive here right about noon in order to take advantage of some pub grub. If you arrive later than 12:15 you may find the crowds of lawyers intimidating.

The Cittie of York is one of the most venerable and intriguing of London pubs and a popular gathering spot for Gray's Inn lawyers. The first alehouse on this spot appears to date from 1430. The current building dates from 1695 and was rebuilt in 1923 using some of the original materials. The front of the pub was remodeled extensively in 1983, but if you go through into the rear bar you will see some older and rather impressive looking wine vats above your head. They were actually used as late as 1940. On the whole this cathedral of

Cittie of York

25

pubs seems an ideal place to start our journey through this part of William Shakespeare's London.

So order up a pint and some hearty food to tide you through an afternoon of hard walking. If you have arrived early enough, you might be able to get one of the little private booths, which were constructed so lawyers could discuss their business discreetly during lunch. Note also the unusual triangular stove in the center of the room. It's been there, working like a charm with its chimney vent under the floor, since 1815. The only change is that it is gas-fired now.

After you finish your lunch, leave the pub, turn right, and then turn right again in about 50 yards at a small gate-like passage called **Fulwood Place***. If you pass by the stoplight at the Chancery Lane intersection you've missed Fulwood Place and should turn around and walk back a bit.* As you enter the archway you are walking into the precincts of Gray's Inn, one of the four London Inns of Court. The four Inns (Gray's, Lincoln's, the Middle Temple, and the Inner Temple) date from the 13th century and exist to provide office space for lawyers and to provide lectures and certificatory examinations to students wishing to qualify for the bar in Great Britain.

Follow the passage until you reach lovely **Gray's Inn Gardens***.* They were a favorite strolling-place for ladies of good and ill repute throughout the 17th and 18th centuries. There used to be two aged catalpa trees up at the far end of the garden that were supposedly planted by Sir Francis Bacon from slips given to him by his friend Sir Walter Raleigh, who had brought them all the way from America. Unfortunately, age or disease took their toll sometime between 1988 and 1992, and they have disappeared. Garden strolling used to be limited to Inn members but these days, whatever your repute, you may sample the delights of the greenery from 12:00 to 2:30 P.M. M–F (May 1 to September 30 only).

Tunnel to Gray's Inn Square

If you go into the garden return to the gate where you entered and turn left when you exit. If you don't go in turn right and walk along the edge of the fence looking ahead of you for a tunnel-like opening labeled **Gray's Inn Square***. Go through the tunnel. The square is on your left as you emerge.* The most famous resident here was Sir Francis Bacon, who lived at Number 1 Gray's Inn Square for almost 50 years. Bacon (1561–1626) was the foremost intellectual and essayist of his time. He even has the distinction of having been nominated by some as the true author of William Shakespeare's plays.

The prize for the most infamous Gray's Inn theatrical connection must go to the Anglican clergyman Jeremy Collier (1650–1726).

Collier made his black mark on theatre history when he published his *Short View of the Profaneness and Immorality of the English Stage* in 1698. When not involved with church affairs or attacking the evils of the Restoration theatre, Collier was a law lecturer at the Inn. Other theatrical residents were the Elizabethan dramatist Thomas Middleton (1570–1627), who was a student at the Inn, and the 18th-century dramatist Oliver Goldsmith (1730–1777), who had lodgings within the Inn precincts. Goldsmith was buried at the Inner Temple and we visit that site in Walk Five.

*Unless you wish to stroll in the square proper, turn immediately to your right and proceed down the lane toward the **South Square**. The building on your left is **Gray's Inn Hall**.* It dates from 1560, although it and several other buildings in the area had to be extensively rebuilt after World War II bomb damage. During the 15th and 16th centuries, students at the Inns of Court provided some of the best audiences for live drama and the Inn halls were ideal locations for performances. Records indicate that William Shakespeare's *Comedy of Errors* was given its first known performance in Gray's Inn Hall in 1594. Unfortunately the hall is still used as the Inn's dining room today and entry is restricted. For some fascinating discussion of the nature and arrangement of performances in the halls of the Inns of Court, you might like to look at Robert Burkhardt's article in *Theatre History Studies* Vol. XII, 1992. If you have more interest in the history of Gray's Inn proper, find **Number 8, South Square.** This is the Treasury Office and they have a selection of postcards and brochures (10–4, M–F).

*Return now to **High Holborn** using the archway on the opposite side of the square from the hall. As you emerge turn left. Walk along past*

Gray's Inn Hall

2

the tube entrances. On your right, across the street is **Staple Inn***, an* Elizabethan facade that escaped the Great Fire of London in 1666 by a fortuitous wind change. (Walk Three starts at Staple Inn, and you can find more information on the building there.)

Cross **Gray's Inn Road** *and continue walking now on* **Holborn***. Shortly, on your left, you will pass the red brick Victorian Gothic bulk of the Prudential Assurance Company.* It stands on the site of Furnival's Inn where Charles Dickens stayed while writing the first part of *The Pickwick Papers*. The playwright James Barrie of *Peter Pan* fame also lodged at the Inn for a short time. *Walk through the arched gate if it is open. You'll find an impressive bridge gallery dead ahead and beyond that a courtyard containing a strange plastic bubble and a World War I monument. Return to the street and turn left.*

Cross **Leather Lane** *and just beyond a large W.H. Smith look for a street called* **Hatton Garden***, which should come up on your left.* This street, now the center of London's diamond trade, is named after Sir Christopher Hatton, Elizabeth I's Lord Chancellor and also her favorite dancing partner. Hatton was apparently no one else's favorite but the Queen's, but in those days that was the one favor that counted.

We will rejoin Hatton in a moment, but for now walk by Hatton Garden and turn slightly to the left at the **Holborn Circus** *"spaghetti bowl." You'll find yourself on the beginning of* **Charterhouse Street***. Almost immediately on your left will be the gates of* **Ely Place***.* This cul-de-sac roughly defines the former palace of the Bishop of Ely. It has been a liberty area, and therefore outside of city jurisdiction, since the 13th century. To this day it is privately guarded at night and in theory not even the metropolitan police can enter uninvited. As you enter the enclave it might be interesting to note that from 1600 to 1624 the Bishop's old palace served as the residence of the Spanish Ambassador to England and during that time one of the last medieval Passion Plays done in England was performed in the house.

But our real interest here is at the back left corner of the close where you will find the enchanting church of **St. Etheldreda***. Walk there now, go in, and climb the stairs to the sanctuary.* This church, formerly the Bishop of Ely's private chapel, is all that remains of this once elegant complex. All, that is, except some interesting memories out of the plays of William Shakespeare. The Bishop's gardens, for instance, were apparently quite well known. In *Richard III*, the Bishop of Ely is a character and Richard, the Duke of Gloucester, says to him: "My Lord of Ely, when I was last in Holborn, I saw good strawberries in your garden there; I do beseech you send for some of them." The residents of Ely Place continue to commemorate this event with a strawberry festival held each year during the last week of June.

The Bishop's Banqueting House also made a footnote for itself in history. Henry VIII and Catharine of Aragon attended a five-day feast there in 1531. The menu has been preserved and consisted of 24 beefs,

100 muttons, 51 veals, 34 porks, 10 dozen capons, 13 dozen swans, 340 dozen larks, and a whole ox.

The church of St. Etheldreda has always been one of our favorite spots in London. *Take a seat and look about you.* It is a 13th-century Gothic building of livable proportions whose major claim to fame is that it was the first prereformation English church to be returned to the Roman Catholics and it is claimed that the chapel at West Point in the United States is pat-terned after it. Even though the building escaped the Great Fire of 1666 as a result of the same wind change that saved Staple Inn, it has still been much restored. Major work occurred in 1870, 1935, and again after World War II. The 500-square-foot west window (modern glass) is one of the largest in London and the chestnut roof is simply superb. Gracing the sides of the walls are painted life-size statues, not of great saints as you might expect, but of ordinary people who rose to martyrdom by sheltering priests or failing to take the oath of supremacy in the dark days of the 1530s. Look particularly at the figure of John Roche, a Thames waterman, and Anne Line, a seamstress. It may be the gen-tle gazes of those quiet, little

St. Etheldreda

known martyrs, or the soft aroma of incense and melted candles, but the sanctuary somehow seems to incorporate and reaffirm their per-sonalities and their faith. It is all that a church should be. Please leave a generous gift in one of the collection boxes. This is not a money-gouging tourist venue.

When you leave the sanctuary make your way back down the ancient stairs and look for the crypt entrance on your left. This space, now a serenely simple chapel (complete with a scale model of the Bishop's entire palace complex), rests on Roman foundations. John of Gaunt, the famous Lancaster, father of Henry IV and brother-in-law of Chaucer, who came to live at Ely Palace in the late 1390s, died in the palace in 1339 and his mortal remains may have reposed for a time in this very crypt. The circumstances surrounding his death were

2

immortalized by William Shakespeare in *Richard II*, act II, scene 1. In that scene Gaunt speaks of his country in as eloquent a manner as has ever been spoken. He says:

> This royal throne of Kings, this sceptered isle
> This earth of majesty, this seat of Mars,
> This other Eden, demi-paradise:
> This fortress built by nature for herself
> Against infection and the hand of war;
> This happy breed of men, this little world;
> This precious stone set in a silver sea
> Which serves it in the office of a wall
> Or as a moat defensive to a house,
> Against the envy of less happier lands:
> This blessed plot, this earth, this realm,
> This England!

With the congenial resonance of those words in your ears, step back outside into Ely Place once more. It is time to pick up the story of Christopher Hatton again. In 1576 Queen Elizabeth was seeking a way to reward her good friend Hatton and thought that some choice Holborn real estate might be ideal. She asked the Bishop of Ely to lease most of his house and grounds to Hatton for a yearly rent of ten pounds, ten loads of hay, and one red rose from the garden. The Bishop demurred and the Queen sent a note which said, "Proud prelate, you know what you were before I made you what you are! If you don't immediately comply with my request, by God, I'll unfrock you." The Bishop, being a practical man, rapidly signed the lease. Hatton got his estate, but later got into financial difficulties, fell from the Queen's favor, and ultimately died a broken man.

*Walk now down the right side of Ely Place (west side). A bit more than halfway back to Charterhouse Street is a small opening in the facade of row houses. It is about four feet wide and has an iron bar down the center of the opening to make it even narrower. It is called **Ely Court** and you should turn right into it. In about 50 paces this tiny alley will reveal one of London's best hidden pubs. It is the splendid **Mitre Tavern** that dates from 1546.* What you see now, though, is the product of an 18th-century renovation. The site of the tavern is supposed to mark approximately the division between Christopher Hatton's garden and the Bishop's remaining piece of garden. It is worth a visit. Inside the tavern in a glass case, you can still see the dried trunk of a cherry tree around which Sir Christopher and the Virgin Queen supposedly danced the Maypole. Ask the barman to see a sheet on the pub's history if you have the time.

Filled with this historical tidbit and perhaps an additional libation of old English bitter, step back out onto Ely Court, turn right, and continue on until you pop out into Hatton Garden. Then turn left and walk back to Holborn Circus at the jaunty hat-tipping statue of Queen Victoria's beloved Prince Albert.

Once at the Circus ignore Charterhouse Street, which would lead you right back to Ely Place, and choose instead the wide **Holborn Viaduct***. Just across from you is the gray stone of the Christopher Wren* **Church of St. Andrew***.* The great fire of 1666 had just reached and destroyed the old church when that sudden change of wind referred to a few

2

paragraphs ago came up and saved Ely Place, Staple Inn, and other buildings on High Holborn from destruction. St. Andrews was destroyed again by the Germans in 1940 and it was not until the 1960s that this fine building was completely restored to its 17th-century glory. *Cross the street toward the church.* Should you wish to visit the interior you will find that William Hazlitt, the Shakespearean critic, was married in the church in 1808. Charles Lamb and his wife were best man and bridesmaid. Both men lived nearby on Southampton Buildings.

Mitre Tavern

Otherwise carry on down Holborn Viaduct, which is the name of the street, but also a real viaduct and one of the truly great large scale Victorian engineering projects that altered the face of London. The viaduct is over 1400 feet long and carries traffic over the ancient "stream in a hollow" (Hole Bourne) portion of the now buried Fleet River. For hundreds of years this valley had been a major bottleneck for horses and wagons attempting to enter the city through Newgate. Finally in 1869 cast iron came to the rescue and the long hill was no more. The viaduct itself is well worth a closer look. The Victorian penchant for uplifting public morality is seen in the statues of Fine Art, Science, Agriculture, and Commerce that grace the structure. *There's a little bit of irony just underneath the bridge where you will find one of the mustiest, but certainly most fascinating, Oddbins' Wine shops in the whole of the city. Should you wish to see it, take the stairs just past the end of the iron bridge down to the lower level and walk back under the bridge. Turn right when you come back up or continue on your way if you can resist the temptation of a demon rum diversion.*

Holborn Viaduct will soon reveal your next landmark on the left—the tower of **St. Sepulchre Without Newgate** *topped by four small spires. For a closer look cross back to the left side of the street at the pedestrian crossing.* This church dates back to the 12th century, but has been

2

remodeled and restored many times since then. Some of the interior work is by Christopher Wren. Unfortunately, aside from concerts and other special events, the church is open only on Wednesdays from 11 A.M. to 3 P.M.

Americans may wish to step inside just to see the grave of Captain John Smith of Pilgrim fame. It is located in the south aisle. Theatre enthusiasts will want to see the famed Newgate execution handbell that was sounded outside a condemned man's cell on the night before he was to die. It was given to the church in 1605 and is now mounted on a pillar in the south aisle. It is alluded to in act IV, scene 2 of John Webster's *The Duchess of Malfi*. The executioners have arrived in the room and Bosola says to the Duchess, "I am the common bellman, that usually is sent to condemned persons the night before they suffer." William Shakespeare also knew of the bell. He would have passed the old church each time he came from Stratford and entered the city through the Newgate. In act II, scene 1 of *Macbeth* he has Lady Macbeth say, "Hark! Peace! It was the owl that shrieked, the fatal bellman which gives the stern'st good-night." St. Sepulchre is also well known today as the musicians' church and is the site of excellent and varied noon-hour concerts.

Handbell

Diagonally across the way from the church stands the gray mass of the Central Criminal Courts Building or, as it is more commonly known, The Old Bailey. The corner itself is the site of the old **Newgate** into the city of London. The gate was large enough to include a prison and it was there that the Elizabethan playwright Ben Jonson was incarcerated after killing Mr. Gabriel Spencer in a duel. It was also where Christopher Marlowe was jailed for suspicion of complicity in a murder. Newgate's real theatrical fame, however, lies in John Gay's *The Beggar's Opera* (1728). The entire play is set in and around old Newgate Prison and its vivid picture of London lowlife in the early 18th century is unmatched anywhere. The escapades of Macheath, Lucy Lockit, and Polly Peachum climax with the tolling of an execution bell (from St. Sepulchre). Bertolt Brecht and Kurt Weill's *The Threepenny Opera* (1928) with its famous title song "The Ballad of Mack the Knife" was based on Gay's play.

In 1783, after a disastrous fire, the architect George Dance designed another and larger prison for the site—a structure that was called "a prototype of Hell" by Henry Fielding. If you wish to soak up some of that building's atmosphere, one of its original cells is on display in the Museum of London. Until 1774 it had been common for prisoners in the old Newgate to be transported to the Tyburn Gallows for execution. Clergymen from St. Sepulchre were traditionally on hand to give each condemned person a nosegay and a blessing as they rumbled by. As late as the 1890s the church bells were rung to mark executions at Newgate itself. If you'd like to pursue the grisly history of these prisons, we'd recommend a book titled *The Triple Tree: Newgate, Tyburn, and Old Bailey* by Donald Rumbelow.

At the intersection, cross Holborn Viaduct and start down the right side of **Old Bailey Street** *with the Criminal Courts Building on your left. Once on Old Bailey Street, look for a sign on the new building to your right for the Magpie and Stump public house.* The current pub is at least the third on the site. Legend has it that a last drink from the Magpie's pumps was offered to all condemned prisoners from the old prison and that the landlord sold upper window seats to the wealthy so they could have a better view of the execution in the square outside. The 19th-century Magpie and Stump was severely damaged in 1973 by a powerful explosion that was attributed to the Irish Republican Army. The pub was literally destroyed and windows in all directions were blown out. You can still pick out some pockmarks and patched areas from the blast on the walls of the Criminal Courts Building. *Walk on a bit until you see on your left a set of doors labeled Central Criminal Court. Cross to the left side of the street here.* The public galleries are open from 10:30 to 1 and 2 to 4:30 M–F if you want to see some real modern English theatre in process. The disappointing thing is that unless you are traveling very light you will have to leave someone outside with your possessions as there are no checkroom facilities available and you may not bring food, cameras, recorders, or bags of any kind into the public galleries. Of course a return is always possible.

Otherwise continue to move down Old Bailey Street toward the intersection with **Ludgate Hill**. *New construction in recent years has erased several interesting features so you'll have to do some imaginative reconstruction as you walk.* First imagine that you are really walking along the banks of that same invisible river you just crossed on the Holborn Viaduct. Fleet Lane (named after the Fleet River) used to cut off to your right and run steeply downhill toward the riverbank. At the bottom of Fleet Lane was Seacoal Lane. During the late middle ages ships brought high quality coal down the coast from Newcastle (yes, that's the origin of the phrase "it's like bringing coals to Newcastle"), up the Thames, and finally up the Fleet River. They tied up along Seacoal Lane to unload their cargo. Alas, it's just a modern and terribly uninteresting office block now.

A short stroll farther and you will intersect with Ludgate Hill. It is cluttered with traffic and tourists, but is a lot more circumspect than it was in the 1500s. At that time it was a downright unpleasant corner of the city. The Fleet River was a fetid, open sewer; the coal yards contributed a layer of grime; and there were at least two prisons in spitting distance of where you are standing. Right in the middle of all this was the infamous Belle Sauvage Inn. Records indicate that companies of players used the inn for performance in the 1570s and 1580s.

2

Richard Tarleton, the most famous of Elizabethan clowns, and most probably the model for the king's jester referred to by Hamlet when he says "Alas, poor Yorick, I knew him, Horatio," played at the Belle Sauvage shortly before he died in 1588. The inn was still embroiled in "evil theatrics" over 40 years later when in 1632 William Prynne (1600–1699), a zealous puritan residing not far away at Lincoln's Inn, published his *Histrio Mastix*, a ferocious 1000-page attack on actors and the theatre. One passage refers to the profane playing at the Belle Sauvage of a play called *Faustus*, which featured an actual appearance by the devil. Mention is also made of some audience members who were sorely frightened by this apparition. Luckily for us the old inn is now long gone and no apparitions have been reported by the chartered accountants who currently inhabit the area. If you are in the mood for a light-hearted treatment of this old superstition and an actor's life around the old Elizabethan innyard theatres, look up Edward Marston's delightful murder mystery titled *The Merry Devils*.

*Turn left now at **Ludgate Hill** and begin your climb toward the grand dome of **St. Paul's Cathedral**, passing on the way the Wren Spire of **St. Martin Ludgate**.* The interior, if open, is not impressive, but it is original as the building escaped German bombs during the Blitz. *You may stop and visit St. Paul's at this time if you wish, but our walk today is merely going to go by the building and plunge immediately into the precincts of Blackfriars.* Walk Five, "A Fleet Ramble to St. Paul's," formally culminates with a visit to this magnificent symbol of the city of London.

*When you reach the open space in front of St. Paul's Cathedral, edge your way off to the right and locate the round **City of London Information Center**. You will need to cross the busy street to reach it. To be safe, walk up to the first stoplight and then return to the Information Center. **Godliman Street** runs just in front of the tourist office. Go about 50 paces along Godliman Street and turn right into **Carter Lane**. Watch carefully on your left now for a sign reading **Bell Yard** and just below it to the right a small, barely legible, off-white plaque that marks the site of the **Bell Inn**.* On October 25, 1598, Richard Quinney of Stratford-Upon-Avon was staying at the Bell Inn. He was in a bit of a financial bind and penned a letter to another Stratford fellow who was doing right well for himself in London. Quinney's

St. Paul's Cathedral

letter is the only known piece of private correspondence addressed to William Shakespeare. It begins, "To my loving and good friend and countryman, Mr. Wm. Shakespeare," and then asks the successful playwright for a 30-pound loan. There is no record of Will's response, but it couldn't have been too negative as some years later Quinney's son married Judith Shakespeare, Will's eldest daughter.

2

*A bit farther along on Carter Lane is **Dean's Court**, where the Dean of St. Paul's Cathedral lives. Just beyond is an extraordinary mock renaissance palazzo that used to house the St. Paul's choir school and is now a youth hostel. Watch closely on your left now as you walk for the narrow arched entrance to **Wardrobe Place**, another of those hidden spots that make London a delight to explore. There is no street sign, just a small metal plate saying Number 1 Wardrobe Place. If you arrive at a street called **St. Andrews Hill** before you find Wardrobe Place you've gone too far and should go back and look again.*

Once in the small shady yard, put your imagination cap on again. Wardrobe Place was the site of the King's Wardrobe where, from the time of Edward the III (14th century) the robes of state were made and stored. In 1604 on this location William Shakespeare signed a receipt for 4½ yards of cloth to be used to make livery for the state entry of James I into London. Shakespeare's company, the Chamberlain's Men, had been invited to become the King's Men after Queen Elizabeth's death and were now entitled to wear royal livery. If you have taken Walk One, you may recall that we mentioned this episode in connection with the possibility that Shakespeare's company might have shown off their new livery at the great celebration at the Bishop of Winchester's palace on Bankside to honor the accession of James I.

Turn left after you leave Wardrobe Place and proceed the few steps to St. Andrews Hill. Turn left again and walk down the hill. The narrow streets are graphic reminders of London's past. This district was burned to the ground in the great fire of 1666 and Christopher Wren's initial rebuilding plans called for wide open streets radiating from St. Paul's. The grandiose ideas never quite made it off the drawing board and ultimately the buildings were rebuilt following the medieval street plans. Thus you walk today through twists, turns, and narrow alleys that would have been totally familiar to Shakespeare and his fellow actors. City planners have continued to argue these questions. World War II bombing destroyed much of a similar rabbit warren of streets on the other side of St. Paul's and the sterile office blocks that were erected in the 1950s destroyed much of the old street plan. Those buildings are already looking shabby and not too long ago the Prince of Wales, who has made the despoiling of London by faceless modern architecture one of his royal crusades, made a speech in which he referred to this part of the city as a sad example of what can happen when commercial interests take precedence over historic and aesthetic interests.

*A little over halfway down St. Andrews Hill on the right side of the road is the **Cockpit public house**.* Its decor today recalls the 16th-century venue that used to occupy the space. William Shakespeare would certainly have known the cockfighting parlor that stood here, for he had a home somewhere within a hundred yards of where you are now standing. On March 10, 1613, Shakespeare purchased a property known as the Blackfriars Priory Gatehouse on Upper Thames Street. The most probable location from today's perspective is somewhere on the north side of Ireland Yard where it joins St. Andrew's Hill and it may have been purchased because of its closeness to the Blackfriars Theatre where the King's Men played during the cold winter months when the open-air Globe across the river was closed. Shakespreare paid 140 pounds for the property and ultimately willed it to his elder daughter Susannah who passed it on to her only daughter—Shakespeare's last direct descendent. It was sold sometime before 1667.

*Cross toward the front door of the pub. From this position you should just be able to see ahead of you and slightly to the left the entrance to the Wren **Church of St. Andrew by the Wardrobe**. It would be to your right if you have just exited the pub. Find the church entrance and if it is open go in. Upstairs there are two almost hidden memorials to William Shakespeare and his contemporary, the musician **John Dowland**.* Although some critics have complained that this kind of attempt to claim the presence of historic luminaries and to impute in them an unproven conventional piety is a shameless catering to the tourist trades, it is difficult to accept this when one sees how these memorials are hidden from the general public view. To locate them you must first find the church open, and then know enough to make your way up the stairs to the back of the West Gallery. They are unadvertised at the church entrance and completely invisible from the floor of the sanctuary below. They are quite unassuming but pleasantly done

Shakespeare plaque in St. Andrew by the Wardrobe

in oak and limewood. The inscription on Shakespeare's plaque reads simply, "Poet Playwright, Parishioner, and owner of a house in Ireland Yard." In the same upstairs room you will find a copy of the Blackfriars Gatehouse deed of sale, thus saving you a trip to the British Museum to see the original.

*Leave the church and return to the Cockpit pub. Just in front of it, on your right, is a small alley called **Ireland Yard**. Turn into this passageway and walk down it until you come to a tiny courtyard containing three trees fighting for life amid the surrounding brick walls. Walk in for a moment.* You are now in the confines of the **Blackfriars**

Monastery, a religious community that occupied this area as early as the 13th century. There was a church, a cloister, a priory, various outbuildings, and even a dock down on the river. At one point, during the tenure of Sir Thomas More as speaker, the English Parliament actually met within the walls of the Priory.

After Henry VIII dissolved the monasteries in 1539, the grounds were held by various nobles as so-called liberty areas, which were free from City of London control even though they were within the bounds of the city. In 1548 the precincts were granted to Sir Thomas Cawarden, who was then the King's Master of Revels. Cawarden rented out parts of the complex for dwelling and business purposes, but also allocated some space to acting companies of young choir boys. More on this in a moment.

Exit the courtyard now, turn right, and step along a little farther on Ireland Yard. You will soon come to a slightly larger space called **Playhouse Yard**. Somewhere near this spot a small monastery building was adapted for theatrical use by Richard Farrant and the Children of the Chapels' Royale. This was the first Blackfriars Theatre. Performances by these young choir boys were popular among court audiences and seem to have been given regularly from 1576 to 1580. Other boys' companies used the space periodically over the next years, but by 1584 it was being let out for lodgings. In 1596 James Burbage, builder of London's first public theatre in Shoreditch (The Theatre—1576), leased another small hall (the nearby former refectory of the monastery complex) with the idea of converting it into a theatre. Even while remodeling was in process, there were complaints lodged against the appearance of professional players in the district. The boys' companies had claimed an educational bent, had close court ties, and were considered to be innocent and genteel amateurs whereas the boisterous and unruly professional players were not thought to be positive influences on neighborhood ambience or property values.

Just before the remodeling was finished Burbage was forbidden to use his theatre. When he passed away in 1597 his sons Richard and Cuthbert decided not to push the question of professional playing in the precinct any further for the moment. They finished the work and leased the building to another boys' company, which played there until 1608. Interestingly this relocation failure plus the continuing lease expiration problems at The Theatre out in Shoreditch put an added premium on finding a good location for the company, which of course turned out to be the Globe in 1599. (See Walks One and Eight.)

In 1608 James I formally disbanded all the boys' companies and the building was left without a tenant. Two years later Richard Burbage, William Shakespeare, and four other King's Men shareholders negotiated a new lease and received permission for adult professionals to use the space. The King's Men used this second Blackfriars

2

Theatre from October to May while returning to the Globe for the summer season. It appears that the King's Men retained possession of the building until the formal closing of all theatres in 1642. A quick look at a map can also tell you just how important the location of this building is. An indoor theatre with a small capacity needs to charge more for seats and thus circumscribes its clientele. The Blackfriars was close to the various Inns at Court and the string of Royal, Ecclesiastical, and Duchal Palaces that ran along the Thames from Westminster to the Tower. For the full story of this remarkable venue see Irwin Smith's *Shakespeare's Blackfriars Playhouse* or chapter six of Jean Wilson's *The Archaeology of Shakespeare.* You can now also see a working reconstruction of this playhouse in Virginia where it is the home of America's Shenandoah Shakespeare Company.

*Opening off to the right from Playhouse Yard is yet another narrow alleyway called **Church Entry**. Cross into it and not far along you will discover a more deeply buried but actually quite pleasant little court-yard that used to be the **graveyard of St. Ann's Blackfriars**, the parish church of the Blackfriars Priory.* Some sources indicate that the church, which bordered closely on the Blackfriars theatres, sometimes had its services disturbed by the sounds of trumpets, uproarious cheers, and loud drums emanating from performances.

*Step back out of the old graveyard and turn left. The next intersection is **Carter Lane**. Turn left and stroll along until you reach a "T" intersection, which is **Blackfriars Lane**. Turn left and follow its winding course down to **Queen Victoria Street**.*

*Our choice for end-of-walk refreshment comes just after you turn right off Blackfriars Lane onto Queen Victoria Street. Walk under the railroad bridge and look on your right for the distinctively shaped **Blackfriars***

*Pub**, decorated inside and out in 1903 by Henry Poole of the Royal Academy.* It is an Art Nouveau masterpiece. There has been a pub on the site since 1600 and the current one, with its marble, bronze, wood, and mosaics, was almost destroyed by redevelopment plans in the 1960s. That story is on a signboard inside. Go in if you can for it is worth a visit by any standard—Shakespearean or otherwise.

*After your libation, a subway (underpass) just outside of the door of the pub will take you under the street to the **Blackfriars tube station** (District and Circle Lines).*

Blackfriars Pub

WALK THREE

LINCOLN'S INN
FIELDS
AND ITS ENVIRONS

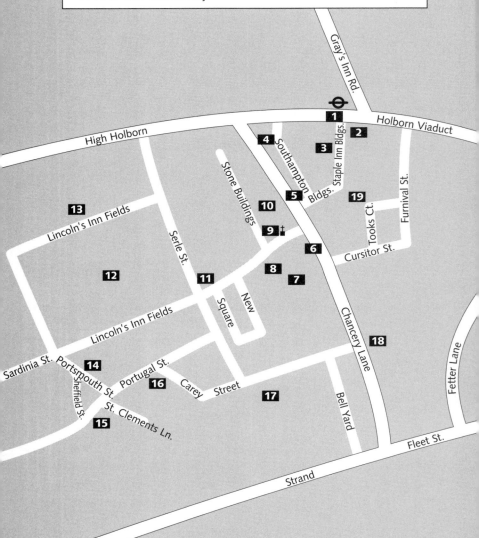

Walk Three

1 Chancery Lane station
2 Staple Inn
3 Society of Actuaries Hall
4 Southampton House
5 London Silver Vaults
6 Lincoln's Inn Gate House
7 #23 Old Buildings
8 Old Hall
9 Lincoln's Inn Chapel
10 Old Square
11 New Hall and Library

12 Lincoln's Inn Fields
13 Sir John Soane Museum
14 Old Curiosity Shop
15 Vere St. Theatre site
16 Lincoln's Inn Fields Theatre site
17 Law Courts Buildings
18 Former Public Records Office
19 Sponging House site
⊖ Tube Station

his walk contains some important Restoration the-
atre history and features as its centerpiece a visit to
Sir John Soane's Museum. This incredible private
home is not to be missed by any serious student of art, archi-
tecture, or theatre. There is also a possible visit to the London
Silver Vaults. Since the Soane Museum visit is a critical part
of this walk, you may want to double-check the current open-
ing hours, usually 10 to 5 Tuesday through Saturday. (No
admission charge at this date.)

Y*our starting point is the* **Chancery Lane tube station** *on the Central*
Line. Exit the station by the Holborn south side stairs (Exit 3). You will
come up right alongside **Staple Inn**. This is one of the very few original half-timbered frontages left in London. The name has designated
a gathering place for wool staplers from as early as the 14th century.
The term "staple" was used to classify the quality of cotton or wool—
indicating that it was of fine, long or short staple. In the 15th century the legal profession began using the Inn and it soon became an
official Inn of Chancery, whose function was to feed young legal trainees
into the advanced courses at nearby Gray's Inn or Lincoln's Inn.

What you are actually looking at here is only a much restored facade,
but it does date from 1568, which qualifies it as one of the few pre-
Great Fire views left in
London. Since we know
that William Shakespeare
visited the Great Hall at
Gray's Inn and the nearby
home of his patron, the
Earl of Southampton, we
can confidently assume
that he would still recognize the view today.

Staple Inn

3

A few feet farther along is a gateway. Turn right between Vodaphone and Sanford's Jewelers. Look carefully at the huge doors and make sure you read the sign underneath the arch as you pass through. We hope you left your horse tied up in the street outside. You will now find yourself in a pleasantly restored 18th-century courtyard. Should you be captivated by it, you are in the very best of company for it has been weaving its magic for some time. Charles Dickens described it this way in his novel *Edwin Drood*:

> [It] . . . imparts to the relieved pedestrian the sensation of having put cotton in his ears and velvet soles on his shoes. It is one of those nooks where a few smoky sparrows twitter in the smoky trees, as though they called to one another, let us play at country.

At the rear and to the right in the courtyard is located a fine little restored Elizabethan hall dating from 1580, which now belongs to the Society of Actuaries. It is not normally open to the public.

For an even more pleasant surprise penetrate into the second courtyard. There you will come upon an enchanting jewel of a garden complete with gurgling fountain and a rainbow of flowers. Here indeed is one of London's secret spots visited only by those who know where to go to escape the noisy ravages of city traffic. Even in winter the spot has a certain charm. Nathaniel Hawthorne, the 19th-century American novelist, also visited Staple Inn and, finding himself in the inner court, where you now stand, wrote in his journal:

> There was a surrounding seclusion of quiet dwelling houses, with beautiful green shrubbery and grass plots . . . and a great many sunflowers in full bloom. . . . I have a sense that bees were humming in the court, though this may have been suggested by my fancy, because the sound would have been so well suited to the scene. . . . In all the hundreds of years since London was built, it has not been able to sweep its roaring tide over that little island of quiet.

When you are fully refreshed, leave the inner courtyard of Staple Inn via the short flight of stairs at the back gate. The first formal street on the right is **Southampton Buildings**. *Henry Wriothesley the young Earl of Southampton lived*

Staple Inn first courtyard

Staple Inn inner court

with his mother in **Southampton House** *just up the way where Chancery Lane blends into Holborn.* We do not know exactly how Shakespeare met Southampton, but we do know he was one of the Bard's early and major patrons.

That Shakespeare was a regular visitor at Southampton House we can also be assured; he may even have lived there in 1593 when the plague closed the theatres. Will's first printed work, the long poem titled "Venus and Adonis," was dedicated to Southampton and some scholars believe that Southampton inspired many of the Sonnets as well. It is also thought that the premiere performance of *A Midsummer Night's Dream* was given in the great hall of the Earl's house on May 2, 1595. If that's not enough for this one little street, we can also note that in much later times the Shakespearean critics Charles Lamb and William Hazlitt both lived on Southampton Buildings.

You want to go straight ahead at this point, as turning right would put you back out onto Holborn. Keep looking at the building on your right for a small sign and a blue awning that says "The London Silver Vaults." Inside and down the stairs is enough sterling silver to keep the Lone Ranger in bullets for a lifetime. This side trip has nothing to do with theatre, but the vaults are well worth a visit; some of the items are priced quite reasonably. *If you do not wish to cross your palm with silver proceed straight ahead until Southampton Buildings terminates at* **Chancery Lane.**

London Silver Vaults entrance

3

**Tudor gatehouse
of Lincoln's Inn**

Directly across from you now is **Lincoln's Inn**, *one of the four London Inns that educate, certify, and provide office accommodation for the British legal profession. If you go about 100 yards to your left you will see a venerable Tudor gatehouse, which was restored in the reign of George V.* Some of the money to construct it was given by King Henry VIII. The playwright Ben Jonson, Shakespeare's friend and contemporary, is said to have worked as a mason on the gatehouse when he was a young man. *Enter the Inn by the gate and walk into the first court. Sir Tyrone Guthrie, the noted stage director, and his wife had their first London home in the attic of Number 23 Old Buildings, which is to your left.* They lived there for many years from early in the thirties until the middle fifties, when he was doing his exciting and pioneering work with the Old Vic Company, including Olivier's Freudian *Hamlet* in 1937, and Ralph Richardson's *Peer Gynt* in 1944. He later founded the Stratford, Ontario, Theatre and the Guthrie Theatre in Minneapolis. This quirky little flat figures often in the Guthrie mythology. *Walk on through the first court, turning a bit to your right, so you are walking along the open undercrofting of the* **Lincoln's Inn Chapel**. *Stop for a moment before moving through the arch ahead of you.*

Lincoln's Inn is the oldest of the four Inns of Court and its formal record books go back to 1422. The name comes from Henry

Lincoln's Inn (Old Hall)

de Lacey, the 14th-century Earl of Lincoln, who once owned some of the land on which the Inn stands. *A bit to the left is the Old Hall, which was built sometime between 1490 and 1520.* Sir Thomas More spent a good deal of his professional life there. Its most famous fictional use was the setting for the opening scene of Charles Dickens' *Bleak House:*

> And hard by Temple Bar, in Lincoln's Inn Hall . . . sits the Lord High Chancellor . . . ; and before him is the great cause, never to be understood, of Jarndyce vs. Jarndyce.

A large arch, separating the Old Hall and the Chapel, will pass you into the Old Square. If the chapel is open, you may wish to pay a visit. It was built in the 1620s, perhaps to plans by Inigo Jones. The dedication sermon was preached by Dr. John Donne, who served as preacher to Lincoln's Inn for six years before moving on to an appointment as Dean of St. Paul's Cathedral. The chapel bell has tolled curfew for Lincoln's Inn every evening at nine o'clock since 1596. It has also been the custom to toll the bell whenever a "bencher" of the Inn dies. Barristers from around the grounds would then send clerks out to discover who had passed away. It was perhaps an echo of this custom that inspired Donne to write in 1624,

Lincoln's Inn (New Hall and Library)

No man is an island, entire of itself; every man is a piece
of the continent, a part of the main; if a clod be washed
away by the sea, Europe is the less, as well as if a promon-
tory were, as well as if a manor of thy friend's or of thine
own were; any man's death diminishes me, because I am
involved in mankind; and therefore never send to know
for whom the bell tolls; it tolls for thee.

3

*If the chapel is not open, continue walking into the large square, skirt-
ing the lovely garden on your left. Head for the large red brick (with
striking cream trim) Victorian Tudor New Hall and Library.* It is not
normally open to the public, but occasionally you can get into a con-
versation with an Inn member, who will offer to take you inside.

*Continue along in front of the New Hall toward an ornate gatehouse
made of the same red brick and cream stone. Exit Lincoln's Inn via that
gate. You will now find yourself on the largest square in central London—
Lincoln's Inn Fields.* It was laid out by the Neoclassic architect and
scene designer Inigo Jones in 1618. *On the south side of the square
(ahead of you and to the left) are the hall and buildings of the Royal
College of Surgeons.* Most of the rest of the elegant premises surrounding
the central park are occupied by law offices, but in the 17th century,
residents like the flamboyant actress Nell Gwynn gave the area a slightly
different tone. The square was also one of London's more popular
dueling grounds before it was fenced in.

*Walk around the square to your right. You will go past some pub-
lic restrooms. You are looking for Number 13, which is Sir John Soane's
Museum.* It is open Tuesday through Saturday from 10 to 5, and
admission is free, but groups must book in advance. This remarkable house contains the quirky and constantly amazing collections
of the distinguished architect whose main claim to fame was the original design for the Bank of England building. The house and its
furnishings were left to the nation and are displayed substantially
as they were left on the day of Soane's death in 1837. Inside is a
wealth of material including a fair number of interesting theatrical
paintings and busts. Make sure you do not miss the little
Shakespearean Recess on your way up to the second floor. You will
also find statuary of all periods, exquisite furniture, jewel-like rooms,
Egyptian sarcophagi, and finally the stunning picture room with
Hogarth's brilliant paintings of the Rake's Progress. Soane
acquired the Hogarth paintings from the actor David Garrick, who
originally had them in his country house along the Thames. Don't
be afraid to ask questions while touring the house. The caretakers
are friendly and well informed.

*Upon leaving the Soane Museum continue to your right around the
square toward the Southwest corner where Portsmouth Street leaves
Lincoln's Inn Fields.*

3

Sir John Soane's Museum

*As you walk down Portsmouth Street you will pass on your left a quaint little building that claims to be Charles Dickens' original **Old Curiosity Shop**.* Most sources put the Old Curiosity Shop somewhere behind the National Portrait Gallery at the bottom of Charing Cross Road, but this one is indeed old and certainly has plenty of old English atmosphere.

The Old Curiosity Shop

Turn to the right a bit at the Old Curiosity Shop and move down **Sheffield Street** *until you reach* **Portugal Street**. It was at this corner that Mr. Thomas Killigrew, with a precious royal patent freshly in hand, installed a company of actors in November of 1660. The building had been remodeled from a tennis court, and was called the Vere Street Theatre. Killigrew and his King's Men opened the theatre on December 8, 1660, with a production of Shakespeare's *Henry IV, Part I*. A bit later came a production of *Othello*, which probably featured the first appearance in an English public theatre of a native-born professional actress in a major dramatic role. We do not know her name or the exact date, but she did apparently act the role of Desdemona sometime before the end of 1660.

Turn left into Portugal Street. It takes a quick bend left, crosses St. Clement's Lane, and then bends left past the **George IV pub**. *Walk on for a short distance along the side of the British Library of Political and Economic Science until you reach* **Carey Street** *coming in from the right.* Had you been walking here in 1660 you would have seen on your left another theatre converted from a tennis court (Lisle's Tennis Court). It's also true that had you been walking here on October 10, 1940, you might have had another kind of theatrical experience during a German air raid. *Look at the shrapnel hole in the old W.H. Smith sign on the corner building to your right.*

But back to Lisle's Tennis Court in June of 1660: It was leased by the second Restoration patent holder, Sir William Davenant. Davenant called his newly converted tennis court the Lincoln's Inn Fields Theatre and opened it in June of 1660, a full five months before Mr. Killigrew got his Vere Street Theatre operating. Davenant's first production was a revival of *The Siege of Rhodes*, an opera that had been done privately at his home, Rutland House, during the Commonwealth.

Its opening here therefore marked the first officially sanctioned public production of a play in London since the closing of the theatres by Oliver Cromwell in 1642. It also introduced changeable wing and drop continental scenery for the first time to the public London stage. Inigo Jones, the architect and designer we have mentioned previously, had brought the Italian scenic ideas to England and used them in his Court Masques in the early 1600s. Davenant's scene designer John Webb, who was a pupil of Jones, carried on the tradition.

Davenant's company played at the Lincoln's Inn Fields Theatre until 1671 when they moved to their Christopher Wren–designed Dorset Garden Theatre (see Walk Five). The Lincoln's Inn Fields Theatre was not vacant for long. Killigrew and his company had moved from the Vere Street Theatre to their Theatre Royal in Bridges Street in 1663. Unfortunately a fire destroyed that theatre in 1672 and they moved into the vacant Lincoln's Inn Fields site for two years until their own Wren-designed theatre, the second Drury Lane (see Walk Twelve), was ready for them in 1674. After Killigrew's departure the building reverted to a tennis court again for a while before being demolished. A new "second" Lincoln's Inn Fields Theatre was built on this same site in 1695 by the playwright William Congreve. It was managed by the actor Thomas Betterton and featured as leading actresses Elizabeth Barry and Anne Bracegirdle. The inaugural production was Congreve's *Love for Love* and King William III was in the audience. This second Lincoln's Inn Fields Theatre was torn down by the theatrical entrepreneur Mr. Christopher Rich and his son, who built another theatre on the site, which opened in 1714 with James Quin as the major star. It was in this "third" Lincoln's Inn Fields Theatre, in 1726, that John Gay's *Beggar's Opera* premiered. It was so successful that the common joke at the time was that it made Gay rich and Rich gay. The third Lincoln's Inn Fields Theatre was finally abandoned in 1732. By this time the Covent Garden area in the West End had been established as the new entertainment center of the city. Theatres and theatrical activity have never penetrated this section of the city again.

After finishing your imaginative reconstructions of the Lincoln's Inn Fields Theatres, you can continue your stroll by turning right on **Carey Street** *and following it to* **Chancery Lane**. *The gray bulk of the rear of the Law Courts buildings will be on your right.* The back doors are often used by members of the legal profession and sometimes by high profile litigants who wish to slip in or out unobserved. *At the Serle Street intersection note the statue of Sir Thomas More on the building to your left.* The building itself is one of those rather attractive little gems that you can often stumble on in the city. It is not ancient (only 1886), but its red brick and creamy Portland stone trim makes for a finely chiseled appearance. Note also how the graceful swag design seems to soften and lighten the upper wall areas. *Just beyond is one of the smallest and oldest pubs in the city, the* **Seven Stars**, *claiming to date back to the early 1600s.* Conversations in there lean heavily to matters legal. If you go in watch out for Tom, the publican's cat. He's often underfoot. *About 50 yards farther along is Number 56, A. Woodhouse and Son, Ltd. (The Silver Mousetrap), that has a fascinating shop front dated 1690.*

When you reach Chancery Lane you will see across the street and a bit to your right the former **Public Record Office**. It was established in 1838 to gather together in one place all of the official records of England since the Norman Conquest including the Magna Carta, the Domesday Book, and the last will and testament of one William Shakespeare. Unfortunately the very size of the collection created a severe space problem and everything has now been moved to a new repository near Kew Gardens (Ruskin Avenue, Kew TW9 4DU). The facilities are available to serious researchers and guided tours can be arranged (Tel 020 8392 5393).

*Since there is little to see there now, you can turn right and walk down to **Fleet Street** to catch a bus or turn left and return to High Holborn and the Chancery Lane tube station where you started. If you do choose to go back up to Chancery Lane, look out for **Cursitor Street**. When you reach it, turn right and then make a left into **Tooks Court**.* Here in this dingy alley the sparkling 18th-century dramatist, Richard Brinsley Sheridan, of *School for Scandal* fame, spent the last days of his life in what was known as a sponging house—a sort of halfway house for debtors that was one step removed from a real prison. *Follow Tooks Court around until you reach a "T" intersection. Turn left on **Furnival Street** which will take you out to **Holborn viaduct**. A left turn here will lead you back to the **Chancery Lane underground station**.*

Holborn viaduct

WALK FOUR

Strolling the Strand: from Trafalgar Square to Aldwych

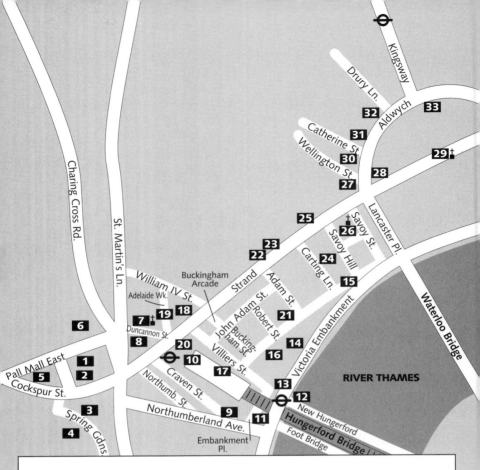

Walk Four

1. Trafalgar Square
2. Nelson's Column
3. Admiralty Arch
4. Old Spring Gardens Area
5. Canada House
6. National Gallery
7. St. Martin-in-the-Fields
8. South Africa House
9. Playhouse Theatre
10. Charing Cross Station
11. Embankment Place
12. Gilbert Monument
13. Embankment Tube Station
14. Embankment Gardens
15. Monument to Sir Arthur Sullivan
16. Water Gate of York House
17. Players Theatre
18. Coutts Bank
19. Wilde Memorial
20. Charing Cross Station Hotel
21. New Adelphi Terrace
22. Adelphi Theatre
23. Vaudeville Theatre
24. Savoy Theatre
25. Strand Palace
26. Queen's Chapel of the Savoy
27. Lyceum Theatre
28. Site of Old Gaiety Theatre
29. St. Mary-le-Strand
30. Duchess Theatre
31. Strand Theatre
32. Aldwych Theatre
33. Bush House
⊖ Tube Station

STARTING POINT: Trafalgar Square (The nearest tube stations are Charing Cross on the Bakerloo, Northern, and Jubilee lines or Leicester Square on the Piccadilly or Northern Lines. A great many bus lines will also deposit you right on the square.)

APPROXIMATE TIME: Two hours.

Nearly every visitor to London will want to cover at least some parts of this route. What we have tried to do is emphasize the theatres and theatrical interest areas while mentioning briefly some of the other more general points of interest. You could do Walk Four and Five on the same day as the end of Walk Four is the beginning of Walk Five, but if that is your plan we would suggest arriving at the Trafalgar Square starting point before 10:00 A.M.

Someone once said, quite aptly, that **Trafalgar Square** is simply seven streets coming together in chaos. *However you arrive, you should make your way through the traffic and pigeons to the center. Once stationed somewhere near the middle you can look at the fountains and the 145-foot-tall* **Nelson's Column.** The spire was in place by 1842 and the huge lions were added in 1864. Edward Landseer made the originals in clay for casting in bronze, not helped by the fact that the aged lion, lent to him as a model by the London Zoo, died before he had completed his task. As he struggled to finish the commission the artist expressed the hope that he would "neither disappoint the country nor the brave Nelson in my treatment of these symbols of our national defenses." *Whitehall runs south directly in front of the column to give you a distant view of the Clock Tower of the Houses of Parliament.* In that tower is the 13-ton bell that is actually called **Big Ben.**

To the right of Whitehall is **Admiralty Arch.** *If you pass beneath it you will find yourself on the Mall and eventually at Buckingham Palace.* That could be your route if you intend to make that grand theatrical spectacle of "the Changing of the Guard" a part of your London experience. The space around the arch was occupied by the Spring Gardens residential area in the 18th century and Colley Cibber (1671–1757), actor, manager, playwright, and Poet Laureate of England, lived there from 1711 to 1714.

ANNO·DECIMO·EDWARDI·SEPTIMI·REGIS·
·VICTORIÆ·REGINÆ·CIVES·GRATISSIMI·MDCCCCX·

4

Admiralty Arch

Continuing to move your eyes around the square to the right, the next major building you will see is **Canada House**, *which was built by Robert Smirke in 1827.* It was originally a gentlemen's club. The entire north side of the square, directly opposite Whitehall, is occupied by the **National Gallery.** The main fabric of the building was designed by William Wilkins in 1838 and a major addition was completed in the early 1990s. It contains one of the truly great collections of paintings in the Western World and should be the subject of a separate visit. It's the ideal choice for that rainy day when walking just seems out of the question. During World War II all the pictures were removed for their safety to underground storage in Wales. But at the height of the Blitz, Dame Myra Hess gave lunchtime piano recitals here to packed houses. Laurence Olivier and Ralph Richardson were released by the Admiralty in 1944 to lead the Old Vic Company when it returned to London and they held their rehearsals in the National Gallery while the V2 rockets were falling all around them. Most members of the company dove for cover when the rocket-engines cut out, but these two ex-servicemen never even flinched, and carried on rehearsing.

Turning to your right again, your eye should fall on the gleaming white spire of James Gibbs' **St. Martin-in-the-Fields** *(1726).* In an older church on this same site the Restoration dramatist George Farquhar (1678–1707) was buried. Even though he died before he was 30, he managed to produce a body of work that included two extremely fine and durable comedies, *The Recruiting Officer* (1706) and *The Beaux Stratagem* (1707). Also buried in the old St. Martin-in-the-Fields was everybody's favorite Restoration actress, Miss Nell Gwynn (1650–1687). Nell's story has been told in any number of books as well as in the popular old melodrama, *Sweet Nell of Old Drury*. Her fame is all the more extraordinary considering she was only on stage for about five years before retiring to become the mistress of Charles II.

St. Martin-in-the-fields

A bit farther to the right is the newest building on the square, South Africa House, built in 1935. Our route today will take us to the right of South Africa House and up the Strand, which is a part of the major ancient route from the political center of London in Westminster to the commercial center in the City of London. The very name of the street recalls its nearness to the river Thames in days gone by. In the Middle Ages the south side of the street was lined with the opulent riverside palaces of the nobility.

Finish your snapshots now and make your way to the south or right side of the Strand. The very first intersection is now a wide sidewalk, which is still named Northumberland Street. The Elizabethan playwright Ben Jonson (1572–1637) may have been born and did spend his boyhood on that street. *If you're already thirsty, the well-known and very touristy Sherlock Holmes pub is about one block down.*

But your route today takes you to the next corner, Craven Street, where you should turn right between Boots and Next. The American statesman, inventor, and printer Benjamin Franklin lived at Number 36 (the sixth door on your left) during his stay in London. There is no longer a number on the door and the bronze plaque, though restored in 1998, is dark and hard to see unless you are looking for it. There is also a bit of a mystery about the Franklin house. During the 1998 restoration some human bones were found under the back garden. Some theorize that Franklin allowed physician friends who were dissecting corpses at the time to use the garden for clandestine burial purposes. *At the lower end of Craven Street you pass an almost lost theatre, the Playhouse, also called The Avenue.* The exterior dates from 1882 and the interior dates from 1907. It was so close to the old Charing Cross railroad station, according to Mander and Mitchenson in *The Lost Theatres of London*, that a part of the station collapsed into the theatre in 1905. George Bernard Shaw's *Arms and the Man* was given its first perfor-

4

The Playhouse

mance here in 1894. Alec Guinness' first professional appearance was in 1934 in a nonspeaking part as a juror in a play called *Libel*, which transferred to the Playhouse after opening in the old King's Theatre in Hammersmith. He was paid £1 a week, and these humble beginnings echo those of many of the other great names encountered in these walks. This part of the city had become unfashionable by World War II and the theatre closed down. In 1951 it became a BBC radio studio. When the Corporation departed in the late seventies it was almost derelict for a few years, but it has now been refurbished and reopened as a café and a periodic performance space.

*Turn left now into **Embankment Place**.* Until the late 1980s this huge arch under the Charing Cross station tracks was a moody, urine-smelling tunnel filled with cheap fish and chip shops and a fair number of the West End's homeless population. It appeared to be in no way altered from the time when a young Charles Dickens worked nearby in a shoe blacking shop. The author's experiences and the place were described vividly in *David Copperfield*. Now most of the homeless have been shooed elsewhere, and the new sanitized tunnel is quite civilized, but rather cold.

*You will emerge from under the bridge at **Villiers Street**. On your right is the **Embankment tube station**, where you can buy lovely and reasonably priced fresh flowers from a cart that has been there since at least the middle 1970s. Turn right into the tube station and walk through the station to the river side. Right across the road and a bit to your left is a nice memorial to W. S. Gilbert of Gilbert and Sullivan fame. Return back across the street and back through the station. Then look for an entrance on your right into the **Embankment Gardens**—a lovely pocket* *park that is always ablaze with exquisite plantings of seasonal flowers.* The park has a bandstand and on nice days is usually packed with tourists and workers from the surrounding stores and offices. *Take the right fork and walk on to the far end of the park just past the rear entrance to the **Savoy Hotel**, where you will find a marvelous **monument to Sir Arthur Sullivan** of the Gilbert and Sullivan partnership.* Note the symbolic accoutrements off to one side—a comic mask, a lute, and a libretto. A grieving classical maiden embraces the plinth that holds Sullivan's bronze bust. Engraved on one side is the following verse attributed to W. S. Gilbert. "Is life a boon?/ If so it must befall/ That death, where'er he call/ Must call too soon." It is rather more romantic than the austerely balanced bas relief tribute to Gilbert you viewed just outside the park.

4

Monument to Sir Arthur Sullivan

We need to finish the triumvirate now; turn around and stroll back down the path about 20 steps. Just at the rear door of the Savoy Hotel turn right into a small open space. There you will find a planter/sundial dedicated to Richard D'Oyly Carte, founder and builder of the Savoy Theatre and the Savoy Hotel and of course the producer of the Gilbert and Sullivan Savoy Operas.

Finish walking back through the park taking the right fork in the path so that the bandstand is on your left as you approach the exit.

*Just before you leave the park, glance to your right at the old **Water Gate of York House**, dating from 1626.* It gives you a good sense

W.S. Gilbert Plaque

Water Gate of York House

of where the river-bank was in the 17th century before the creation of the Victoria Embankment. York House was the city dwelling place of the Archbishop of York and fronted on the Strand. Sir Francis Bacon was born there in 1561 and was baptized and buried in the old St. Martin-in-the-Fields when it was really in the fields. If you have taken the earlier walks you will also already have visited the enclaves of the Bishop of Winchester in Southwark and the Bishop of Ely near Chancery Lane. Remember that it was common for the outlying bishops to have significant estates and dwellings in London convenient to the political and commercial power centers of the country.

*If you leave the park now, you will find yourself back out on **Villiers Street**. Turn right up Villiers Street and look on the left for a large opening labeled "The Arches—Shopping." It is approximately across from a pub now called the Princess of Wales, formerly known as the Prince of Wales. Diana, it seems, has been recognized as a better draw than Charles.*

*Turn left into the Arches arcade, which again is a poor substitute for the soot-stained gloom that used to grace the station approaches, but at least this one is dark enough to convey some small bit of mood. About halfway down on the left you will come across an arched doorway that led to the **Players Theatre**, which was the only purveyor of traditional British music hall entertainment in the West End.* As this book goes to press, the Players Theatre is closed. The new lessees and their artistic director, Michael Kirk, have promised to work with the Players board to refurbish the space and to continue a bill of varied entertainment including traditional music hall and a seasonal pantomime. The theatre will be renamed the Villiers Theatre and will reopen sometime in 2003. The theatre history buff should make arrangements to see a show here if possible.

Music hall, as a genre, seems to have begun in the upper rooms of neighborhood taverns in the 18th century. It spread to larger clubs or halls such as Sadler's Wells in the 19th century after gas lighting made longer evening journeys safer and more practical. It reached the peak of its popularity in the later years of the 19th and the early years of the 20th century. In format the music hall show is a jingo-

Players Theatre

istic blend of song, comic patter, dance, and occasional circus-style acts, all held together by a master of ceremonies called the Chairman. Like American vaudeville it fell victim to those electronic upstarts, the cinema and the wireless.

Getting back to the Players Theatre itself—the original space was back down Villiers Street about 100 yards just across from the exit to the Embankment Gardens. It was destroyed when the new Charing Cross station complex was built. Various live theatre enterprises occupied that old building from 1867 to 1903 when the theatre closed down. It was a cinema off and on over the next 35 years, was mostly derelict during the World War II and then reopened as the Players Theatre in 1947. Its most memorable show was the premiere production of Sandy Wilson's musical *The Boy Friend*, which opened in 1953. The reconstructed interior is a careful copy of the old one and should continue to provide you with an appropriately Victorian evening. As the holder of the only music hall license in London, the Players was the only theatre in town where you could legally bring your drinks into the auditorium. This was a definite help when you needed to wash down the official Players Club gourmet interval repast of a huge banger on French bread. This restriction has been relaxed recently as we have noticed a number of West End theatres serving up drinks in plastic glasses and allowing them to be taken into the auditorium.

Retrace your steps back out of the arch now and turn left on Villiers Street. When you reach the Strand again, you may cross the street and examine the startling home of **Coutts Bank**. The exterior walls of this building are by the great Georgian architect, John Nash. In the 1970s the entire building was gutted and inside the old walls the new bank was built. During regular business hours you can enter the three-story glass frontage and take a gleaming silver escalator up to the main banking level. There, in what their historical brochure describes as "one of the first landscaped, atrium-styled, banking halls" in the country, you can conduct your financial affairs amidst ferns, flowers, fountains, and fishponds. In 1994 there were persistent reports of the sighting of a ghost in Elizabethan dress wandering about the bank. This led to historical investigations into who lived on the site in the 16th century. One apparent occupant was the Fourth Duke of Norfolk, who rashly attempted to marry secretly Mary Queen of Scots, for which Queen Elizabeth had him tried for treason and beheaded in the Tower of London in 1572. His troubled spirit was exorcized in a Roman Catholic ceremony attended by members of the present Duke of Norfolk's family, and it seems was laid to rest, as there have been no further sightings of his ghost.

The bank itself, which has occupied several sites on both sides of the Strand since 1692, has had and continues to have theatrical connections. George Campbell, an early partner, was an investor in Rich's Covent Garden in the 1730s. Several 18th-century theatrical figures banked with Coutts including John Phillip Kemble, Richard Brindsley Sheridan, Edmund Kean, and Madame Vestries. Thomas Coutts, who headed the bank for over 50 years in the late 18th and early 19th century, held permanent boxes at most of the major West End theatres. He lent money to Augustus Harris, the manager of Covent Garden, and was given in gratitude a sterling silver free pass disk good for 83 years. His second wife, Harriot Mellon, was an actress. They married only four days after the funeral of his first wife. He was 80, she 40 and strangely no love was lost between her and the remainder of the family. The banker's association with theatre folk was tolerated, but marriage was quite another matter.

Greeters at Coutts Bank

Other important 19th-century bank customers from the world of the theatre were Sir Henry Irving, the great actor-manager of the nearby Lyceum Theatre, the actor Charles Kean, and the manager-impessario Richard D'Oyly Carte, who produced the Gilbert and Sullivan operettas and built the Savoy theatre and the Savoy Hotel. The theatrical associations continue to this day. Sir John Gielgud was thought to have been a customer and Sir Andrew Lloyd Webber is rumored to be a present client.

Back down on street level, notice the large ficus tree growing in the lower lobby. It was imported from Florida and does not lean toward the light because it is planted in a huge slowly rotating drum.

Outside again turn to your right back toward Trafalgar Square. You will shortly come to a pedestrian path named **Adelaide Street.** *Turn right a few paces and note a dark coffin-shaped granite block surmounted by an equally ghoulish bronze of Oscar Wilde.* This unusual tribute to the great playwright is by Maggi Hambling. The poignant inscription on the top of the sarcophagus reads, "We are all in the gutter, but some of us are looking at the stars."

After meditating for a moment on this macabre stone stuck in the middle of a busy footpath, return to the **Strand.** *You are now in a position to take note across the way of the old frontage of E. M. Barry's* **Charing Cross Station and Hotel.** In the open space in front of the building is the Victorian monument, also by Barry, that commemorates the last of the twelve Eleanor crosses that were built by Edward I in the 13th century. Eleanor of Castile, Edward's wife, died near Lincoln in 1290 while accompanying her husband on a campaign. Her body was carried back to Westminster and Edward erected a cross at each place where the bearers rested on the journey back to London. The original London Cross, destroyed by Cromwell's forces in 1647, actually stood at the top of Whitehall where the equestrian statue of Charles I stands today.

Recross the Strand now back to the station side of the street and turn to your left. Walk back past the station, across Villiers Street, and watch for a tiny passage called **Buckingham Arcade** *(just past McDonald's), which when taken through to the right, will lead to* **Buckingham Street** *and several fine original 17th-century houses.* An extraordinary number of famous men visited or lodged on this short street, but for our purposes the man of most interest was the great diarist Samuel Pepys, who lived at both Number 12 and Number 14 during the years 1679 to 1700. (The brown plaque resides on number 12 on your right.) His diaries give us some of our most revealing accounts of 17th-century theatrical and social life. *At the bottom of Buckingham Street there is a nice view of the back side of the York House Water Gate and the Embankment Gardens.*

E. M. Barry Victorian Monument

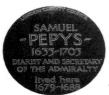

Retrace your steps now back up Buckingham Street and take the first turn to the right, which is John Adam Street. You are now in the area known as the Adelphi. It is a Greek word for "brothers" and was chosen by the Scottish architects and developers Robert, James, and William Adam as the name for their residential and commercial development on the site beginning in 1768. A lot of the current building in the area is from the 1930s and later, but much of it still sits on the gigantic foundation arches designed by the Adam brothers to level off and use the riverbank.

As you pass up John Adam Street, a modern apartment block now appears on the right about where Number 17–19 used to be. The actor, playwright, Shakespeare scholar, and friend of George Bernard Shaw, Mr. Harley Granville Barker (1877–1946) lived in a house on this site as did the modern actor Sir Cedric Hardwicke.

At Number 16 on the left is a blue plaque marking the site of the home, from 1803 to his death in 1827, of the caricaturist Thomas Rowlandson. His work included some fascinating scenes of 18th-century theatrical life that have become standard illustrations in theatre history textbooks.

When you reach Robert Street (named for brother Robert Adam), pause for a moment and look to your left. This is now an office block called the Little Adelphi, but the historic Little Theatre occupied the site

Adam Adelphi Terrace

from 1910 until the late 1940s. The Little Theatre was a tiny band-box of a place with 250 seats and an Adam-inspired interior. It was built on the site of the very first Coutts Bank building and had the most secure dressing rooms of any theatre in the world, since they were constructed inside the old bank's strongrooms.

The original leaseholder was the well-known actress, feminist, and suffragette, Gertrude Kingston (1866–1937). Her first offering was, most aptly, *Lysistrata*, and Miss Kingston apparently played the leading role for all it was worth. So that female authors could be produced without prejudice, she had the unusual policy of withholding the playwright's name from the public until after the first reviews appeared. According to Mander and Mitchenson in *The Lost Theatres of London*, George Bernard Shaw's *Fanny's First Play* was given its original production at the Little Theatre in 1911 and directed by Shaw himself. Even though the author's name was listed as Xxxxxxx Xxxx, it was so successful that it was moved to another house, where it continued to run on for a total of 622 performances, making it Shaw's longest original run. Shaw knew Gertrude Kingston well and wrote the part of Catherine II in *Great Catherine* for her. Another 1911 event in the Little Theatre was Noël Coward's first stage appearance as Prince Mussel in a children's fairy tale called *The Goldfish*.

Although a balcony was added in 1912 to expand the seating capacity, the original Adam gold and wedgewood blue auditorium was kept intact. The theatre was damaged during a German air raid during World War I, rebuilt, and then severely damaged again by bombing in World War II. Even the safest air raid shelters of any theatre in London (the old Coutts bank vaults again), could not save the Little Theatre. After standing derelict for more than four years after World War II, the building was finally demolished and replaced by an office block.

*Turn to your right now, away from the Little Theatre, and walk a few paces up Robert Street. On your right, stretching down toward the river (note the square—not round—blue plaque), was the **Adelphi Court**, an apartment and hotel complex, where several literary figures lived at one time or another.* At Number 1, young Master William Betty lived from 1833 to 1845. As a child of ten, Betty played major tragic roles like Hamlet and Macbeth, made a small fortune, and retired to live a life of ease. Sir James Barrie, author of *Peter Pan* and *The Admirable Crichton*, and John Galsworthy, author of a series of real-

Detail from the current New Adelphi

istic social problem plays such as *Strife* (1909) and *Justice* (1910), were both tenants in this block. *When you reach the end of the street turn left and cross in front of the Art Deco New Adelphi Terrace, which was built after the grand Adam terrace of that same name was demolished in 1936. Stop at a convenient place about halfway down the length of the building and read the following:*

4

> From the 1770s the original Adelphi was one of London's smartest addresses and it attracted a bevy of glittering names. One of the very first and most distinguished of the old Adelphi residents was the 18th-century actor/manager David Garrick. He moved into the center apartment facing the river in 1772 and lived there until his death in 1779. The cream of the world of arts and letters passed through his drawing room, including Dr. Samuel Johnson, Sir Joshua Reynolds, Robert Adam, Dr. Charles Burney, and Fanny Burney, his vivacious daughter. Mrs. Garrick lived on after her husband's death for another 43 years and died in the front drawing room that looked out over the Thames.

Other theatrical residents of the old Adelphi were William Terriss, an actor we will hear more about in a few pages, Richard D'Oyly Carte, who lived in apartment number 4 from 1888 to 1901 while he was producing the Savoy Operas; and George Bernard Shaw, who occupied apartment number 10 from 1900 to 1919. The Adam brothers themselves kept apartment number 4, right next to Garrick's, for several years. The occupant of number 9 in 1775 was a Mr. John Robinson, Secretary of the Treasury. His rather whimsical theatre connection occurs as a result of the acid tongue of dramatist Richard Brinsley Sheridan. It seems that Robinson had been given the task of disseminating ministerial bribes from his treasury position. Sheridan got wind of it and attacked the government's corruption in Parliament. When challenged to name the wrongdoer, Sheridan gazed at the Treasury Bench and replied, "Yes, I could name him as soon as I can say Jack Robinson." And we remember old Jack to this day.

Finish your cross in front of the length of the 1936 Adelphi Terrace now. Turn the corner at the end of the building and you will be on Adam Street. The Adam brothers were definitely not given to modesty when it came to naming streets. *Keep your eye out on the right for Number 7 Adam Street, with its dark brick and cream trim.* Designers, take note, as this is a virtually unspoiled Adam house and gives you a superb sense of the distinctive Adam decorative style. *Number 9 became the new home of the Green Room Club in 1997.* The original club was founded by David Garrick and it has traditionally catered for the more proletarian end of the acting profession, rather than for the distinguished leading actors who frequent the club actually named after Garrick. The Green Room has also been forced to be much more peripatetic in its premises; its most recent previous home was opposite the stage door of the Haymarket Theatre.

Otherwise the solid blocks of newer buildings today even cover up old streets such as the now vanished Salisbury Street, where Oscar Wilde once lived. Cecil Street was also once located somewhere to your right. The actor Edmund Kean (1790–1833) lived there while a young unknown. The story is told how after his first big success he ran up the stairs at number 21 Cecil Street and shouted to his wife and son, "Mary! You shall ride in your carriage, and you Charley, shall go to Eton."

Adam house

You have now almost circumnavigated the new Adelphi Terrace with its sleek 1930 style streamlining. If you want to view another lovely Adam frontage, turn left on John Adam Street and look on the right for Number 2, which has been the home of the Royal Society for the Encouragement of Arts, Manufactures, and Commerce since 1774. Prince Philip is the current president. The society is housed in Numbers 2–8 on this street and Number 18 Adam Street around the corner, the basement of which contains some of the old storage vaults upon which the whole Adelphi development was built.

Retrace your steps back to Adam Street, turn left and walk on up to the Strand. You will be passing on your left the site of another one of those lost theatres so lovingly described by Mander and Mitchenson. This time it is the **Tivoli Theatre of Varieties**, which was built in 1890 on the site of a beer garden and restaurant at the corner of Adam Street and the Strand. It operated as a music hall until 1914, then stood derelict for a while, and was finally demolished. The Tivoli Cinema was built on the site in 1923, but it was damaged during the Blitz and it too was pulled down to make way for a department store and finally the current New South Wales House.

*Back out on the Strand proper you can see, directly across the busy street, the facade of a surviving theatre: the **Adelphi**.* This is the fourth theatre on the site since 1806. The current Adelphi seats more than 1400 people and opened in 1930 with the Rogers and Hart musical

Adelphi Theatre

Evergreen. There is little of real historical import to note about the shows that filled the theatre up to the late 1950s. Then Bea Lilly opened *Auntie Mame.* That success was followed by the scenically spectacular production of Lionel Bart's *Blitz* in 1962. The motorized platforms and moving bridges of its scenic design had a seminal influence on the modern, mechanized designs of John Bury. Anna Naegle played herself in a musical called *Charlie Girl* beginning in 1965 and it ran for almost 2000 performances until 1971. In recent years the theatre has seen a string of musicals including *Sunset Boulevard* and *Chicago.*

The Adelphi has the melancholy distinction of being the only theatre in the country where an actor was assassinated at the stage door. This was William Terriss (1847–1897), a leading member of Henry Irving's company for some years, who was stabbed in the back by a crazed small-part actor with an imagined grievance. Terriss was known affectionately to the British public as "Breezy Bill," and also as "Number 1 Adelphi Terriss," as much of his best work was done when he was living there. On the centenary of Terriss' death Sir Donald Sinden unveiled a plaque commemorating the event at the stage door on Maiden Lane. (You will have a chance to inspect it and hear a bit more about poor Mr. Terriss if you take Walk 12, Part III.)

Not too far to the right of the Adelphi, you will also see the front of the Vaudeville Theatre. This is the third theatre built on that site since 1870, although the frontage now visible was retained from the second rebuilding in 1891. The interior has seen some major redecoration since the 1926 rebuilding but no real structural changes. Its fare has been mainly light comedy and musical revue, but in 1911 it had a true blockbuster when Sarah Bernhardt played Pelleas to Mrs. Patrick Campbell's Melisande. The longest run in the house was the musical *Salad Days*, which carried on for over 2300 performances from 1954 to 1960.

You should still be standing at the intersection of the Strand and Adam Street. Turn right and continue your walk down the Strand. At the corner of Carting Lane is the Coal Hole tavern. The site was originally the coal cellars for the Savoy Palace and later may also have been a brothel. In the early 19th century it was already a tavern frequented by the coal heavers who unloaded barges on the Thames. The actor Edmund Kean, who as we just noted lived nearby, frequented the tavern and, according to John Wittich, founded the Wolf Parlour Club there in May, 1815, for "repressed husbands who were not allowed to sing in their baths." There is a sign in the back of the pub noting the event. According to Elizabeth Sharland in *A Theatrical Feast*, Kean was also noted for varying his diet depending on the

Vaudeville Theatre

type of role he played. He ate roast pork before playing tyrants, raw beef before playing a murderer, and boiled mutton if playing a lover. No record exists of what he played if he had ham for dinner.

There are many atmospheric nooks in the Coal Hole, especially in the basement, and a late night visit might easily find you in the company of Savoy Theatre actors partaking of an after-show libation. Sharland mentions that it was a favorite haunt of Richard Harris and Richard Burton when the latter was playing Hamlet at The Old Vic just on the other side of Waterloo Bridge.

*Moving on another few steps will bring you to the head of **Savoy Court**, the only two-way street in London which you enter and drive on the right-hand side. To learn more about the Savoy, cross the Court and read the series of metal plaques that are mounted along the side of the building. When you finish the story you will be almost at the entrance of the luxurious, world famous **Savoy Hotel**. To your right will be the equally famous **Savoy Theatre**.* Richard D'Oyly Carte built the first Savoy Theatre in 1881 and looked convincingly to the future by making it the first theatre in London to be lit by incandescent light. A plaque in Carting Lane on the back of the theatre declares that it was the first public building in the world to be completely lit by electricity. D'Oyly Carte's remarks at the opening, as cited by Mander and

4

Savoy Court

Mitchenson, did show, however, that he regarded the experiment with some fear and trepidation. In lines that are amusing today, D'Oyly Carte assured his patrons that the entire building had also been piped for gas and that the pilot light on the central chandelier would always be kept lit so that if the new lights failed, the whole interior could be illuminated within seconds by reliable gas mantles.

The Savoy Theatre opened on October 10, 1881, with Gilbert and Sullivan's *Patience*. The Prince and Princess of Wales were in the audience. From then on until 1907, it saw a set of now classic pearls with softly glowing names like *Iolanthe*, *The Sorcerer*, *The Mikado*, and *The Gondoliers*. Apart from what became known generally as the Savoy Operas, there was also success with an historical piece titled *Merrie England*. Then the theatre fell on hard times and was closed for a while, until in 1907, the Vedrenne/Grandville-Barker partnership had a run of successful Shaw and Shakespeare revivals. Most spectacularly Barker and Vedrenne staged seasons in 1912–1914 of *The Winter's Tale*, *Twelfth Night*, and *A Midsummer Night's Dream*, which revolutionized the presentation of Shakespeare.

In the 1920s there were several long-run hits culminating with R. C. Sheriff's highly charged war drama *Journey's End* in 1929. The story of this show could occupy a book by itself. It had originally been scheduled for a two-performance trial run at the Apollo Theatre. A struggling young actor by the name of Laurence Olivier took on the role of Capt. Dennis Stanhope for the princely sum of five pounds. The short run was impressive enough for the producers to book the Savoy Theatre and try a regular run. Olivier, however, had another offer—to play a leading role in a production of *Beau Geste* at a guaranteed 30 pounds a week—and dropped out of the cast. The role was recast with an actor named Colin Clive. Needless to say, *Journey's End* opened to acclaim, ran for over 600 performances, and made a momentary star of the young man who took Olivier's place. *Beau Geste* ran only four weeks and Sir Laurence would have to wait a bit longer for fame and fortune.

When *Journey's End* closed, the theatre was completely rebuilt in the smooth, sleek, 1930 streamlined Art Deco style that you see on the frontage today. Throughout the next two decades the Savoy was primarily the home of comedies with occasional light opera seasons thrown in for good measure. Tom Conti changed this frivolous image in 1978 when he opened in Brian Clark's stimulating and controversial *Whose Life Is It Anyway?* It was back to light-hearted fun in 1982 when the farce of the decade, Michael Frayn's *Noises Off* opened its four-year run. Tragedy struck in 1991 when a disastrous fire destroyed the entire theatre. *Look for some pictures of the damage at the Theatre Museum.* The building and its decor were faithfully restored and it reopened on July 19, 1993. One new twist is that the Savoy Hotel swimming pool is now located on top of the reconstructed theatre. One wonders if provision has been made to simply pull a drain plug if there is another blaze.

For a remarkable and deliciously detailed portrait of Gilbert, Sullivan, D'Oyly Carte, and the creation of the Savoy Theatre and its famous productions, rent a copy of the 1999 Mike Leigh film *Topsy Turvy.*

While we are here we might also mention that D'Oyly Carte built the Savoy Hotel in 1903 with profits from the theatre. This elegant hostelry, just next door to the theatre, was constructed with a bathroom and lavatory for each room, which was an unheard of extravagance at the turn of the century. Cesar Ritz was the first manager and the famed Escoffier was an early chef. The first martini is said to have been mixed in its American Bar and of course you may still dine in the Thameside restaurant where the peach melba and Melba toast were created in honor of the famed singer Nellie Melba. Theatrical links to the hotel are many and include things as varied as its being the site of one of the first altercations between Oscar Wilde and the Marquess of Queensbury as well as the place where Laurence Olivier first met Vivien Leigh. It remains today one of the finest hotels in London and the preferred stopping and dining place for the stars of international business, politics, and entertainment.

Return now to the Strand and take a right turn to continue your stroll. Across the street another hotel should catch your eye. Not quite the Savoy, but elegant still, the **Strand Palace** stands on the site of Exeter Hall, a 19th-century meeting and recital hall that once was graced by the likes of the inimitable Jenny Lind, the "Swedish Nightingale." *Note on your right the venerable restaurant Simpsons-in-the-Strand where the traditional English dinner of roast beef and Yorkshire pudding is king.*

About ten paces on at the street sign for Savoy Buildings is another Edmund Kean association. According to the wall plaque, this was the site of the Fountain Tavern wherein met the Fountain Club, of which Kean was the leading member.

*At **Savoy Street** Gilbert and Sullivan fans might wish to take a side trip. Turn right to find the **Queen's Chapel of the Savoy**, built in 1501, and the only surviving part of the ancient Savoy Palace.* There is a stained glass window in the church dedicated to Richard D'Oyly Carte, but the chapel is open only from 11:30 to 3:30 Tuesday through Friday and during Sunday services.

*Otherwise continue your stroll in the Strand for one more short block to the busy intersection of **Lancaster Place** where traffic is fed over the **Waterloo Bridge** and toward the South Bank arts venues such as the Old Vic, the National Theatre, and Royal Festival Hall (see Walk Thirteen).*

*Cross this congested artery. If you look back slightly across the Strand to the north up **Wellington Street**, you will see the classical portico of the historic **Lyceum Theatre**.* The first Lyceum opened in 1772 and actually faced out into the Strand. It hosted exhibitions, concerts, and assorted entertainments including the first waxwork shop of Madame Tussaud. Strangely, its survival seems to have been built on the one major enemy of historic theatres—fire. From its inception the Lyceum had no license to perform plays, which accounts for its potpourri programming. But in 1809, when the Theatre Royal Drury Lane burned down, the Lyceum owner got a performance license to receive the Drury Lane's homeless company. He also managed to retain the license on a periodic basis after the Drury Lane company moved back to their new premises.

In 1830 fire caught up to the Lyceum itself and ultimately a new building was constructed slightly west of the old and this time fronting on Wellington Street. This second theatre hung on for several years, but by 1855 it was bankrupt. Once again a fire saved the day. The Covent Garden theatre burned in 1856 and the company was moved to the Lyceum for two years.

From here it was not long until the arrival of Henry Irving, born John Henry Brodribb, who became

Lyceum Theatre

70

the chief actor and manager of the theatre in 1878. With his leading lady Ellen Terry, he gave Londoners a distinguished series of productions for the next 24 years. His long and enterprising tenure at the Lyceum is generally acknowledged as one of the major reasons for the rise in status and respectability of the acting profession in the minds of the British public. In 1896 Mr. Irving appeared on Queen Victoria's Honors List and thereby became Sir Henry Irving, the first ever of his profession to be knighted in Great Britain.

The theatre itself did not survive Irving's departure by much and was razed to the ground, except for the portico and rear wall, in 1904. A rebuilding as a music hall apparently did nothing to rid the house of its bloody resident ghost, a woman who sits calmly in a box with a severed head on her lap, or to recapture its old luster.

The last actor to tread its boards before the outbreak of World War II was John Gielgud, whose *Hamlet* then went on to appear at Kronborg Castle in Elsinore itself, as the war clouds gathered.

The Lyceum stood derelict for much of the war and was then adapted for use as a dance hall and later as a site for rock concerts. In 1985 the National Theatre's successful restaging of *The Mysteries* there created new interest in its survival, and after a major rebuilding and redecoration the Lyceum reopened in 1996 with a revival of *Jesus Christ Superstar*, not perhaps quite approximating the classical tradition of Irving, but still a live theatre production. At publication date the Elton John/Julie Taymoor/Walt Disney version of *The Lion King* was comfortably ensconced for a long run and it appears that this grand old house has a new lease on theatrical life.

Look now past the rounded facade of Number 346 Strand to the little island created between the curve of **Aldwych** *and the Strand, dominated now by the facade of Citibank. You are gazing at the site of another famous lost theatre—the (second) Gaiety.* The first one was destroyed when the Aldwych development was created. When the second theatre opened in 1903, Edward VII and Queen Alexandra were in attendance and it remained one of the most stellar showplaces of the city until it closed in 1939. It then sat vacant for almost 20 years before being demolished in 1957. As a sidelight, one of the offices in the Gaiety building housed the Wireless Telegraph Company of one Mr. Marconi, who operated a station and studio there until 1922 when it became the British Broadcasting Company.

Another piece of the past that doesn't have to be imagined is visible just ahead down the Strand. The church of **St. Mary-le-Strand** *was built by the same James Gibbs who designed St. Martin-in-the-Fields in 1714.*

Let your eyes wander to the left now and up the gentle curve of **Aldwych**. You are looking at one of the major urban redevelopment projects of turn-of-the-century London. In order to get a better route from the West End to the river and to widen the Strand, the crescent ahead of you and the broad expanse of Kingsway at the top of the crescent were literally carved out of 30 acres of densely popu- lated urban real estate. Some of the leveled land was unmistakably filled with slums, but several commercial properties, including some legitimate theatres such as the first Gaiety and the Olympic were also destroyed. There were actually a number of theatres with a number of names on the Olympic site but the second one had a particular theatrical cachet. In 1831 the actress Madame Eliza Vestris took over management of the theatre and became the first female theatre man- ager in London. Over the course of the next eight years she became known for the verisimilitude of her productions. Historical accuracy in settings, costumes, and properties was her watchword and she is today given credit for using the first "box" set (walls and ceiling) in the English theatre.

*Cross the Strand now, toward the gray stones of Number 346, and start up the left side of the Aldwych crescent. At **Catherine Street** on the left you can look up toward the tiny **Duchess Theatre** (747 seats),* which dates from 1929. Two of Emlyn Williams' best plays opened here and ran for over a year each. They were *Night Must Fall* (1935) and *The Corn is Green* (1938). T. S. Eliot's *Murder in the Cathedral* had its first West End production here in 1936 and Noël Coward's *Blithe Spirit* had already run a year at the Piccadilly Theatre before it transferred to the Duchess in 1942, where it continued through 1945, running up a total of 1997 performances.

In 1974 Kenneth Tynan's nude review *Oh Calcutta!* transferred into the theatre and for the next four years the house was filled with high-class bodies and low-class jokes. The Duchess also holds the West

End record for shortest run ever. *The Intimate Review*, which premiered in 1930, did not even survive its open- ing night. The curtain was dropped and the audience dismissed before the conclu- sion of the show.

A bit farther on up Cath- erine Street was the site of the first Gaiety Theatre, whose name became the watchword for burlesque and musical comedy from 1864 to its close in 1903. The first Gaiety was one of the the- atres that was destroyed in order to create the Aldwych

Duchess Theatre

and Kingsway. In those days elegant young ladies received the night's program engraved on a perfumed fan and the chorus girls of impresario George Edwards were as famous in London society as they were in the theatre. The "Gaiety Girls" were a vibrant symbol of the Gay Nineties in London.

As you stand here you will also be able to see at the top of the street the facade of London's oldest and arguably second-most famous theatre after Shakespeare's Globe, the Drury Lane (1812). We will deal with its fascinating history in Part Three of Walk 12—the Covent Garden Promenade.

Directly across **Catherine Street** *is the* **Strand Theatre** *(1905).* It has an identical exterior to its partner on the other side of the Meridien Waldorf Hotel, The Aldwych Theatre. The Strand has not known a good deal of important activity, although the great Italian actress Eleanora Duse did perform there with her company in the inaugural season of 1905. The major long runs have been light comedies such as *Arsenic and Old Lace,* which ran for 1337 performances beginning in 1942 and a rather mild comedy with a saucily provocative title, *No Sex Please We're British.* This show opened at the Strand in 1971 and was shifted to the Garrick Theatre in the 1980s where it continued to play, building up a run of more than 5,000 performances. When it closed it was billed as the world's longest running comedy and the second-longest running play in the West End. *The Mousetrap,* at 50 years in November of 2002 and still going, should have no trouble staying in first place.

To get back to business, Ivor Novello (1893–1951), lived in a flat above the Strand Theatre for many years. There's a blue plaque above the door of Number 11. Novello, like Noël Coward, was an actor, playwright, composer, lyricist, and producer. He wrote more than 20 plays, most of them comedies or musical reviews, and starred in a vast majority of them as well. Unlike Noël Coward, Novello never did become a major celebrity in the United States. He is remembered, however, as the composer of one of World War I's most popular songs, "Keep the Home Fires Burning."

Strand Theatre

*Walk on now past the Meridien Waldorf Hotel to the **Aldwych Theatre**, which was for several years the London home of the Royal Shakespeare Company.* The RSC now resides at the Barbican for parts of each year. Like its companion theatre, the Strand, the Aldwych has American associations. The brothers Shubert were the original lease holders of the Strand and the Aldwych was built by a partnership that included Mr. Charles Frohman, another financial giant in the 19th-century American theatre.

In the 1920s the Aldwych was most famous for a series of productions now known as the Aldwych farces. Many of them were by Mr. Ben Travers, whose name was given new life by a successful revival of *Plunder* (1928) at the Royal National Theatre a few years back.

4

To recount the successes at the theatre just during the RSC tenure would take a book itself, but two modern events do bear noting. From 1964 to 1973, Mr. Peter Daubeny and the RSC presented what was known as the World Theatre Season at the theatre. They brought the best theatre companies of the world to London to perform in their native languages. Thus this house has not only seen the best that the Royal Shakespeare Company has to offer, but it has also seen companies from most of Western Europe, the United States, Africa, Eastern Europe, Canada, and the Far East. The Aldwych was also home to the RSC's original eight-hour production of *Nicholas Nickleby* in 1980. In recent years it has housed transfers from other theatres ranging in size from the Almeida to the National, as well as productions by West End commercial managements.

*Continue your stroll along the crescent toward the broad expanse of Kingsway, which you will reach shortly. On your right, dominating the end of Kingsway is the vast building known as **Bush House**, which contains the offices and studios of the BBC's World Service.*

You are now at the ending point for this walk. Public transportation is available by turning left on Kingsway and walking up to the Holborn tube station. There are also plenty of buses running on the Strand that will take you back to Trafalgar Square or Piccadilly.

Should you still have shoe leather and stamina left, you could turn immediately to Walk Five and continue on toward St. Paul's Cathedral. If this is your choice, continue on around the rest of Aldwych until it rejoins the Strand. From there, move toward the courtyard in front of St. Clement Dane's church where you can pick up Walk Five.

WALK FIVE

❁

A FLEET RAMBLE TO ST. PAUL'S:
FROM TEMPLE BAR TO THE CATHEDRAL

Walk Five

1 St. Mary-le-Strand
2 St. Clement Danes
3 Royal Courts of Justice
4 Temple Bar
5 Middle Temple Hall
6 Inner Temple Hall
7 Temple Church
8 Oliver Goldsmith gravestone
9 St. Dunstan-in-the-West
10 Johnson's Court
11 Bolt Court
12 Dorset Garden Theatre site
13 Salisbury Court Theatre

14 Bridewell Theatre
15 St. Bride Church
16 Ye Olde Cheshire Cheese
17 Fleet Prison site
18 Bridewell (Prison) site
19 St. Martin Ludgate
20 Stationers' Hall
21 St. Paul's Cathedral
22 St. Paul's tube station
23 Mansion House tube station
⊖ Tube Station

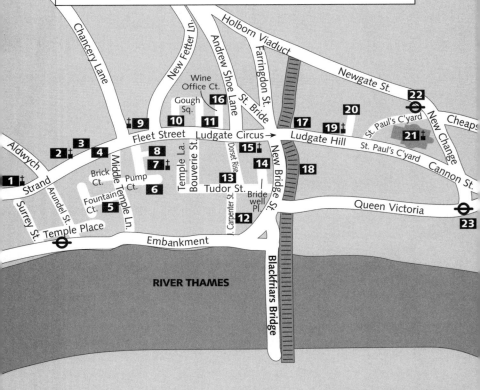

This is essentially a continuation of Walk Four, and in it you will visit the Middle and Inner Temple, Fleet Street, Dr. Johnson's house, the Cheshire Cheese, St. Bride's Church, the sites of some long-forgotten theatres, and St. Paul's Cathedral. Take this walk on a weekday, as Middle and Inner Temple, like the other Inns of Court, are closed on weekends.

5

From **Temple station,** make your way left out of the exit on **Temple Place,** past the river frontage of the Howard Hotel, and then turn right on **Surrey Street** and proceed up to the **Strand** where you will turn right. William Congreve, the playwright (1670–1729), lived on Surrey Street for some years. Nearby was the home of Anne Bracegirdle (1663–1749), the actress who was an extremely close friend of his. (This walk used to start at the now closed Aldwych station on the Strand, which was built on the site of the Royal Strand Theatre. The theatre was demolished in 1906 to make way for the construction of a bizarre little spur line on which trains ran back and forth to Holborn station. It was in this deep dead-end tunnel that some of the art treasures of the National Gallery were stored during World War II.)

St. Clement Danes

You should be able to see ahead of you a traffic island in the middle of the street on which the Wren church of St. **Clement Danes** (1682) is perched. The famous bells that rang out "Oranges and Lemons" were destroyed during a World War II bombing. (A recent guide to literary London by Ed Glinert notes that it is more likely that the famous reference belongs to St. Clement's Eastcheap, which was nearer to the docks where oranges and lemons were unloaded.) We are a bit surer about some of the theatrical connections. Falstaff's line to Justice Shallow in Shakespeare's *Henry IV Part II* "We have heard the chimes at midnight," does refer to the bells of St. Clement Danes. Orson Welles used the line as the title for his film on Falstaff— *Chimes at*

St. Mary-le-Strand

5

Midnight. The dramatist Thomas Otway (1652–85), whose most famous play was *Venice Preserv'd* in 1682, was buried in an older church on the site. Mrs. Sarah Siddons, the preeminent 18th-Century tragic actress, had lodgings somewhere nearby as well.

Back up the Strand and behind you is the graceful and delicate church of St. Mary-le-Strand (1717) designed by James Gibbs. Farther back at Trafalgar Square is another Gibbs church St. Martin-in-Fields. We mentioned both in Walk Four. You may now wish to compare all three as Gibbs also did the steeple on St. Clement Danes in 1719. *Pass St. Clement Danes on either side. Pause and enter if you wish.* This is now the official Royal Air Force church so behind the large and imposing statue of the great Victorian statesman, W. E. Gladstone, you will see those of the wartime RAF chiefs, Fighter Command's Lord Dowding, and Bomber Command's Sir Arthur Harris.

Just past the church, on another little island, are some underground, but clean and well-maintained public loos. They are open from 10 to 6, seven days a week and might be handy for those who have chosen to continue on with this walk immediately after Walk Four.

*Coming up shortly on your left you will see the grounds of the **Royal Courts of Justice** where civil court cases are tried.* Courtrooms here are open to the public, just as at the Old Bailey (Central Criminal

Royal Courts of Justice

5

Twinings; Wig & Pen Club

Courts Buildings on Walk Two) and you can check for details on visiting at the main entrance if you wish. *You will also want to cast your eyes on the rather agreeable frontages to your right. There is a lovely narrow old pub called the George and just a few steps beyond Number 216, the site of Twinings original tea salesroom dating from 1706. Number 230 is the Wig and Pen Club.*

About 100 yards ahead, a stone plinth surmounted by a strange beast known as a Griffin will catch your eye. This is the site of **Temple Bar**, a former gate into the City of London. To this day, when the Sovereign wishes to visit the City of London, she pauses at this boundary and requests permission of the Lord Mayor to enter. Inside the boundaries of the City of London, the Lord Mayor ranks ahead of even the Queen's own family in terms of protocol. It is also at this point that the Strand becomes **Fleet Street**, taking its name from the now covered Fleet River that runs into the Thames at the bottom of the hill ahead of you.

*At Number 1 Fleet Street just inside Temple Bar and to your right is the office of **Child's Bank**,*

Temple Bar

79

5

Child's Bank

England's oldest private bank (1671). Pretty Nell Gwynn, the actress and mistress of Charles II, was a customer of Child's as were Samuel Pepys, John Dryden, Oliver Cromwell, Horace Walpole, and indeed even royalty including Charles II, James II, and William III. At an earlier time this was also the site of the Devil Tavern, where Ben Jonson met with his "Apollo Club" cronies to eat, drink, and jest.

Just a few more steps on your right you will find the 1684 Christopher Wren gatehouse into **Middle Temple Lane**. *Enter it. Once through this gate you are in the precincts of the Middle Temple.* There are four so-called Inns of Court in London (Lincoln's Inn visited in Walk Three, Gray's Inn visited in Walk Two, Middle Temple, and the Inner Temple). The Inns have the exclusive pre-rogative to call persons to the Bar. They provide lec-turers and examinations for students and office space for barristers. In earlier years they also provided lodging for members and other pri-vate citizens.

**Gatehouse into
Middle Temple Lane**

On your right shortly after entering is **Brick Court**. Oliver Goldsmith (1730–74) lived out the last nine years of his life here. The actual building is now demolished. We will visit his grave outside the Temple Church shortly. *Continuing down Middle Temple Lane, the next open space on the right is* **Fountain Court**. *The dominant building on the court is* **Middle Temple Hall**, *which used to be open to visitors, but now appears to be permanently closed to the public.* The hall, built originally in 1570 and restored after heavy bomb damage in World War II, has one of the finest double hammerbeam roofs in all of England. Its theatrical interest comes from a February 2, 1602, diary entry by John Manningham, a barrister of the Temple. Manningham saw a play in the hall called *Twelfth Night* and a character named Malvolio caught his particular fancy. Four hundred years later, in the winter of 2002, the Shakespeare's Globe Theatre Company, under the direction of Mark Rylance, produced *Twelfth Night* in the hall once again. That production went on to anchor the Globe's 2002 season and achieved the fancy of most of London's theatrical community.

Manningham's diary is also the source of the only contemporary anecdote about Shakespeare. He reports a story that a young lady was so taken by Richard Burbage's performance in *Richard III* that she invited him to come to her chambers in costume after the performance. Shakespeare apparently overheard the plan, went on ahead, and was himself being entertained when came a knock at the door and the announcement that Richard III was at hand. Whereupon Shakespeare sent down the message: "William the Conqueror was before Richard III."

Middle Temple Hall

Brick Court fountain

5

Stroll into the interior of the court toward the ancient fountain (1681) where Ruth Pinch met her brother Tom in Dickens' Martin Chuzzlewit. *At the rear of Fountain Court turn left down the stairs into* **Garden Court.**

From here you can look out to your left over the Middle Temple Garden and believe if you will the legend that this was the very garden where Richard Plantagenet (who becomes the Duke of York) and the Earl of Somerset quarreled and ordered their supporters to show their loyalties by plucking a red rose or a white rose. There is no hard evidence suggesting that the War of the Roses actually did begin here, but in Shakespeare's *Henry VI, Part 1,* act II, scene 4, Plantagenet leaves with a group of four to eat dinner. This was the traditional number in a "mess" at the Middle Temple Hall.

Since the garden is not open to the public, you must retrace your steps back to Middle Temple Lane. Look but do not turn to your right. If you went that way you would soon pass by the former residence of poet and playwright William Butler Yeats and Crown Office Row where the critic and author Charles Lamb was born. But our route today takes us back to the left. Cross the lane and move back up toward Fleet Street looking out on the right for a small passage leading to the **Pump Court.** *Henry Fielding (1707–54), novelist and playwright* (Tom Thumb), *rented chambers in this court.* Fielding's prime reputation today rests on his novels, but in his early years he had a significant influence on the London theatre scene. His satirical plays were among the main reasons for the passage of the Licensing Act of 1737.

Walk on through the Pump Court and out through the cloisters at the other end. You are now in another court and on your right is the **Inner Temple Hall.** The ancient hall on the site (the current one is a reconstruction of a 19th-century building) saw the production of

Temple Church

many plays in the 16th and 17th centuries. Thomas Norton and William Sackville were both members of the Inner Temple when their play *Gorboduc*, the first English tragedy in blank verse, was produced in the Inner Temple Hall in 1561. The records indicate that Queen Elizabeth I was in attendance.

To your left is a true architectural treasure. The **Temple Church,** dating from 1185, is one of five surviving round churches in England. Entrance hours appear to be changeable. If you find it open, take advantage of the opportunity. In the older circular portion of the church there are some fine recumbent effigies of 12th- and 13th-century knights. On the interior walls, just above head height, is a series of exquisitely carved faces. Some are calm and beatific, but others are fanciful or grotesque. The only theatrical figure buried in the church is John Marston (1575–1634) a minor Elizabethan dramatist and satirist.

Leave the church and turn right circling the rounded end of the building. You will pass the great west doors (now sealed) and be moving up **Inner Temple Lane**. *Make a right turn at the first opening labeled* **Goldsmith Building** *and move down the walk parallel to the north side of the church.* Several feet to the right of the statue of a semi-recumbent and long forgotten magistrate named Johannes Hiccocks is a low, moss-covered slab with the barely legible sentence, "Here Lies Oliver Goldsmith." Goldsmith, like Fielding and Swift, is perhaps best known as a novelist today, but his *She Stoops to Conquer* (1773) remains one of the true classics and most often produced of all 18th-century British dramas. If you have ever read John Mortimer's "Rumpole of the

Gravestone of Oliver Goldsmith

Bailey" stories or watched the television series based on them, Rumpole's firm had offices overlooking this yard at the fictional address Number 3 Equity Court. In "Rumpole and the Children of the Devil" the resolution hinges on a bet made as to whether it is Dr. Johnson or Goldsmith who is buried in the court below. Many of the exteri-

ors for the series were filmed in and around the Middle and Inner Temple.

Return to Inner Temple Lane, turn right, and head back toward Fleet Street. You will be exiting the Inner Temple beneath **Prince Henry's room.** If you look back above your head after you reenter Fleet Street, you will see one of the few pieces of original half-timber work left in London. It dates from 1610 and you may visit one of the rooms associated with Henry, the elder son of James I, between 11 and 2, Monday through Saturday. Admission is free. The stairs are to the left of the archway and if you go up you will find a cosy little room and a small exhibit of Samuel Pepys memorabilia.

A right turn out of the Inner Temple or Prince Henry's Room will send you once again down Fleet Street. Shortly you will note across the way the interesting octagonal church of **St. Dunstan-in-the-West** *(1832). Cross the street now to examine it more closely.*

St. Dunstan-in-the-West

The figure of Queen Elizabeth I over the east vestry porch was taken from the old Lud Gate into the City of London. Two figures associated with the Elizabethan theatre, Philip Massinger and Thomas Campion, were buried in an older church on the site. Massinger's best known work is a play titled *A New Way to Pay Old Debts*, which was written in 1625. One of its leading roles, Sir Giles Overreach, was a particular favorite of actor Edmund Kean. It was frequently in the 19th-century repertoire, but has fallen out of favor in the 20th; the last great exponent was Donald Wolfit in his post-war tours. Campion was a poet and court masque composer who touched the theatre briefly via his friendship with Philip Rosseter, who directed a company of boy actors at the Whitefriars Theatre not too far from here. Congreve mentions the church by name in his *Love for Love*. The clock (1761) is also worth a look as you pass by.

Continue on down the left side of the street past Fetter Lane into what used to be the very heart of the British newspaper industry. The call of the open spaces and cheaper rentals of Docklands has denuded the

5

area of publishers, but the streets seem no less busy now. It's only the character that has changed.

Keep your eyes ahead as you move around a slight bend in the street and you will see ahead of you a famous view of **St. Paul's Cathedral** *with the small slender spire of St. Martin Ludgate in front of it and acting as a foil for the massive dome.*

Right about at this point (Number 167) you should also find on your left **Johnson's Court**, *which will lead you through a number of intriguing twists and turns to* **Gough Square** *and the nicely preserved 18th-century home of Dr. Samuel Johnson.* Although Johnson did not have a great fondness for actors, he did know many of them. The house has several nice theatrical prints and an old chest that David Garrick used for costume storage. It is open from 11 to 5 except Sundays

St. Paul's Cathedral with St. Martin Ludgate in foreground

5

Top: Statue of Dr. Samuel Johnson's cat
Bottom: Home of Dr. Johnson

and Bank Holidays. *There is an admission charge for visiting the interior, so if paying to see the very attic where the ubiquitous Dr. Johnson composed his famous dictionary does not move you, walk down to the bottom of Gough Square where you can at least view the fanciful statue of Johnson's cat, Hodge. Leave by taking a right at the cat, then a right at the next fork, and then a left. You should emerge back out onto Fleet Street at* **Bolt Court.**

When you get back to Fleet street, you should see a traffic light almost in front of you. Cross back over to the right (south side) of the street. Turn right and look for a sign into **Bouverie Street.** *Turn left into it. The critic William Hazlitt lived at Number 3 (no longer there, but the site is marked by a blue plaque about shoulder high). A little farther on there is a dead end street to your right that leads back to the Inner Temple. If you walk along for another 30 paces or so, across from 11–12 Bouverie Street, you will find on your left a small unmarked alley.* This used to be called **Magpie Alley** and was once a part of the Whitefriar's Monastery complex.

Somewhere near Magpie Alley was the small theatre called the Whitefriars that we alluded to a few paragraphs ago. It appears to have been a private theatre built within the refectory hall of the old monastery. The entire building was approximately 35 feet wide and 85 feet long. Refectory halls appear to have been an optimum size and shape for theatrical conversion. Burbage's second Blackfriars, which we noted in Walk Two, was also converted from one of these large, open, rectangular rooms dedicated to a monastery's meal service. Little is known about this theatre, but the Children of the King's and Queen's Revels played there under their director Philip Rosseter. Rosseter apparently left to take another hall in 1614. Lady Elizabeth's Men and later on the Prince's Men struggled on at the theatre until 1629. Samuel Pepys records a visit there in 1660, but he may have meant the Salisbury Court Theatre, which had opened nearby.

Residents of the Whitefriars precinct objected strenuously to the presence of actors and entertainments. They felt that the theatre attracted rough and unsavory people into the district and also created massive traffic jams in the narrow streets. That also parallels the complaints heard from residents of the Blackfriars area. It appears that then and now there is nothing like a theatre to spoil the neighborhood. One wall of Magpie Alley is now covered with a tile mural depicting important events in the history of English printing. It is an incongruously hidden reminder of the quite public media who made "Fleet Street" a synonym for journalism in our language.

Move along now to the intersection of **Tudor Street** *where a glance to the right will reveal the third (eastern) entrance to the Inner Temple. Our route takes us to the left on Tudor Street.* John Dryden (1631–1700) lived along here, as did the minor dramatist Thomas Shadwell (1642–1692). Shadwell wrote a play called *The Squire of Alsatia* in 1688 in which he took his characters from the low life types that lived around his house.

Move along Tudor Street for two blocks until you reach **John Carpenter Street**. *Take a right turn. On your left is a new monolithic gray stone building housing the Morgan Guarantee and Trust, an American bank. The older building on the right is the former home of the Guildhall School of Music and Drama, which has now taken up facilities in the Barbican Arts Complex.*

If you look closely at the facade of the building you will see a series of classical composers' names staring rather incongruously down into the street. Busts used to occupy the empty circles below the names.

It is of course theatre and not music that brings us here. There used to be a nice blue plaque on the wall of an old London primary school that stood across from the Guildhall School before J. P.

Former Guildhall School of Music and Drama

Morgan invaded. It announced that this was the site of the **Dorset Garden Theatre** (1671–1706). Plans for this famous and historic theatre were initiated by Sir William Davenant who, along with Thomas Killigrew, held one of the two patents for dramatic performances issued by Charles II when he returned to the English throne in 1660. (See Walk Three for more information on the first patent theatres opened by Davenant and Killigrew.) The ground for the Dorset Garden was leased in 1670 and tradition indicates that Sir Christopher Wren was hired to design it. Davenant died before its completion and his widow and a group of investors headed by the actor Thomas Betterton finished and opened it in 1671. Betterton went on to manage the theatre for a number of years and actually lived in a flat on the premises.

According to all accounts, the Dorset Garden was the most lovely and fashionable theatre of its time. Several prints of its proscenium facade and 140-by-57 foot exterior are available. One of its most attractive features was the fine river frontage and private landing stage built to enable patrons to arrive and depart by boat, thus avoiding the crowded and dangerous streets of the area. Today if you look for a block or so down John Carpenter Street you can make out a line of buildings that mark the far side of the river. If you had been standing here in 1671, you would be poised on top of the Dorset Stairs with the muddy banks of the Thames at your very feet. The difference is that in the 19th century the Victoria Embankment was constructed and the extensive tidal mud flats of river were claimed for a roadway and new buildings.

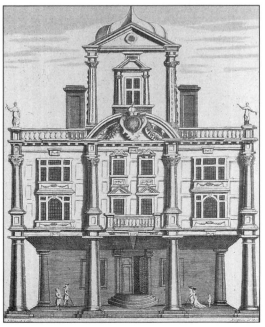

With Betterton as manager the Duke's Company at the Dorset Garden provided stiff competition for the Drury Lane company until 1682. At that time the two groups combined and moved into the more commodious Drury Lane Theatre. From then on the fortunes of the Dorset Garden receded and it was demolished sometime early in the 18th century.

Turn around now and return to Tudor Street. Turn right for about 20 yards and then jog left on **Dorset Rise**. *Climb the hill until you reach*

Dorset Garden Theatre

a small square with a signpost that says "Bridewell Theatre." Turn around and look back. You should see a street marker that says **Salisbury Square**. *Walk back to that sign and peek around it and high to the right. There you should discover one of the most carefully hidden blue plaques in London. Walk back across the street to see it better.*

Bridewell Theatre

The **Salisbury Court Theatre** was built in 1629 as a private theatre and cost only 1000 pounds as compared to the Dorset Garden's 8000 pounds. It was on a site 140 by 40 feet and was initially occupied by the King's Revels (1629–31). Prince Charles' Men were there from 1631–35, and the Queen's Men from 1637–42. Apparently some clandestine performances were given there after the closure of the theatres in 1642. In 1649 its interior fittings were destroyed by soldiers, but it was restored to usable condition by William Beeson in 1660. Beeson's own company used it briefly followed by a group of players led by George Jolly. Jolly had toured in Germany during the Commonwealth period and had also managed to perform before the future Charles II and secure a special license to do plays in London should Charles ever be able to regain the throne. Davenant and Killigrew, however (See Walk Three), outmaneuvered poor old Jolly after 1660, and he ended up fading out of the picture even before the Great Fire of 1666 burned the Salisbury Court to the ground.

If you are facing the plaque turn right and make your way back into Salisbury Square. On your right is the entrance to **St. Bride's Passage**. *Step through it and into a small courtyard. At the far end, on the site of Henry VIII's Bridewell Palace, is the 1893 building of the St. Bride Foundation Institute.* This was apparently a typical Victorian charity dedicated to providing both physical and intellectual stimulation to area residents. In 1994 the basement of this building was converted into the **Bridewell Theatre**. Doesn't sound too odd yet, does it? Just wait. The basement of the building contained swimming baths. They were used until the 1950s. After 30 years of collecting dust, the pool was remodeled into a theatre. On Walk Four we learned that the Savoy

Church of St. Bride

5

Theatre had a pool on top of it; now we have a theatre in one. In recent years the Bridewell has achieved an excellent reputation for finding and producing both new and older small-scale musical theatre pieces.

Unless you feel compelled to examine it, turn around and step back out of the courtyard. Turn right and a few more steps will bring you to **St. Bride's Avenue.** Samuel Pepys, the great diarist, was born in a house nearby. *Turn right into this passage and go through an anachronous set of modern plate glass doors. You will find yourself in the* **Church of St. Bride,** *burned in the 1660s, rebuilt by Wren in the 1670s, bombed to a smoking shell in the 1940s, and restored again in the 1950s. Take a good look at the rear wall behind the altar as you enter. Then walk up close to it for a theatrical surprise courtesy of the artist Glyn Jones.*

The history of this exquisite Wren church is told eloquently in the basement museum. Theatrically we can mention that Thomas Sackville, co-author of that unreadable tragedy *Gorboduc*, was buried in an older church on the site and our friend Samuel Pepys and all of his brothers and sisters, who were born just a few steps away, were baptized in the old church.

Leave St. Brides by the north exit rather than the glass doors. A tiny remnant of the graveyard is to the right. Go straight ahead and out the entrance gates. When you

Trompe l'oeil wall behind the altar at St. Bride's

arrive at Fleet Street take another look back and up at Wren's lacy spire. It is his tallest at 226 feet.

Cross the busy street somehow and turn left on the opposite side. About 150 yards back up Fleet Street past Shoe Lane is a major London tourist attraction, **Ye Olde Cheshire Cheese,** *an inn and chop-house that was rebuilt in 1667 after the great fire and survives today with a good deal of its 17th-century atmosphere intact.* It was much frequented by Dr. Samuel Johnson, James Boswell, Oliver Goldsmith, and most of the literary figures of the day. The entrance is around the corner down the narrow **Wine Office Court.** Johnson's own chair and the brass door knocker from Goldsmith's front door are even exhibited, but these particular items may just belong in the category with pieces of the true cross and beds that George Washington slept in. Despite the excess of tourists, it's worth a stop. Food in the sit-down restaurant is a bit dear, but the pub grub in the fascinating cellar bar is reasonable. Of course the price of a half-pint will give you access to all the ambience and it may be just about time for a sit and a little libation.

After your visit to the Cheshire Cheese return to Fleet Street, cross to the other side again, turn left, and continue on down toward the main intersection at the bottom of the hill. You'll pass a couple more interesting pubs, the Olde Bell and the Punch Tavern. Once at the corner you are on the banks of what was a stinking ditch and open sewer until the latter part of the 18th century when the Fleet River was finally arched over and turned literally into what it had already become.

To your left up **Farringdon Street** *you can just see the cast iron arches of the Holborn Viaduct, which was constructed in 1863 to carry traffic over the course of the river. You crossed that bridge if you took Walk Two. Kitty corner across the road used to be the Old King Lud Pub.* It is now an eatery called the Hogshead, but castings of Old King Lud still remain above the doors. The former name was a more apt reminder that you were approaching the old Lud Gate out of the City of London.

Behind the Hogshead on what would have been the opposite bank of the Fleet River would have stretched the sinister walls of the **Fleet Prison.** Its existence has been traced back to the 11th century. It was continually destroyed and then rebuilt until it was finally pulled down for good in 1846. Its primary occupants were petty criminals and debtors. We have a vivid portrait of its 18th-century interior in Hogarth's *Rake's Progress* paintings, which you may have seen at Sir John Soanes' museum on Walk Three and a slightly different rendering of the prison by Charles Dickens who placed Mr. Pickwick there for debt in the 19th century. The playwrights Thomas Dekker (1572–1632) and Thomas Nash (1567–1601) spent time there.

William Wycherley (1640–1716), author of *The Country Wife*, was imprisoned there for debt for seven full years.

To your right down New Bridge Street toward the Thames was located another equally infamous prison—Bridewell. Thomas Kyd (1558–94), the author of the most popular and influential Elizabethan play of the 16th century, *The Spanish Tragedy*, was imprisoned and tortured there as a result of his connection to the playwright Christopher Marlowe. In May of 1593 constables searching for the authors of verses written against the immigration of Flemish Protestants searched Kyd's rooms and found instead some items that seemed to point to the even greater crimes of blasphemy, atheism, and other political and religious heresy. Kyd, who was rooming with Marlowe at the time, was arrested and under torture attributed the authorship of the incriminating papers to his flatmate. Marlowe was then arrested, but he had better political connections and was released on bail. Unfortunately for Kyd, Marlowe was killed in a tavern brawl a month later, and the affair was never resolved, though recent historical research suggests he was the victim of a deliberate political murder. Kyd remained imprisoned in Bridewell and was a broken man by the time he was finally released. He died in total poverty within a year. Thus it was that two of the finest and most promising young playwrights of Elizabethan England left a fast growing, talent hungry, and beckoning theatre scene to a young "Shakescene" in the early 1590s. Fictional treatments of this marvelous and mysterious story have tempted several authors. Try reading Anthony Burgess' *A Dead Man in Deptford* or Robin Chapman's *Christoferus or Tom Kyd's Revenge.*

*It is now time to make the last leg of our journey. Cross **Ludgate Circus** and begin your climb back up the opposite bank of the Fleet River onto **Ludgate Hill** imagining as you do that you are exiting the City of London through the old Lud Gate. The gate actually stood somewhere between here and the **St. Martin Ludgate** church which is just ahead on the left side of the street. As you climb the hill you might turn back and take another glance at the frosty white spire of St. Bride's behind you.* A baker named William Rich had a shop on this hill in the 18th century and is said to have modeled the wedding cakes he baked on the steeple he could see from his shop window. It began a style that is still followed today.

Stop and visit St. Martin's Church if you wish. It is normally open. William Penn, founder of Pennsylvania, was married in an older building on the same site. *About 50 paces beyond the church is a small passage that leads to the courtyard in front of the **Stationers' Hall**.* This guild or company (founded in 1402) was given the royal charter for copyright. Until 1911 every book published in Britain had to be registered at the Hall. A good deal of our hard knowledge about Elizabethan literature and drama comes from the Stationers' Register that was kept by this guild. *Their hall is not open to visitors, but the courtyard is another of those little isles of calm in the midst of the crowded city. To the left of the hall you can sometimes see into an even more secluded inner garden shaded by a large spreading sycamore tree. Return to the street and turn left.*

You have now reached the top of Ludgate Hill and one of the great symbols of London awaits your exploration. Theatrical names are not associated in any great numbers with **St. Paul's Cathedral** although its architect, Sir Christopher Wren, designed both the Second Drury Lane and the Dorset Garden theatres. Hard by the walls of the cathedral and close to the Stationer's Company were the offices and shops of the major printers and publishers. The first edition of Shakespeare's *"Venus and Adonis"* and *"The Rape of Lucrece"* as well as the quartos of some of his plays were all published by printers working under the shadow of the (old) cathedral.

Our walk ends here with the hope that you will now visit the masterpiece of Sir Christopher Wren. If you arrive before 3:30 P.M. (the crypt usually closes then), be sure to visit Wren's tomb where one of the most moving epitaphs ever composed is found. It says:

> "Lector, si Momentum, requiris, circumspice"
> "Reader, if you seek a monument, look about you."

Since you are seldom out of sight of one of Wren's creations in the whole of London, it is more than fitting.

After exploring St. Paul's, leave by the same exit you entered, turn right and then right again so you are walking parallel to the north side

Stationers' Hall

of the cathedral. Jog a few steps to your left as you come to the iron fencing of St. Paul's Churchyard. Walk along the outside of the fence until you pass through two large barrier posts in the pavement. Turn left and you should be able to reach the St. Paul's tube station (Central Line) shortly. Several bus routes also run on the south side of the Cathedral and they can take you back toward Trafalgar Square and the West End.

5

WALK SIX

PICK A DAFFY IN PICCADILLY AND BEYOND

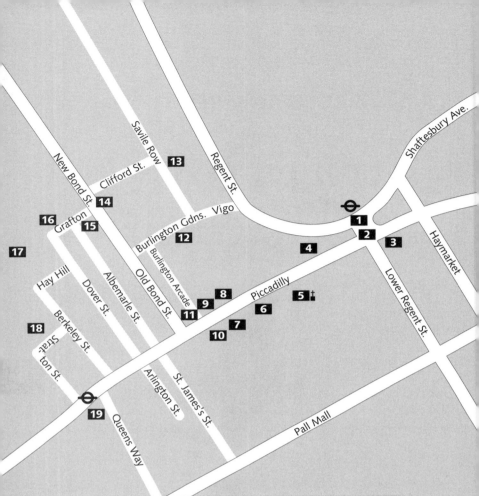

Walk Six

1 Piccadilly Circus tube station
2 Piccadilly Circus and Eros statue
3 Criterion Theatre
4 Meridien Hotel
5 St. James Church
6 Hatchard's
7 Fortnum & Mason
8 Albany Courtyard
9 Burlington House; Royal Academy
10 Piccadilly Arcade
11 Burlington Arcade
12 Former Museum of Mankind
13 Sheridan Houses
14 "Allies" statue
15 Irving House
16 Medici Galleries
17 Berkeley Square
18 Mayfair Hotel; Mayfair Theatre
19 Green Park tube station
⊖ Tube Station

STARTING POINT: Piccadilly Circus tube station (Piccadilly or Bakerloo Lines). Many bus lines will also deposit you at Piccadilly Circus.

APPROXIMATE TIME: One and one-half hours.

T his walk covers mainly vanished theatrical pleasures, but you will visit a nice variety of busy shops as well as the classy and quieter district known as Mayfair. Potential visits include some of Oscar Wilde's haunts, Henry Irving's house, Hatchard's bookstore, Fortnum and Mason's, the Royal Academy, and the Medici Galleries. Schedule this one for a regular shopping day (Monday through Saturday) and do not start before 10 A.M.

W e begin this walk at **Piccadilly Circus**, the hub of London's West End. If your arrival is by tube look for an exit labeled Subway Four after you have cleared the ticket gates. Once in that subway you will see some stairs labeled **Shaftesbury Avenue** on your right. Go right on by and keep looking for a sign saying "Haymarket and Eros." This stairway will deposit you aboveground at a point convenient to the famous fountain with its graceful archer that has been casting its spell over the crowds since 1893. Several generations of hopeful romantics have insisted upon calling the figure Eros, but it was actually intended to represent the Angel of Christian Charity and to memorialize the philanthropy of Lord Shaftesbury—a 19th-century industrial reformer and evangelical. You can remember the true honoree if you note the direction the arrow has flown, i.e., Shaft's buried in ground thus Shaftesbury. Unfortunately the missile is heading more toward Lower Regent Street

Shaftesbury Avenue

6

97

than Shaftesbury Avenue, so it doesn't help your geographical orientation one bit.

As you scan the square from the fountain, search for the marquee of the **Criterion Theatre**, *the only legitimate theatre remaining on Piccadilly Circus. It is just to the left of Lillywhite's.* The architect Thomas Verity developed the site beginning with a large restaurant on the south called the Criterion in 1873 and then expanded a planned small concert hall into a full-fledged theatre by 1874. The frontage is unassuming but pleasant with the name picked

6

Above: Criterion Theatre entrance
Below: Criterion Theatre interior tilework

out in white letters on blue tiles. Notice also the grotesque comic mask that crowns the marquee. *Cross toward it now and enter the foyer if it is open.* This is London's only completely underground West End theatre. Just the box office is at street level. It is a lovely space with

tiled walls and painted ceiling panels and also holds a portrait of Mary Moore, the Criterion's actor/manager from 1919 to 1931. She inherited the theatre from her second husband, the actor/impresario Charles Wyndham. (See Walk Twelve.) When you are in the stalls of this theatre the tube literally runs beside you and even the upper circle is reached by going downstairs. The underground location was used to advantage during World War II when it was turned into a safely sheltered radio studio by the BBC. The house today, which holds fewer than six hundred seats, is warm and intimate. The decor is soft pink and gold, and the graceful curves of the circles are pleasantly sinuous. The foyer and stairs have been enhanced with exquisite tile work by William De Morgan, some of which is visible from the entrance hall.

Small cast dramas, comedies, and revues have been its usual fare. The current long-run champion is *The Complete Works of William Shakespeare Abridged* with a run of over seven years as of 2002. Other successes have been Ray Cooney's *Run for Your Wife* (1,600 performances beginning in 1983), Terrence Rattigan's first play, *French Without Tears*, Iris Murdoch's *A Severed Head*, Simon Gray's *Butley*, and Alan Ayckbourn's *Absurd Person Singular*.

More important from a theatrical history standpoint might be the fact that Peter Hall's landmark production of Samuel Beckett's *Waiting for Godot* transferred here in 1955 from the Arts Theatre and went on to run for a full year.

The theatre went dark for a period in the late 1980s and early 1990s while the old restaurant and much of the rest of the building were demolished, restored, and rebuilt. The theatre was also refurbished and just before it reopened to audiences in 1992 it was the location for Kenneth Branagh's film of Chekhov's *Swan Song*, starring John Gielgud and Richard Briers. A huge party celebrating the opening of the Branagh film was held in the newly renovated Criterion "Marco Pierre White" restaurant, which some have called the most beautiful in London. Sir John was the guest of honor and feted by over three hundred of the major figures of the London stage.

*If you have peeked into the Criterion's lobby, turn left upon exiting and cross **Lower Regent Street** toward the Clydesdale Bank sign to reach the south side of **Piccadilly**. On your right across the street is the Tower Records store and shortly the flags and marquee of the Meridien Hotel.*

If you could put yourself into the 19th century you might be able to conjure up an image of Charles Dickens striding up this street in 1870 and entering St. James Hall to deliver his last public reading. That hall stood where the hotel stands today.

Or you might imagine a jaunty Oscar Wilde parading up Piccadilly through Knightsbridge to Belgravia where the actress Lillie Langtry lived. Wilde is purported to have carried a lily, a symbol of the Aesthetic Movement and of Miss Langtry's name, on these journeys. In Gilbert

6

St. James Church Piccadilly

and Sullivan's operetta *Patience*, which poked fun at the Aesthetic Movement, the character Reginald Bunthorne was patterned after Wilde and one of the lyrics goes:

"Though philistines may jostle
You will rank as an apostle
In the high aesthetic band
If you walk down Piccadilly
With a poppy or a lily
In your Medieval hand."

You may not be carrying a lily today in honor of Oscar Wilde, but you will certainly be jostled on these busy sidewalks. *On past the hotel there will shortly appear on your left the thin rapier-like spire of Christopher Wren's **St. James Church**.* Its particular theatre connection is that it has become the most favored venue now for actors' and writers' memorial services. It also hosts many lunchtime and evening music events. On Wednesdays through Saturdays the churchyard is filled with delightful market stalls ranging from souvenirs to antiques. The merchants are friendly and the prices are reasonable. *Go on through the yard and take a look at the spare, cool interior of the church.* It's not original, but the reconstruction after World War II bomb damage was faithfully executed right down to reproduction of the actual plaster mouldings from surviving fragments.

*When you leave the churchyard turn left and continue your perambulation past the offices of BAFTA—the British Academy of Film and Television Arts—to the facade of one of London's oldest booksellers—**Hatchard's**.* They have been in business since late 1797 and in that building since 1801. If they are open, there is no penalty for taking a look.

*A few steps farther on is the home of **Fortnum and Mason**, where some of the most elegant foodstuffs in the world can be found.* A visit

Albany

6

should be mandatory, if only to see the staff in their fancy dress coats and to register shock at the prices of things like wild boar paté and 100 year old balsamic vinegar.

When you exit the store, cross **Piccadilly** *and turn to your right, until you reach* **Albany Court** *directly opposite* **Hatchard's** *bookshop. Find it and go in. At the rear of the courtyard is the entrance to the luxury lodgings known as* **Albany.** They were created within the framework of an earlier house designed in the 1770s by Sir William Chambers. What was built in 1802 was a row of apartments all facing onto a long covered passage, called the Ropewalk, that passed all the way through to **Vigo Street** and **Burlington Gardens.*** If the door is open you can clearly see the long line of delightful columns. It has been and continues to be a most desirable address. Theatrical occupants have included Dion Boucicault, the prolific author/adaptor of at least 150 plays including *The Corsican Brothers* (1852), *The Octoroon* (1859), and *London Assurance*, which was first performed in 1841 and memorably revived by the RSC at the Aldwych in 1970, with Donald Sinden and Judi Dench; the playwright, J. B. Priestley; the actor/manager Herbert Beerbohm-Tree; and the playwright, Henry Arthur Jones. Other famous residents have included Lord Byron, William Gladstone, Aldous Huxley, and Graham Greene. And perhaps we should not forget an important fictional resident—Mr. Earnest

---

*According Ann Saunders, *The Art and Architecture of London,* Alexander Copeland did the conversion work on the Albany apartments. Other sources indicated that Henry Holland, the architect of the third Drury Lane Theatre, designed the conversion.

Worthing. Oscar Wilde gave him the fashionable address of B4 at the Albany in *The Importance of Being Earnest. Return now to Piccadilly and turn right.*

Almost immediately the massive gates of **Burlington House**, *a 17th-century Palladian villa that now houses the Royal Academy, come into view.* Major art exhibitions are mounted here throughout the year and the current show is usually advertised prominently. *Walk into the courtyard and take a peek at the statue of its first president, the great painter Sir Joshua Reynolds, while you make up your mind whether a visit is in order.*

Turn right as you exit from the **Royal Academy courtyard**. *Note shortly just across the street the entrance to the* **Piccadilly Arcade**, *an upscale mini shopping mall.* This is the former site of the Egyptian Hall. Numbers 170–173 just beyond the Arcade are still labeled Egyptian House. *Walk on until you are even with 170–173.* There is a bizarre story connected with the old Egyptian Hall. It seems that an obscure painter by the name of Benjamin Haydon had a display of his work in a front gallery of this hall in 1846. Unfortunately the central part of the hall was hired by the great showman P. T. Barnum, who was exhibiting his famous dwarf General Tom Thumb. This event so submerged Haydon's exhibition that the distraught artist cut his throat three months later. The great showman may not have been much of an art critic but he clearly knew what an audience would buy.

Turn around now and you should see on your side of the street an entrance to another arcade. This is the **Burlington Arcade**. Dating from 1818, it was built originally as a buffer to keep the riffraff from throwing trash into Lord Burlington's elegant gardens. Today it's the prices that keep the riffraff away. *Turn to your right into the arcade and take a leisurely*

Royal Academy

stroll into the past. Keep an eye out for the top-hatted and waistcoated Burlington Beadles with their amusingly anachronous two-way radios. They were formed to protect the customers and to keep them faithful to the laws of Regency London. They may legally forbid you to whistle, sing, or hurry. And hurry we certainly do not want you to do. The shops are little theatrical jewels in and of themselves and deserve to be savored even if you cannot afford to buy.

As you come up on the far end of the arcade note the two sturdy posts set in the pavement. Early one morning in 1964 a blue Jaguar jumped the curb and roared down the deserted arcade. It

Burlington Arcade

screamed to a stop at Goldsmith's Jewelers, some men leaped out, and 60 seconds later sped off toward the Picadilly entrance with 150,000 pounds-worth of loot. The posts may not prevent another theft, but the next getaway vehicle will have to be on two wheels.

*The street at the top of the arcade is **Burlington Gardens** and if you turn to the right you will walk past the imposing building that used to house the **Museum of Mankind**.* This ethnographic collection has now

Former Museum of Mankind

been moved back to the British Museum in Bloomsbury, leaving the images of Francis Bacon, John Locke, and Adam Smith staring rather forlornly out of their

103

niches onto the almost deserted street.

*A bit farther on is the rear entrance to the Albany and then **Savile Row**, the famous street of quality tailors. Turn left there and look for Number 14, the plain but sturdy Georgian house where the playwright Richard Brinsley Sheridan lived.* It is only barely marked with a dim brown plaque above the Hardy Amis sign on the doorway. Number 17, a few doors down, is also an attractive building in spite of the addition of wrought iron trim from another period. Sheridan died in 1816 in the front bedroom of this house, though the blue

Richard Brinsley Sheridan house

plaque commemorates a reasonably obscure architect, George Basevi.

*You are now almost to **Clifford Street**. When you reach it, turn left.* There are some lovely Georgian houses along this street. Number 8, on your right, is particularly fine. *Continue walking until you reach **New Bond Street**, then take a jog left. Stop and be pleasantly amazed for sitting quietly on a park bench are lifesize bronzes of Sir Winston Churchill and Franklin Roosevelt.* Haul out your camera and have

Jim De Young with bronzes of Franklin Roosevelt and Winston Churchill

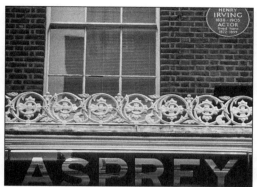
Henry Irving residence site

someone take a few snaps of you hob-nobbing with your famous friends. You will see where to perch by the highly polished left knee of Roosevelt and right elbow of Churchill. *After you finish your Kodak moment, take a quick right into* **Grafton Street**. On the corner at 15A, above what is now the premises of Asprey & Garrard, a merger of two of the most famous names in international jewelry, lived Sir Henry Irving, the greatest of the 19th-century actor/managers and the very first English theatrical figure to be knighted in 1895. You'll see a blue plaque there. He occupied the flat for almost 30 years from 1872 to 1899 and we can confidently assume that almost every notable theatre personage of the late 19th century must have passed some time at this location.

6

The right side of the street now contains a slim new gray marble office block, but at Number 13 (now the location of Wartski, jewelers of distinction) was the **Albemarle Club**. It was here that another notable theatrical figure of the 19th century, Mr. Oscar Wilde, received a fateful note left for him by the Marquess of Queensbury. The allegations prompted Wilde to sue for defamation of character. He won the first case but the publicity led to a morals charge, which ultimately sent him to prison and to his ruin. The year 2000 was the centenary of Wilde's death and occasioned several major exhibitions on his life and art in London and an Oscar Wilde Week at the Royal National Theatre.

Continue on down **Grafton Street** *until it takes a sharp left when it turns into* **Dover Street**. Huddled at the corner here are the main offices of the **Medici Galleries**—distributors of fine cards and prints. You may wish to stop in and browse a bit. It is normally uncrowded and the staff are friendly.

Upon coming out of the Medici Galleries follow Dover Street one short block to **Hay Hill**. *Turn right there and go down the hill to* **Berkeley Street**. This name is pronounced "bark-lee" by the way. To your right is **Berkeley Square**, immortalized during World War II in a song by Vera Lynn entitled "A Nightingale Sang In Berkeley Square." *Unless you feel a need for a rest, turn left away from the square and walk on along Berkeley Street until you reach* **Stratton Street**. Just in case you hadn't realized it, you are now in Mayfair—a district of the city that Michael Elliot in *Heartbeat London* called "one of the bolt-holes of old money." *Take a right past the posh **Mayfair Intercontinental Hotel**. As you walk*

under the main marquee, there is a glass door on your right labeled **Mayfair Theatre**. This pleasant and well equipped 300-seat house was constructed inside the Candlelight Ballroom of the hotel. It opened in 1963 with a highly successful production of Pirandello's *Six Characters in Search of an Author* starring Sir Ralph Richardson. It housed Christopher Hampton's *The Philanthropist* in the 1970s; a thriller entitled *The Business of Murder* had a five-year run in the 1980s; but in recent years it had been primarily used for business conferences. The summer of 2001 saw the reopening of the theatre with a production of the musical, *Song of Singapore,* but it remains doubtful that the venue will be returned to full-time legitimate theatre activities.

A bit farther along on Stratton Street at Number 17 is a fine five-story red brick building tucked in among more modern neighbors. Henry Irving occupied rooms here briefly in 1900 just after he gave up his flat on Grafton Street and Sir James Barrie of Peter Pan fame lived in the building in 1908.

*Stratton Street then curls back to Piccadilly and the **Green Park** underground station. You can terminate your stroll here or walk back down to Piccadilly Circus stopping at places you may have passed up on the outbound journey. Another alternative is to go on to Walk Seven— "Clubland Is also Playland: From St. James to the Haymarket." It originates at the Green Park underground station and takes you back to Piccadilly Circus via a more theatrical route.*

6

#17 Stratton Street, where Henry Irving and James Barrie occupied rooms

WALK SEVEN

CLUBLAND IS ALSO PLAYLAND:
FROM ST. JAMES TO THE HAYMARKET

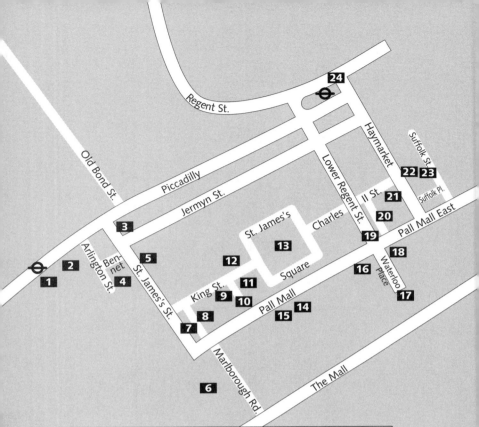

Walk Seven

1. Green Park station
2. Ritz Hotel
3. White's
4. Brooks Club
5. Boodles
6. St. James' Palace
7. Berry Brothers & Rudd; Lock & Company, Hatters
8. Crown Passage & Red Lion Pub
9. St. James' House
10. Angel Court
11. Golden Lion pub
12. Christie's Auction House
13. St. James' Square

14. Royal Automobile Club
15. Peninsular House— Nell Gwynn House site
16. Reform Club; Travelers Club; Athenaeum Club
17. Duke of York monument
18. Institute of Directors
19. Crimean War Memorial
20. Royal Opera Arcade
21. Her Majesty's Theatre
22. Haymarket Theatre
23. Oscar Wilde plaque
24. Piccadilly Circus & tube station
⊖ Tube Station

STARTING POINT: Green Park station (Victoria, Jubilee, or Piccadilly line).

APPROXIMATE TIME: One hour.

his *walk takes you past a royal palace, several old London clubs, the site of the historic St. James Theatre, and finally closes with a look at two of the West End's best known and still operating theatres—Her Majesty's and the Haymarket.*

Take *the underground to* **Green Park** *(Victoria, Jubilee, or Piccadilly line). Select a Piccadilly south side exit. Once on the surface locate the gray bulk and covered arcades of the* **Ritz Hotel** *(1906), where afternoon tea is still a production number.*

If you are continuing on from Walk Six, you will end at the entrance to the Green Park station and need only look across the street to find the Ritz. Cross busy Piccadilly and you are ready to begin.

Walk along the side of the hotel under the arches. Visit the lobby if you are reasonably well dressed. Just to the right at the next corner— down **Arlington Street**—*is one of London's most eminent show business restaurants.* Le Caprice was opened in 1947 by Mario Gallati, the head waiter at another still famous theatre eatery, The Ivy. Over the years it has been frequented by Orson Welles, Charlie Chaplin, Vivien Leigh, Robert Morley, Maria Callas, and the playwright Terrence Rattigan. Unless your wallet is well padded, it will probably not be frequented by you. *Go past Arlington Street and on to* **St. James Street**. *Take a peek in the windows of the exclusive shops and restaurants as you walk.*

7

When you reach St. James Street turn right and let your eye roam down one of London's most pleasant streetscapes. Within a scant third of a mile there is a wealth of artistic, political, commercial, and social history. Since the 18th century this street has been the heart of London clubland.

As you start down the hill, the second building on your left is **White's**, *the oldest London Club, founded in 1693.* (You will soon

The Ritz

109

**White's famous
bow window**

observe that none of the long-established gentlemen's clubs do anything so vulgar as to put their name on their door.) The present building dates from the 1750s and contains a famous bow window on the
first floor that should be of some interest to costumers. It was there
that Beau Brummel and his friends displayed themselves in the garb
that set the fashions for the day. Colley Cibber, the 18th-century actor
and theatre manager, was a member of White's. His interest to theatre
historians now is that he added some embellishments of his own to

Shakespeare's *Richard
III*, a couple of which
Laurence Olivier included
in his film portrayal: "Off
with his head, so much
for Buckingham," and on
the morning after the
King's nightmare, "Rich-
ard's himself again."
Edmund Kean was
famous for his effects
with these interpolated
lines, and Olivier was not
averse to following his

Brooks Club

St. James' Palace

example, though none of the film critics seemed to notice.

Continue walking and pass Bennet Street. A bit farther along on your right, just past Number 60, is Brooks Club, founded in 1764. The current building dates from 1788 and is stolid though finely porportioned. Richard Brinsley Sheridan and David Garrick were both members of Brooks, as were men like Edmund Burke, David Hume, Sir Robert Walpole, Charles James Fox, and Sir Joshua Reynolds. If the light is just right you can occasionally see a perfectly suited gentleman in the front room sipping a coffee or reading the paper.

On the left side of the street, across and back a bit from Brooks, at Number 28, is Boodles (white stucco ground floor and brick above) founded in 1762 and in the building since 1783. The building is more airy and gracious than Brooks. *Several other clubs occupy premises on the right side all the way down to St. James' Palace at the far end of the street.* (Clarence House, within the palace complex, was the official home of Queen Elizabeth the Queen Mother until she passed away in 2001 at the age of 101.) *By the way, if you want to see a mini changing of the guard up close and don't want to fight the crowds at Buckingham Palace, station yourself in front of this 16th-century brick gatehouse shortly after noon. Bad weather, state occasions, and seasonal variation can alter or cancel guard changing times so do check on the day of your walk if this is a priority for you.*

Turn around now and walk back up the opposite side of St. James Street. There you will find some of London's most venerable and exclusive shops. Number 3 is **Berry Brothers and Rudd, wine merchants**. Just past their shop, you should see the tiny passage called Pickering Place. Nothing theatrical down there, but it is an enchanting little nook and also the spot where the fledgling Republic of Texas had their official ambassadorial digs from 1842–1845.

Number 6, **Lock and Company, Hatters** always has an extraordinary display of specialized headgear. Number 9 is **John**

111

Berry Brothers & Rudd

Lobb, Bootmaker. Lobb usually exhibits period footwear, including the very lasts used to make Queen Victoria's shoes. Construction is done right in the front of the shop and you can watch their craftsmen work on handmade boots just as they have for two hundred years.

*Continue to walk back up the hill until you reach **King Street**. Then turn right. Locate and take a side trip into gas-lit **Crown Passage**.* There are a number of shops, restaurants, sandwich bars, and a tiny pub called the Red Lion tucked away down there. They are primarily for the locals and reasonably priced. The Red Lion boasts that it holds the second oldest pub license in the West End and if you make your way down the steep stairs to the men's loo, you'll find a door labeled **Nell Gwynne's Cellar**. It's close to the famous Restoration actress' Pall Mall house but not quite worth a cigar; the actual spot is coming along a bit later in this walk.

*Return to King Street, turn right, and continue on to Number 23–24 where you will find **St. James House**.* For theatre historians the name calls up sad reminders of the all but forgotten St. James Theatre. It was built on this site in 1835 by Mr. John Braham, a well-known tenor and good friend of Charles Dickens.

Lobb craftsmen at work

At one point in the lobby of an older St. James House, you could find a handsome bound volume that preserved pictures and programs from the old theatre. It was also possible to obtain from the security guard a small self-congratulatory pamphlet that described the new building that replaced the theatre. The document proudly proclaimed that "the actual site of the stage was now a balcony at the south end of the staff restaurant." How's that for respectful veneration of the past? By the late 1980s a functionary at the door of the building could produce only a badly photocopied version of the original bound scrapbook.

By 1994 a new building had appeared but the old photocopy had disappeared. A frosted glass panel above the door, like a strange ghostly image of the past, is now the only reminder of this site's theatrical past. At the top of the panel is an image derived from a sculpted figure of Fame that appeared above the stage of the old theatre, flanked by two unexplained winged beasts. The side panels are meant to portray a metaphoric family group looking toward Fame and an abstracted curtain with various symbols of culture and business intended to convey a sense of the international cross-fertilization of commerce and art. You may now be the only person within hailing distance who has ever noticed those images or knows what they allude to.

*At this point you need to walk on a few steps further and find a small alleyway opening, just past a ramp leading down to the parking garage entrance. This is called **Angel Court**. Walk down this alley about 50 yards looking on your right for three slabs of stone mounted on a wall over the point where the parking ramp enters the building.* These slabs are three bas-relief panels commemorating people who contributed to the noble history of the St. James Theatre. They used to decorate the front of the 1960 building that replaced the demolished theatre, and have now been moved to their present position of prominence. *Get yourself to a point where you can best see the panels.*

The top one honors Sir George Alexander, the actor-producer, who was in charge of the theatre from 1892 to 1918. His sculpted head is flanked by figures from two of his most famous roles in *The Prisoner of Zenda* and *If I were A King*.

The middle panel featuring bas relief of Oscar Wilde

The middle panel alludes to Alexander's premiere productions in the theatre of Oscar Wilde's *Lady Windermere's Fan* and *The Importance of Being Earnest* in 1892 and 1895 respectively. For some reason, known only to the sculptor, Wilde's portrait is flanked by representations of Dorian Gray and Salome rather than figures from the two famous plays associated with the theatre. Jonathan Sutherland in *Ghosts of London* reports that Wilde's ghost may still haunt the site. A séance held in the theatre in the 1920s apparently materialized a phantom hand that wrote out Wilde's name when given a pen. Other important first nights during this period were Arthur Wing Pinero's *The Second Mrs. Tanqueray* and George Bernard Shaw's *Androcles and the Lion*.

The bottom panel depicts Mr. Gilbert Miller who acquired the theatre lease in 1918 and managed it throughout the twenties and thirties, when a galaxy of West End stars paraded across its boards. A quick sampling of names would include Sybil Thorndike, Edith Evans, Claude Rains, Noël Coward, Cedric Hardwicke, the Lunts, Gerald du Maurier, and Gladys Copper. Miller went on to buy the theatre outright after World War II and controlled its fortunes up until it was sold for redevelopment in 1954.

At this time turn around and go back toward King Street. Just before you reach the street you enter a small covered area containing some tables for the pub next door. On the wall of this little nook you will find a brown wooden plaque commemorating the St. James Theatre, put up by the City of Westminster and the Society of West End Theatres. Set in the wall above it is the fourth bas-relief stone frieze from the 1960 building, featuring the heads of Laurence Olivier and (his then wife) Vivien Leigh, flanked by full length figures of them as Antony and Cleopatra.

The Oliviers took out a four-year lease on the St. James theatre in 1949 with the idea of restoring the grand old 19th-century actor/manager tradition. The figures on the ends of the frieze honor the successful 1951 Festival of Britain productions in which Olivier and Leigh appeared alternately in Shaw's *Caesar and Cleopatra* and Shakespeare's *Anthony and Cleopatra*. Unfortunately the management

Fourth frieze panel featuring Olivier and Leigh

venture proved unsuccessful, and the theatre went dark. There was a last-ditch campaign to save the theatre from the wrecking ball in 1957. Vivien Leigh led the public demonstrations against its closure. She strode along the Strand in a protest march while swinging a large hand bell. Then she interrupted a House of Lords debate from the Visitors' Gallery and had to be escorted from the chambers. Her activities captured the front pages of the newspapers, but they were not enough to save the St. James, and London lost another piece of its glorious theatrical past.

Before leaving you should take a short tour of the **Golden Lion pub.** It has been here long enough to preserve signs of its lost theatrical neighbor. There are little tragic and comic masks in its leaded glass windows. The stairs to the second floor and the luncheon room above are decorated with prints and programs associated with the St. James.

Upon leaving the pub turn right. At or around number 28 (Almack House) once stood Mr. William Almack's Assembly Rooms. From 1705 until 1863, this semi-auditorium was the home of fashionable fine arts, music, and drama soirees. *We should probably also mention that opposite Angel Court is the home, since 1823, of the famous auction house* **Christie's.** Drama of another kind goes on there daily. The sale rooms are open to the public and may be visited.

Moving along King Street you will soon come to the green oasis of **St. James Square.** *Move around the square clockwise using the narrow pavement closest to the park fence. You are entering at six o'clock and will be making an almost full circuit and leaving by the exit at four o'clock.* You can stroll the perimeter of the square solely to admire the facades including some by Adam and Hawksmoor. Along the way you should be able to see the house where three British prime ministers have lived (Chatham House), the Georgian townhouse of Nancy Astor, the first woman member of the British Parliament (a blue plaque), and General Dwight Eisenhower's World War II Allied forces headquarters (Number 3, Norfolk House).

Our choice for a stopping point in the square is at the 11 o'clock position kitty corner from Number 5. It is hard to believe that some years ago this elegant and peaceful location was the scene of an international terrorist incident. On April 17, 1984, demonstrators outside the Libyan embassy (it was Number 5 in the 11 o'clock corner of the square) were fired on from an embassy window. A British policewoman, Yvonne Fletcher, who was guarding the demonstrators, was shot and killed. After several days of negotiating,

Fletcher memorial

115

with the square completely cordoned off, the entire Libyan embassy staff, including the unidentified presumed killer, was escorted to the airport and deported. There is a moving little memorial to Fletcher on the inner corner of the square marking the spot where she was struck down. Fresh flowers are often present even today. *Continue your circuit now and exit the square in the southeast corner at the four o'clock heading. Just a few steps and you will be on Pall Mall.*

Across from you is the Royal Automobile Club building. Cross the street, turn to the right, and stroll along Pall Mall until you locate Number 79, Peninsular House. This 1890 office block now houses the P & O Steamship Line, but in the 17th century this site contained the home of the Restoration actress, Nell Gwynn. As Arthur Mee noted in his *London: The City and Westminster*, all of the south side of Pall Mall is crown property except for this tract. When Gwynn became Charles II's mistress, she insisted that she would not live in a house that was not her own and the King acceded to her demands and deeded the freehold over to her. Two other long term mistresses of Charles II, the Duchess of Cleveland and the actress Moll Davis, also lived nearby.

There is much more to tell here, of course. The lovely Nellie lived at 79 Pall Mall from 1671 until her death and her house became one of the most convivial centers of London political and social life. Though she was never officially raised in status, both of her sons by Charles II were elevated to the peerage. One of them, the Duke of St. Albans, successfully negotiated the British political scene after his mother's death and was installed as a Knight of the Garter by George I. For the full story of this remarkable woman and actress, check out Roy MacGregor-Hastie's biography titled *Nell Gwynn.*

Back across the street from where you are now standing was the bizarre Shakespeare Gallery of London alderman John Boydell. He used a good share of his fortune to commission 18th-century artists to paint and sculpt scenes from Shakespeare's plays. The gallery ended in failure, but the works commissioned for it continue to be exhibited throughout the country. For instance the well-known Fusili Shakespeare drawings, which were originally commissioned by Boydell, are now exhibited at the Tate Britain Gallery.

Reverse your steps and walk back down Pall Mall. You will repass, on your right, the Royal Automobile Club, then a faceless, graceless building (Number 100), then shortly the ornate classical bulk of the Reform Club (Number 104), then the slightly more austere Travelers Club (Number 106) where the intrepid adventurer Philias Fogg set out around the world in 80 days, and finally, at the corner of Pall Mall and Waterloo Place, the creamy stucco site of the Athenaeum Club (1830). At Waterloo Place, the monument to the Duke of York is on your right. Cross the wide boulevard toward the building on the opposite side, John Nash's 1827 United Services Club (now the Institute of Directors) and then turn

7

Athenaeum Club

back. Although there is also a classical frieze on the Nash building, the one by John Henning on the front of the Athenaeum Club is a bit nicer and can best be admired from here. To your right now is **Lower Regent Street** *heading back up toward* **Piccadilly.**

Walk that direction, past the monument for the Crimean War dead, until you come to **Charles II Street.** *Turn to your right here and focus on*

another lovely Neoclassic city view planned and executed by the architect John Nash. Ahead of you at the far end of the street is the gleaming, columned, white facade of the **Haymarket Theatre.**

Nash (1752–1835), the dominant figure in Regency architecture, was the town planning genius who conceived the idea of linking London's West End with Regent's Park via the creation of Regent Street. *His serene style*

Old United Services Club (now Institute of Directors)

117

can also be seen on your right as you walk down Charles II Street. Look for the entryway to the **Royal Opera Arcade** *(1817) which recedes splendidly into the interior of New Zealand House in a series of graceful lighted domes and hanging flower baskets.* Visit some of the pleasant and ever-changing shops if you wish and try to see if you can imagine the scene as it might have been in 1911 when Herbert Beerbohm-Tree organized a gala production of *Julius Caesar* in honor of the coronation of George V and Queen Mary at His Majesty's Theatre just next door. According to Patricia Dee Berry in *Theatrical London* the show featured a huge cast and 300 actors were assigned this Arcade as their dressing room.

If you entered the arcade turn right when you re-emerge. Otherwise just continue to walk straight ahead on Charles II Street.

Four different theatres have stood in the area just past the Royal Opera Arcade moving up toward Haymarket. The first of these was known as the Queen's Theatre and was built in 1705 by the playwright and architect, Sir John Vanbrugh. William Congreve was the first manager. It was a huge barn of a place and not too successful until 1709 when the acting company moved to the Drury Lane Theatre and the vacant theatre was taken over by the producers of Italian opera. Thus it became the cradle of Italian opera in England and the first theatre in the country given over solely to opera production.

After a fire laid the first building to waste, a second and larger theatre took its place in 1791. A remodeling of that building in 1816 resulted in a classical colonnade on three sides with Nash's Royal Opera arcade built to occupy the fourth side. From 1830 to 1850 it was the musical social center of London. Fire took this building as well, and in 1867 a third structure was erected. The next twenty years were checkered, but the theatre did see the London premiere of *Carmen* in 1878, the first complete performance of Wagner's *Ring* in England in 1882, and two Sarah Bernhardt tours in 1886 and 1890.

As you finish your walk toward Haymarket now, you will be alongside the fourth theatre. At the corner note the rather dull plaque and then turn right and view the facade of **Her Majesty's Theatre**, *which was built in 1896 by the great actor-manager* **Sir Herbert Beerbohm-Tree**. Carrying on in the tradition of Henry Irving, Tree was also famous for lavishly mounted Shakespeare productions, with live rabbits in the Forest of Arden and Richard II entering on a real horse. After his first performance as Hamlet, W. S. Gilbert said to Tree, "My dear fellow, I never saw anything so funny in my life, and yet it was not in the least vulgar."

Plaque in lobby of Her Majesty's Theatre

Irving's own view of Tree's clear ambition to succeed him as the pre-eminent actor-manager of the late Victorian era is best exemplified by their famous public encounter on this spot. Tree was simultaneously leasing the Haymarket Theatre and building Her Majesty's for his own use; viewing progress on the latter he was greeted by Sir Henry who said "Mornin' Tree, working?"

In 1904 Beerbohm-Tree started a drama school in connection with his theatre. That school is still functioning, though not here, and is now known as the Royal Academy of Dramatic Arts, commonly abbreviated to RADA.

The Tree tenure from 1897 to 1917 can make up a book alone, as indeed it has, and the stories

Her Majesty's Theatre

abound. One of the most intriguing is that of Hubert Carter, a lumbering giant of a man, who was a supporting player for Tree over many years. According to MacQueen-Pope in his *Ghosts and Greasepaint,* Carter was famous throughout the town as a prodigious eater. He would buy two pounds of steak, have the butcher cube it, eat it raw right there on the spot, and then go in search of lunch. One of Carter's favorite roles was Claudius in *Hamlet*. His interpretation called for a fiercely masculine king and in marvelous pre-Method diligence he would purchase a pint of ox-blood before each night's performance and drink it down just before stepping on stage.

Another story told about him concerned a post-performance visit with a friend to an out-of-the-way pub. Immediately upon their entrance, Carter and his companion attracted the attention of the shady clientele. It was clear immediately that robbery, mayhem, or worse was being contemplated. Carter sized up the situation and strode over to the fireplace, picked a poker out of the grate, and bent it to the shape of a horseshoe. Then, smiling apologetically, he bent it back straight again, and replaced it. He and his friend, unbothered, then finished their drink calmly and left.

In 1916 a show called *Chu Chin Chow* started a 2,238 performance string at Her Majesty's and that was London's long run champion until 1958 when it was passed by the current and still running champion, Agatha Christie's *The Mousetrap*. The post-war years saw the house occupied mainly by musicals, many of them from America, including *Brigadoon, West Side Story, Bye Bye Birdie, Fiddler on the*

Roof, and *Applause. Tree's ghost has been sighted on a number of occasions moving between his top-floor flat under the copper dome and his favorite box. This just might have something to do with the theatre's occupant.* Since 1986—Andrew Lloyd Webber's *The Phantom of the Opera.*

As fascinating as the story of Her Majesty's is, it pales into insignificance, when compared with the history of the Haymarket Theatre, just across the street.

The first Haymarket, or Little Theatre in the Hay, was built in 1720 with the hope of breaking the royal patent monopoly that dated all the way back to Thomas Killigrew and Charles Davenant in the 1660s. But this did not happen and the theatre operated on and off for the next fifteen years as a sort of fringe home for a potpourri of entertainments, some of them legal and some of them not.

In 1733 more notice came to the tiny theatre when Theophilus Cibber, son of the manager and comedian Colley Cibber, brought in a company of disgruntled actors who had revolted against the management of Drury Lane. The patent companies were becoming more than a little disturbed now, and this turned to open warfare when the playwright Henry Fielding took over as manager in 1735. His lively, but crude, satires began to attract positive attention in the town and negative attention from some of the key politicians, who were the butts of Fielding's jokes. Sir Robert Walpole was particularly incensed. Before the fray was over the Licensing Act of 1737 was on the books and Fielding decided that writing novels was a more promising field of endeavor than the theatre.

Briefly, the Licensing Act limited the number of theatres to those currently holding patents, required all new productions to get an authorization from the Lord Chamberlain, and gave the Lord Chamberlain power to prohibit any individual theatrical performance. We do not have time to deal with government censorship of the English theatre here, but suffice it to say that what was initiated primarily by the happenings at the Little Theatre in the Hay remained a part of English law until 1968, when the function of the Lord Chamberlain to approve manuscripts and license plays for performance was finally abolished.

Haymarket Theatre

The effect of the Licensing Act on the Haymarket was immediate and telling. It was closed and remained so for a good deal of the time over the next several years. Finally in 1747, a second-rate actor, Samuel Foote, gathered a company and reopened the building. His gambit to evade the licensing laws was to advertise the sale of tea or chocolate. Musical and dramatic entertainment just happened to be included in the price of the drinks. Things were still touch and go, however; and Foote finally got his official patent the hard way. While at a party he was boasting of his prowess as a horseman. The Duke of York was quick to produce a lively animal. Foote mounted, was thrown, and broke his leg in so many places that it had to be amputated. The contrite Duke offered a favor in order to make amends, and Foote asked for some intercession with the King to get a patent for the Haymarket. Thus in 1766 he was finally granted a license to perform legally during the summers when the other theatres were closed. So in essence Foote got his patent as a result of a lucky break.

Many years later, in 1820, it was decided to rebuild the theatre as a part of John Nash's grand plan for the West End. It was moved a little to the south (the present position) in order to create a pleasing vista from St. James Square down Charles II Street. It is that exterior, completed in 1821, that you still see today making it the second oldest functioning theatre in the city. The interior has been completely renovated several times since then, with the present Louis XIV style dating from 1941. You also came quite near to reading about the second Haymarket Theatre in the past tense. Early in October of 2002, a fire destroyed the building on the corner of Haymarket and Suffolk Place. Only a narrow 30 foot wide structure between the theatre and the burning building kept the flames from spreading.

It is impossible to catalog the list of famous productions and stars that have appeared at the Haymarket over the past 150 years. Even a limited list would have to be a very personal choice. There were Phelps, Macready, Tree, and Ellen Terry in the 19th century, along with plays by Tom Robertson, Shakespeare, and Wilde. In the early 20th century there was the first English production of Maeterlinck's *The Blue Bird*; the original scene designs for that production now decorate the walls of the Upper Circle Bar in the theatre. The year 1914 saw the first licensed public theatre performance of Ibsen's *Ghosts*. In 1944 there was a major repertory season under the direction of John Gielgud. In 1948 Helen Hayes made her first London appearance in Tennessee William's *The Glass Menagerie*. Other successes in recent years have included Thornton Wilder's *The Matchmaker*, *The Heiress*, *The Chalk Garden*, *Two for the Seesaw*, and any number of Shakespeare, Wilde, and Shaw revivals. The latter's *Heartbreak House* starring Paul Scofield, Vanessa Redgrave, and Felicity Kendall was a sellout in 1992. So was Tom Stoppard's *Arcadia* in 1994. A more current and bizarre story centers around the shortlived December,

7

2000 production of Jeremy Archer's crime thriller, *Accused*. Archer, known primarily as a novelist and part-time politician, was at one point acting in his own play at night while appearing as a defendant in a real bribery case at the Old Bailey by day. His understudy was ecstatic as he was guaranteed performances on matinee days when the crime-story author/actor had to appear in a real courtroom. Archer was ultimately convicted and sent to jail.

We shouldn't leave this historic site without mentioning Mr. John Baldwin Buckstone, an actor and manager of the Haymarket from 1853 to 1878. His ghost still allegedly haunts the theatre and has been seen by many actors and stage personnel over the years. He is a benign presence and usually opens and shuts doors, walks the corridors, rests in dressing rooms, or sits quietly in the royal box. His presence is supposed to signal a long run. When Donald Sinden was a young actor he made his West End debut in the 1953 production of *The Heiress*, starring Ralph Richardson and Peggy Ashcroft. One night, descending the stairs from his dressing room to the stage, he passed a frock-coated figure with his back to him. He said, "Good evening Sir Ralph," but received no reply, and was astonished when he reached the wings to find that the great actor was already there, in an identical Victorian costume. He is convinced that as he bounded down the stairs the figure he had passed was the legendary ghost of Buckstone.

*Should you wish to look for him yourself, perhaps you should step across the street and purchase a ticket for the current production. At a minimum, step into the lobby for a moment to soak up the atmosphere. Exit the lobby and turn left. Then go left at **Suffolk Place**, and left again at **Suffolk Street**. Walk all the way to the end of this architecturally perfect cul-de-sac. On your left is the Haymarket Theatre stage door and just to the left of that a nice little plaque honoring the premiere productions of two of Oscar Wilde's plays:* A Woman of No Importance *in 1893 and* The Ideal Husband *in 1895. The plaque was unveiled by Sir John Gielgud in 1995.*

*Retrace your steps back to the Haymarket now and turn to your right. A short stroll will take you to **Piccadilly Circus** and convenient transportation back to your hotel or flat.*

WALK EIGHT

LONG GONE BUT NOT FORGOTTEN:
TOWER HILL TO ST. LEONARD SHOREDITCH

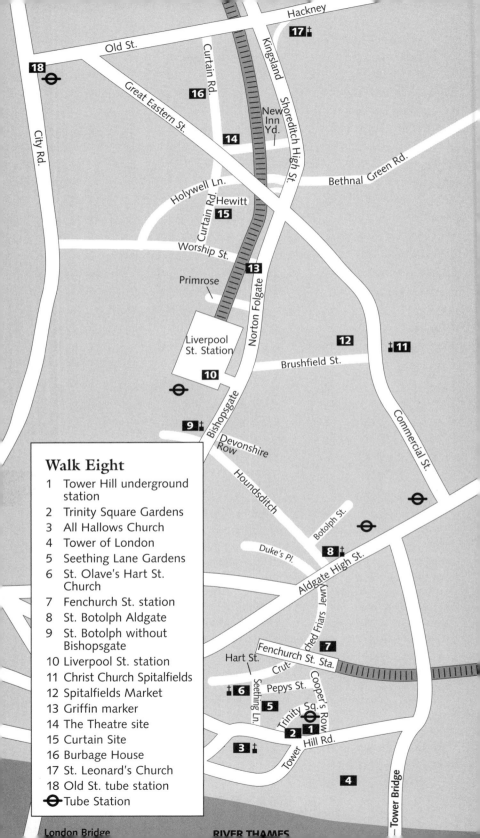

Walk Eight

1 Tower Hill underground station
2 Trinity Square Gardens
3 All Hallows Church
4 Tower of London
5 Seething Lane Gardens
6 St. Olave's Hart St. Church
7 Fenchurch St. station
8 St. Botolph Aldgate
9 St. Botolph without Bishopsgate
10 Liverpool St. station
11 Christ Church Spitalfields
12 Spitalfields Market
13 Griffin marker
14 The Theatre site
15 Curtain Site
16 Burbage House
17 St. Leonard's Church
18 Old St. tube station
⊖ Tube Station

STARTING POINT: Tower Hill station (Circle and District lines) or Liverpool Street station for the abbreviated version (Circle, Central, Metropolitan, or Hammersmith and City lines).

APPROXIMATE TIME: Two hours (30 minutes less for truncated version).

T*his walk is not the stuff that most tourist brochures are made of; the traffic is horrendous, the streets are gritty, the construction sites seem endless and the delights are rather farther apart than in most of the other rambles. It is recommended only for the most dedicated theatre history buffs. The prime reward is a visit to what is arguably still the site of the first permanent, purpose-built, public theatre in London—James Burbage's The Theatre. Its ancillary purpose is to give you a physical sense of exactly what kind of journey it would have taken to get to a performance way out in Shoreditch in the 1580s. There are also a number of other items of thespian interest along the route.*

An abbreviated version of this walk, covering just the journey out of the city gates and to the theatres, can begin at the **Liverpool Street station***. If you choose to start there, exit the tube station into the main concourse of the railroad station. Go up the escalator at the end of the concourse and out onto* **Bishopsgate** *where you will turn left.* Rejoin the text at the appropriate point on page 130.

Rejoin the text at the appropriate point on page 130.

The "full monty" of this walk starts at the **Tower Hill underground station**. It would combine nicely with a visit to the **Tower of London**, which has inspired enough drama to qualify hands down as a premiere theatrical site. The walk does grow out of the Tower's medieval heritage and in addition gives you a chance to get off the main tourist paths. This may be quite welcome if you have spent the morning amid the mobs fighting for your very own 20-second view of the Crown Jewels. (*Remember, if you have visited the Tower, you will need to return to the underground station to begin the walk.*)

Walk dead ahead as you pass through the tube ticket gate and you should be able to see over the busy **Tower Hill Road** the copper green spire of a church called **All Hallows by the Tower**. That's where you are heading. Take a left at the iron fence and look for a gate into **Trinity Square Gardens**. Cross into the park, stop, and take in the vista. Across Tower Hill Road and a bit to the left is the Tower of London itself. To the right, dominating the quiet of the Gardens, is the rather vulgar bulk of the **Port of London Authority building**. And out in front of you is the church spire.

Tower of London

Step quietly along the walk through the **Seaman's Memorial** *and remember that you are also quite near the site of the Tower Hill Scaffold where large numbers of the not-so-lucky met their maker.* It was regarded a privilege to be executed inside the Tower where the public was normally barred and the victim, as William Chambers said, was spared the final indignity of having his head held aloft by the headsman who announced "Behold the head of the traitor." Actually a majority of the condemned prisoners held at the Tower were dispatched at the public scaffold, including that man for all seasons Sir Thomas More. The short stairs leading to the gallows were apparently rickety and More is reputed to have said to the Lieutenant by his side, "See me safely up, for my coming down I can shift for myself."

Exit the park on the opposite side. Then jog left down **Trinity Square** *and finally right onto busy* **Byward Street.** *When you are about even with the church, a subway (underpass) should come up on your right. Use it to cross the road if you value your life.*

All Hallows by the Tower is an extremely old church with even older Roman paving stones in the crypt. *Enter it for a visit if it is open.* From its tower (the current copper spire in the

8

All Hallows by the Tower

Wren style is post World War II), Samuel Pepys watched the Great Fire of London spread in 1666. The church was saved from the ravages of the fire by Admiral William Penn Sr., a parishioner and father of the founder of Pennsylvania. Penn Sr. is said to have instructed some seamen to blow up houses in the path of the fire thus creating a break and saving the church. Strangely enough the same story is told by a warden at nearby St. Olave's Church in Hart Street, but this time the hero was Samuel Pepys, who was trying to save his own parish church. In either case both men lived in the area and would have been concerned about their homes and their respective parish churches. Penn's young son William Jr. was baptized here in 1644. You can see the actual font used, with its carved Grinling Gibbons cover, in the baptistry. One other interesting feature is a Saxon arch dating from 675 A.D. and actually containing some Roman tiles.

If you need a ghost for comfort in old churches, this one apparently has the cat of a former organist according to Jonathan Sutherland. The lady wished to have the cat buried on consecrated ground when it died; the request was turned down; and the animal now restlessly roams the church in the early morning hours.

The church also has one other non-theatrical American association. John Quincy Adams was married here in 1797. Its present theatrical connections stem from its use by the City of London Festival every July as a performance venue for dramatic recitals, which are usually well worth catching if your visit coincides.

Leave All Hallows by the same door you entered. Directly across from you is the entrance to **Seething Lane**. *Take the subway again back to the opposite side of the street. Turn right as you emerge and right again into the Lane. About one block up Seething Lane is a small park called appropriately* **Seething Lane Gardens**. *At its center is a pleasant bust of the neighborhood's most famous resident—Samuel Pepys. A little farther on, again on the right, is* **Pepys Street** *where the great 17th-century diarist lived for many years.* We should perhaps say a bit about this man whose name occurs almost as often as Shakespeare's in these walks. Pepys, who lived from 1633 to 1703, spent most of his adult life as an administrator in the British naval service and in the course of his duties achieved an extraordinarily wide background of travel, knowledge, and social contacts. He was, amongst other things, an avid theatre-goer and his extensive diaries remain one of the best sources for firsthand information about the Restoration theatre in particular and life in 17th-century England in general.

On your left now you will see **St. Olave's Hart Street**, *another fine old church that had to be almost completely rebuilt after destruction by German bombs. Enter the churchyard beneath a macabre gateway of skulls with its Latin motto, "Mors mihi lucrum", which translates as "Death is a light to me."* Dickens in *The Uncommercial Traveller* referred to it as his "best beloved churchyard St. Ghastly Grim." *If*

8

St. Olave's Hart Street

the yard is not open proceed to the next corner and turn left to find the other door to the church. We hope one of the doors will be open so you can view the memorial to Samuel Pepys in the right aisle. Look also at the bust set in a niche high on the left beyond the pulpit. It is of Pepys' wife Elizabeth, who died at the age of 29, and seems to be positioned so that he could look at her as he sat in his pew.

Both husband and wife are reunited now in the crypt beneath the altar. Lunchtime concerts take place here on some Wednesdays and Thursdays.

Leave the church through the exit opposite the churchyard and you will find yourself on **Hart Street**. *To your left a splash of color and a pub sign of a clipper ship in full sail should catch your eye.* It is the front of an art nouveau pub called the Ship dating from the 1890s. It must be one of the most fanciful tavern fronts in the city. Don't bother to go in as the interior has been remodeled into nondescript brewery modern.

After a glance at the pub front retrace your steps back past the church and across Seething Lane. You are now on a street called **Crutched Friars** *and moving toward the bleak stone arch of* **Fenchurch Station**. This unusual street name comes from the 13th-century friary of the Holy Cross that stood in Hart Street. The monks wore a cross as their emblem and were known as the "crossed" or "crutched" order.

Once under the arch of Fenchurch station, you may notice a pub called the Cheshire Cheese. This is not the famous one, which is just off Fleet Street (see Walk Five).

Continuing on in gentle curves you will cross **Lloyd's Avenue** *and then reach* **Rangoon Street**. *At that corner, set into a building wall, you will find a modern statue of two crutched friars. Just beyond that Crutched Friars becomes* **Jewry Street** *and then shortly intersects with* **Aldgate**, *the site of another one of the four original gates into the city.*

Geoffrey Chaucer occupied apartments above this gate from 1374 to 1385. *Make your way as best you can across this busy intersection toward St. Botolph Aldgate, by George Dance the elder.*

Our route takes us along the east side of the church (i.e., the church is on your right) and up Houndsditch, which is the street dead ahead of you. This is a maddening intersection. Unless you are insane enough to vault the metal barriers, you will have to work your way over to Houndsditch via a subway. (That's an underpass, remember.) There's one on the corner labeled Exit 7. If you miss that one there's another labeled Exit 5 around the

The Ship

corner in back of the church. No matter which one you enter make sure you leave by Exit 3. When you emerge just keep walking straight ahead on Houndsditch.

With a bit of imagination, if you have any left after negotiating that intersection, you can see yourself now walking on Houndsditch parallel to the old city wall that ran from Aldgate to Bishopsgate. Your feet are treading on the moat or ditch constructed outside the walls for additional safety. The name apparently comes from some well-known 12th-century kennels for hunting dogs that were located just outside the walls of the city. *After a fair walk you will see*

8

Crutched Friars

St. Botolph Without Bishopsgate

the spire of **St. Botolph without Bishopsgate.** *Keep going until you reach the intersection.*

*Houndsditch ends at **Bishopsgate,** which stood until 1760 at a point to your left.* The church is a bit to the right of that as it stood "without" Bishopsgate. The elder George Dance had a hand in the design of this church as well as the one back at Aldgate. *Cross to the church and go in if it is open.* It's an interesting irony that the older church escaped the great fire of 1566, and this one survived World War II with only one window lost, only to fall victim to an IRA bomb in 1993. Repairing that damage took four years. Our theatrical connection is that we are now in Alleyn country. In an older St. Botolph without Bishopsgate on this site, Edward Alleyn (1566–1626), the actor and co-owner/manager of the Fortune Theatre, was baptized. His family home was up Devonshire Row, a small side street to the right off Bishopsgate. An infant son of Ben Jonson was also buried in the old church. There's also a resident ghost according to Jonathan Sutherland in *Ghosts of London.* A photographer took a picture of his wife in the church in the 1980s and when it was developed there was also the image of another woman in period clothing in the photo. Try it if you have a wife handy.

On your right as you leave is the pleasant churchyard garden complete with a jewel box hall and, would you believe it, a tennis court. Take a bit of a rest here if you feel the need. There will be precious little greenery for the final leg of the walk.

*As you leave the garden, or the church if you have not visited the garden, turn left onto Bishopsgate and move along past the Victorian Gothic pile of the old Great Eastern Hotel. Next is **Liverpool Street station,** where people doing the truncated version of the walk will join up.* The station was originally built in 1874 on the site of the old Bethlehem Hospital for the insane. The current glass and steel entry canopy is obviously newer. The old Bethlehem Hospital had another and more familiar name. It was known as Old Bedlam. It gave the word "bedlam" to our language and provides one of the sites of action in the John Webster play, *The Changeling.* Directly behind Liverpool Street station is Broad Street, which was built on a graveyard where the ill-fated playwright and pamphleteer Robert Greene (1560–1592) was buried. Greene is today remembered more for his bitter attack on Shakespeare, ". . . an upstart crow beautified with feathers . . . the only Shakescene in the country," than for his one major dramatic work, *The Honorable History of Friar Bacon and Friar Bungay.*

Keep moving now past the station and through the present-day bedlam. People beginning the walk here will already be on the station side of the street. As you go by **Brushfield Street** *to your right, you should be able to see clearly the newly restored tower and exterior of* **Christ Church Spitalfields** *built by Nicolas Hawksmoor in the early 1700s.* It is well worth a side trip and a photo if you have an interest in church architecture. Restoration of the interior still has a long way to go, but it was open on our last visit. This is also the way to the once famous Spitalfields Market; it is a shadow of its old self, but area residents are working on its renewal as well.

Turn right again on Bishopsgate if you have taken the diversion; otherwise just keep walking past Brushfield Street. [**Both building and road construction in this area remain a problem for walkers. Unanticipated detours occur and street signs disappear or get relocated.**] *The*

Christ Church
Spitalfields

8

next through street on your left should be **Primrose Street** *where Bishopsgate becomes* **Norton Folgate** *or just Folgate for a scant few yards.* This marks the end of the City of London and a Griffin marker that used to sit astride the center of the road has been relocated now to the corner of Worship Street just ahead.

Although the surroundings may be of little help, it should not take too much imagination to see yourself riding or walking out through the old Aldgate, or Moorgate or Bishopsgate on a sunny, spring afternoon in the late 1570s. Your destination might have been the waving flag of a playhouse. Today you might use the barely visible spire of St. Leonard Shoreditch out ahead as a marker for where you are headed. If you gaze at any 16th-century map of London you will see how the main egress routes flow out past the old city gates and then along familiar strip-mall-like developments into the country. Finsbury Fields, which is where you are in 16th-century geography, was one such parcel of open space that was decidedly rural yet contiguous to the growing city and the roads that led out of it.

Griffin marker signals exit from City of London

Keep walking. Somewhere in this area was a street on which that maker of the mighty line, dramatist Christopher Marlowe, once lived. The next cross street on the left, where the Griffin is now perched, is **Worship Street***, and William Shakespeare is said to have lived there—"six doors from Norton Folgate."*

After you cross Worship Street you are on **Shoreditch High Street** *and facing the next great task, which is to cross the ferocious traffic on the* **Great Eastern Street.** *Two little streets beyond is* **Holywell Lane.** Richard Burbage (1567–1619), the Elizabethan tragic actor, lived near here as did John Webster, author of *The Duchess of Malfi.* Note the narrowness of these lanes even today. The buildings have changed but the basic configuration is still from the 16th century. As we have said, London, like any modern urban area, was growing, ribbon-like, along the main roads out into the countryside. Beyond Holywell Lane, Shoreditch High Street would have been lined with shabby lodging houses, inns, and small businesses. And of course each main thoroughfare would spawn a network of tiny vein-like side streets.

Walk on for one more short block, then take the next left turn at the Texaco petrol station into a clearly ancient and narrow course called **New Inn Yard***. Walk on the right side of the street. Follow it. Go under the railroad tracks and then another block until you reach* **Curtain Road.** *Don't cross the street; just walk a few steps to your right.* A neglected and now almost illegible plaque marks the approximate site of the first permanent public theatre in England—**The Theatre.** A few yards to the left is a newer plaque noting that Shakespeare had acted in The Theatre when it was there.

The Theatre was constructed in 1576 for about 650 pounds by James Burbage, a carpenter turned actor, and his brother-in-law, John Brayne, a greengrocer. It was set back from the road, was round or polygonal, was made of wood, had a paved yard like an inn, a stage supported by posts, a cover or "heaven" over the stage, a "tiring room" for actors, and

THE SITE OF THIS BUILDING FORMS PART OF WHAT WAS ONCE THE PRECINCT OF THE PRIORY OF S. JOHN-THE-BAPTIST. HOLYWELL. WITHIN A FEW YARDS STOOD FROM 1577 TO 1598, THE FIRST LONDON BUILDING SPECIALLY DEVOTED TO THE PERFORMANCE OF PLAYS, AND KNOWN AS "THE THEATRE."

"galleries" for spectators. That is what we know about the first permanent commercial theatre building in London even though it functioned for more than 20 years. It is likely that in addition to all of the plays of Shakespeare up to 1597, the best works of the age were produced here. When this building was dismantled in 1598, the timbers were dragged to Bankside, probably along the route you have just walked, and there reused to construct a new theatre called the Globe. (See Walk One.)

This general area also marks the site of the second purpose-built public theatre in London, The Curtain. *It is nearby on the same Holywell Priory land and totally unmarked, but if you wish to visit it, turn back to the south toward the **Old Blue Last** pub and cross the busy **Great Eastern Street** once again and pick up Curtain Road by a high rise carpark on the other side. On the left side of the road just beyond **Hewitt Street** (and again no doubt back in the field and off the road) was the Curtain, cleverly built in 1577 by Henry Lanman in a location just a bit closer to the city gates than The Theatre.*

Little is known of its shape but Rosemary Linnell has done an excellent job of marshaling the available facts in a tiny 1977 volume titled *The Curtain Playhouse*. Some people have ascribed theatrical significance to the name Curtain Road, but the name Curtain probably refers to an old curtain wall that ran parallel to the original lane, which in those days was called Hog Lane.

Judith Cook in *The Golden Age of the English Theatre* describes an incident that occurred on Hog Lane near the Curtain in 1589. The playwright Christopher Marlowe was accosted there by one William Bradley. Bradley was apparently looking for another poet (Thomas Watson), but ran into Marlowe and decided that he would do. Perhaps it was a case of "any poet in a storm." Weapons were drawn and Marlowe and Bradley were mixing it up when the tardy Mr. Watson arrived on the scene and joined in. Cook reports that, although Watson was not a good swordsman and was soon bleeding from two wounds, Bradley dropped his guard and was run through and killed. Watson and Marlowe were both held for a while, subsequently released on bail, but not officially pardoned for some months. Cook feels that Shakespeare, who also lived nearby at the time ("six doors from Norton Folgate"), might have seen or at least must have heard of the fight and used it in *Romeo and Juliet*. She even goes so far as to speculate that the "brilliant, articulate, and misogynistic Mercutio" was based on Marlowe.

During its existence the Curtain seemed to have had no predominant company in residence and never had the reputation of The Theatre, though the Lord Chamberlain's Men used the building between 1597 and 1599 before they moved into their new home, the Globe, on Bankside. In later years, when the Curtain was the sole surviving playhouse in Shoreditch, it was used by Queen Anne's and Prince Charles' Men. It was destroyed in 1627.

8

You have now completed a true journey back into time. You have walked the route that an average Elizabethan groundling would have taken in order to attend The Theatre or the Curtain. We think it is fair to say that not many 20th-century theatrophiles have made this pilgrimage.

If you have visited the site of the Curtain, retrace your steps back to the site of The Theatre and continue on up Curtain Road. You will pass a building (Number 83) labeled Burbage House. You are probably the only person in the neighborhood who knows what that name refers to. *At the first stoplight, which is **Old Street**, turn right and walk on until the tall, elegant, 192-foot spire of **St. Leonard Shoreditch** appears. That should happen just before or just after you reach a railway bridge. Keep walking until you reach the corner across from the church.* Shoreditch High Street ends at this intersection and Kingsland Road continues to the left. The current church is another George Dance the elder design dating from 1740. The bells of the 15th-century church were still impressive enough in the 16th-century to garner praise from Queen Elizabeth I and to be included for posterity in the famous "Oranges and Lemons" rhyme: "when I grow rich,/say the bells of Shoreditch." Our theatrical interest also centers on the older church for it was the parish church for many of the actors at The Theatre and the Curtain.

8

Cross into the churchyard of St. Leonard and check to see if the building is open. At our last visit this striking edifice was accessible only at odd hours during the week. If it is open you should be able to treat yourself to a memorial tablet in the stairwell to the second floor dedicated to the "players, musicians, and other men of the theatre" who were members of the parish or were buried in the church. The tablet was placed in the church in 1913 by the London Shakespeare League and moved to its current location fairly recently. If you cannot get in, take a seat in the churchyard or on the steps while you read the next section.

The main honorees on the stone are members of the Burbage family. James Burbage (1530–1597), actor, entrepreneur, and builder of The Theatre was buried in the old church, as was his

St. Leonard Shoreditch

elder son Cuthbert, the manager and builder of the Globe, and his younger son Richard (1567–1619), the great tragedian. They all lived and worked in the Shoreditch area.

Richard Burbage began his career in 1585 with the Admiral's Men. Around 1588 he joined Lord Strange's Men and probably made the acquaintance of a young actor and budding playwright named William Shakespeare. By 1598 both men were shareholders in the Chamberlain's Men. Burbage would, in the next few years, create among others the roles of Hamlet, King Lear, Othello, and Richard III. When he was buried at old St. Leonard in March of 1619, "people flocked from all parts of

Plaque inside
St. Leonard Shoreditch

London, in honour of the first sovereign of the English stage."

In addition to the Burbage dynasty, the church memorial also pays homage to a number of other local players who were buried there. There is William Somer (?–1560), a court jester for Henry VIII, and Mr. Richard Tarlton (?–1588), the foremost comic actor of the Elizabethan period. Tarlton was best known for his performances of Elizabethan jigs (medleys of rhymes and songs that were sung and danced to the tunes of popular melodies). Like many gifted comedians, he was an inveterate improviser and the *Oxford Companion to the Theatre* suggests that Shakespeare had Tarlton in mind when he referred to poor Yorick, the King's jester, in *Hamlet*. He may also have been thinking of him when he has Hamlet, in his speech to the players, say, "Let those that play your clowns speak no more than is set down for them." His natural gifts are thought to have inspired Shakespeare to create such popular comic parts as Launce, Bottom, and Dogberry; a drawing of him may be found preserved in a manuscript at the British Library. He died in Shoreditch near the Curtain theatre in the house of his mistress Emma Ball.

In 1598 Mr. Gabriel Spencer, a player at the Rose Theatre on Bankside, was buried in the church. He was not a parish resident but was dispatched during a duel at Hoxton Fields, which was just to the north. His killer was none other than the playwright Ben Jonson.

Also honored are William Sly (?–1608), another principal actor in Shakespeare's company, and Richard Cowley, a bit-part player. A final theatrical burial, just before the old church was destroyed, was that of George Lillo (1693–1739), best remembered as the author of *The London Merchant; or, The History of George Barnwell*. The play was immensely popular both in London and on the continent. It has come to be known as one of the early examples of middle class sentimental tragedy.

At this point the walk is done. You have two main transportation options. From the front of the church you can get on almost any Shoreditch High Street bus [35, 47, 78, 67, 242, or 243] to take you back to **Liverpool Street station** *and connect you with the tube. If totally committed to underground travel walk back down Old Street to the* **Old Street tube station**. *Walk Nine does start at the Old Street station and will deposit you at the Barbican Center (sometime London home of the Royal Shakespeare Company) in fairly short order.*

If you have more time on your hands and are interested in period furniture or design, it is about six blocks up **Kingsland Road** *to the* **Geffrye Museum** *[buses available Number 67, 149, 242, 243].* You will find an attractive building and a series of period rooms arranged in chronological order. As the *Guide to London Museums and Collections* says, "Its scale is untiring, its displays approachable, and its contents immediately apparent." Also in this part of the city is the **Bethnal Green Museum of Childhood** on the Cambridge Heath Road E2. It features toys, doll houses, and model soldiers. *Return down Shoreditch High Street to Bethnal Green Road and from there take an 8 or 8a bus east to the Cambridge Heath Road.*

[See a standard museum guide for more detailed descriptions of these museums.]

8

WALK NINE

DOING BATTLE
AROUND THE
BARBICAN

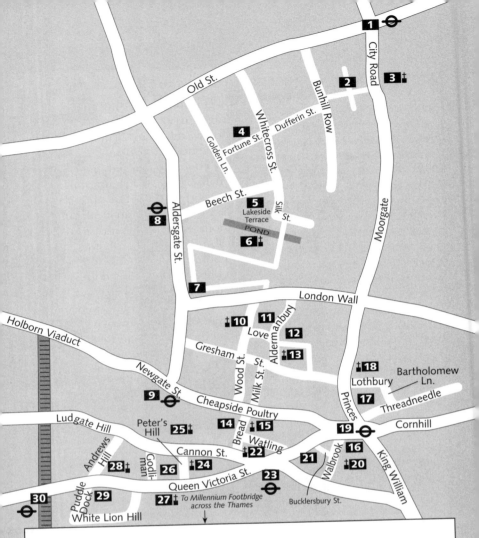

Walk Nine

1 Old Street tube
   station
2 Bunhill Fields
   Cemetery
3 Wesley Chapel
4 Fortune Theatre site
5 Barbican Centre
6 St. Giles without
   Cripplegale
7 Museum of London
8 Barbican tube station
9 St. Paul's tube station
10 Church of St. Albans
11 Site of Wren Church
   of St. Mary Alder-
   manbury & the
   Hemminge-Condell
   monument

12 Guildhall
13 St. Lawrence Jewry
14 Mermaid Tavern site
15 St. Mary-Le-Bow
16 Mansion House
17 Bank of England
18 St. Margaret,
   Lothbury
19 Bank tube station
20 Church of St. Stephen
   Walbrook
21 Temple of Mithras
   remains
22 Church of St. Mary
   Aldermary

23 Mansion House tube
   station
24 St. Nicholas Cole
   Abbey
25 St. Paul's Cathedral
26 College of Arms
27 St. Benet
28 Church of St. Andrew
   by the Wardrobe
29 Mermaid Theatre
30 Blackfriars tube
   station
⊖ Tube Station

STARTING POINT: Old Street station (Northern Line).

APPROXIMATE TIME: Actual walking time is less than three hours, but the better part of a day if you do all three parts and spend some time at the Barbican and the Museum of London.

P art I of this walk takes you to a fascinating cemetery, the site of the Fortune Theatre, a lively street market, and finally on to the now only occasional home of England's Royal Shakespeare Company at the Barbican. The walking part of this section can be polished off easily in 45 minutes. If you are planning a full day, you might begin between 10:00 or 11:00 A.M. This will get you to the Barbican complex in time to check for facility tours, book tickets if there is an appealing musical or theatrical offering available, and have a leisurely lunch on the patio. If you are on a tight budget and the weather is pleasant, grab a sandwich and drink at the tube station. There's a nice spot for a picnic at the little park in Bunhill Fields or on benches around St. Giles without Cripplegate.

Part II takes you to St. Giles Church and the Museum of London. [Note: the museum is now open daily Monday to Saturday from 10 to 5:30 and also on Sundays from noon to 5:30.] Even with a stop at the church, the walk to the Museum of London won't take more than 20 minutes. But the museum visit could be lengthy. We often have difficulty getting out of the bookstore in less than an hour.

Part III visits several Wren churches, the Guildhall, a Roman Temple, some Shakespeare sites, and ends at the Mermaid Theatre. This part involves a fair hike and could be scheduled separately if you spend a lot of time in the museum. There are several tube stops along the route so it can be truncated if you get tired or the hour gets too late.

Part I
(Less than an hour)

O ur starting point is the **Old Street tube station** (Northern line— City Branch). Take Exit 5 out of the station. Walk straight ahead down

Bunhill Fields Cemetery

City Road as you emerge. You are on the right track if the first crossing is Featherstone Street. You'll then shortly pass an office block called Monmouth House. Keep a sharp eye out for the welcome greenery of the **Bunhill Fields Cemetery.**

Just before you reach the cemetery, there is an interesting diversion to your left. The **Wesley Chapel,** *mother church of world Methodism, and* **John Wesley's home,** *now a museum, are available for inspection should you so choose.*

Otherwise turn right into the Bunhill Fields Cemetery opposite. The name is thought to be a corruption of "bonehill" after the piles of bones that would be exposed as the burial ground was reused in successive generations. The cemetery is also unusual because its position, outside of the old city walls, allowed it to accept Jews and other "non-conformists" for burial. The walk through the cemetery is now fenced in to keep you out of the burial grounds proper, but several of the important markers have been moved to the open area at the center of the cemetery. *On your left at the main path crossing is the grave of John Bunyan (1628–88) author of* A Pilgrim's Progress. *On your right is the obelisk for the novelist, Daniel Defoe (1660–1731), and next to it the stone of poet and engraver William Blake (1757–1827). A bit farther to the right is a pleasant little pocket park.* Picnic here if you purchased some food at the tube station.

As you enter Bunhill Fields the city recedes and birdsong takes over. The soul of London is not in the buildings or the traffic; it is in the history and memories of its people. Here in Bunhill Fields the "silent majority" reasserts its power. The stones—chipped, flaking, broken,

9

stained with age, dappled with moss—are eloquent in their silence. They march in measured rows like ghostly gray soldiers over a green carpet. William Blake rests easily here. Mortality and faith repose in quiet equilibrium.

Return from the little park to the crossing at the middle of the cemetery and turn right down the path between the graves. At the next open avenue to your right, walk down to the sarcophagus of Dame Mary Page. Make sure you read the side opposite her name for the rather macabre finish to her life. Cross back to the center path and turn right again. You will ultimately emerge from the cemetery onto **Bunhill Row**. *Take a few steps to the left on this street and then go right on* **Dufferin Street**. *In about two blocks Dufferin Street reaches* **Whitecross Street**. *If you arrive before 2:30 or 3:00 on a weekday afternoon, the intersection marks the bottom end of a colorful local street market. Make a right turn and check out the wares for a bit.*

When you are ready to leave, return to the intersection where you started. To your right Dufferin Street becomes **Fortune Street**. *Make that turn and keep your eyes high and to the right. You will see a blue plaque marking the approximate site of what some might say was the second most famous Elizabethan theatre after the Globe—the* **Fortune**. (The recent stained glass window in St. Giles without Cripplegate pictures the Fortune and gives its location as Golden Lane, which is the next street down from where you are standing.) In any case, it was built near here in 1600 for Richard Henslowe and Edward Alleyn by Peter Streete, a carpenter who had recently done a similar job on Bankside's Globe Theatre for the Burbage brothers. The building contract for the Fortune survives in Henslowe's papers, but at several key junctures the contract unfortunately tells Mr. Streete to simply follow the model of the Globe. Once again the answer to the nagging question, "What did the interior of an Elizabethan theatre really look like?", eludes the researchers. Interestingly, however, some of the measurements that do occur in the Fortune contract have been used in working out the dimensions for the new Globe reconstruction.

The first Fortune burned in 1621 and was replaced by a circular brick amphitheatre that

9

Fortune Theatre window in St. Giles without Cripplegate

The FORTUNE THEATRE GOLDEN LANE

Fortune Theatre site

survived until 1649. For thorough discussions of this theatre and many of the others mentioned in this book refer to Jean Wilson's *The Archaeology of Shakespeare* published in 1995.

Step back to the intersection and turn right. Think of this busy corner as the nexus of a conduit that fed people out of the city through Cripplegate or Moorgate into the more open spaces of the Finsbury Fields area. Henslowe and Alleyn were not fools when it came to business. Small villages were growing and suburbs were springing up in the area. Travel all the way through the city and across the river to reach Bankside was less than convenient. And out here they would not have to compete so directly with their chief rivals, The Chamberlain's Men, with their sumptuous new Globe and their well known and respected playwright William Shakespeare.

Continue walking now away from the street market. On the left are more markets, a covered mall, and a large Safeway food store. Ahead of you rise the brutal towers of the Barbican Estate. If you want a brief respite and a chance to see the Barbican towers more clearly, turn right into Shrewsbury Court just past the pub on the corner. You'll find a little playground, some green space, and several benches. If you take this

9

The Barbican Centre entrance

*diversion turn right again when you return to Whitecross Street. It is then just a brief walk on down Whitecross and across busy **Beech Street** and into **Silk Street**, which will take you to the main **Barbican Centre** entrance.*

As you move down the curved drive you will see the Barbican Theatre's stage door on your left. Just beyond is an enclosed rectangle about 12 by 50 feet in size. This is the lift used to deliver scenery to the scene docks. A fully loaded lorry drives on and then is lowered down into the bowels of the building. If you are lucky enough to find the lift down, it is quite a sight. You peer over the railings and wonder just what a truck is doing down there in a hole that appears to have no exit.

Just past the huge lift is the main entrance. An information desk and ticket office are located to your right. You can book tickets for any event right here.

The Barbican Arts Complex contains two theatres, a concert hall, an excellent public library with a fine theatre and general arts collection, restaurants at all price ranges, a cinema, art galleries, exhibition halls, conference rooms, book stalls, and special facilities for the Guildhall School of Music and Drama. Even without the RSC in full residence the facility is well worth a thorough exploration. Unfortunately, the organization of the interior space is not transparent, and the signage gives little help. A massive reworking of the interior lobbies has just been announced and perhaps the future will see a clearer, more friendly layout.

Part II

(20 minutes plus any time spent at the church)

With some exploration of the Barbican and possibly lunch out of the way, pick up your walk again at the church of **St. Giles without Cripplegate**. You can see your destination clearly from the **Lakeside Terrace** on the ground floor; getting there takes a bit of doing. To reach the church take the stairs or lift up to level two, turn right, go out through the heavy doors. Then turn right again onto **Gilbert Bridge**, which is the causeway across the lake. At the far side you will find some stairs that will descend into **St. Giles Square**.

The ancient church that sits on St. Giles Square is the only building in the 600-acre Barbican site that pre-dates World War II. The main fabric, much restored after the World War II bombing that leveled the surrounding area, dates from 1545. John Bunyan and Daniel Defoe, whose graves you passed a short time ago in Bunhill Fields cemetery, were worshipers here. So were Sir Thomas More and the musician, Thomas Morley. Edward Alleyn, actor and co-owner of the nearby Fortune Theatre, is also said to have attended services here and is honored by a stained glass window donated in 1996 by the trustees of the Dulwich Estates and the St. Luke's Trust. The win-

St. Giles Without Cripplegate

dow is to your left after you enter.

Alleyn is declared a "Benefactor of the Parish" and his picture is flanked on one side by the Fortune Theatre and on the other by the almshouses he built for the parish. Oliver Cromwell, the Great Protector, was married here, as was Ben Jonson.

The most famous grave in the church is that of the poet John Milton, whose gravestone is set in the floor just to the right of the pulpit as you face the altar. You must look carefully as it is almost illegible in the dim light. A lifesize statue of him also gazes at you from the north aisle. Also worth a look is the wall memorial to John Speed (1552–1629). Though touted first as a citizen, merchant tailor, and historian on his marker, today he is remembered best for his capabilities as a mapmaker.

Several members of the family of Sir Thomas Lucy are also buried here. Lucy, you may remember, was the landowner and magistrate of Stratford who supposedly caught and punished the young Shakespeare for poaching and literally helped drive the boy out of Stratford and to his better fortunes. Justice Shallow in *The Merry Wives of Windsor* is felt by some to be a satirical portrait of Sir Thomas.

Jonathan Sutherland, in his *Ghosts of London*, reported on a strange incident in the church when a thief attempted to steal a ring by cutting off the finger of a newly buried female corpse. The corpse apparently sat up and cried out in pain. The thief fled and the revived woman ran back

Edward Alleyn window in St. Giles without Cripplegate

9

home, where after giving everybody a good fright, she was received back into the family. The incident recalls the nasty murder committed by the villain De Flores in Middleton and Rowley's *The Changling*. The corpse did not wake up in this case, but the cutting off of a finger to retrieve a ring is a central element in the bloody plot.

More information about this fascinating church can be found on several historical display boards in the church and there are additional pamphlets available at a modest cost.

Upon leaving the church walk around the building to your left where you will find a pleasant paved terrace overlooking a pond and a splendidly preserved section of the medieval London Wall. Continue around the church until you are back at the stairway where you entered the square. On your left is a pub called Crowder's Well.

To head for the Museum of London climb back up the stairs and turn right at the top, away from the Barbican complex. Take another right at the next passage labeled Wallside. From now on it's as if you were patrolling the parapets of the great wall around the city of London itself. Each step gives you another striking view of St. Giles and the Barbican estate. Continue to follow the yellow brick line on the floor. Walk on until you reach Thomas More Highwalk. Bend a bit right and continue through a small court and go left at John Wesley Highwalk. This walkway will wind and twist, but will ultimately deposit you at the entrance to the Museum of London, which was built just outside the old city walls and on the site of an old Jewish Cemetery. [Note: Major reconstruction of the entrance to the Museum of London was taking place late in 2002. You may need to do some improvisation to find your way into and out of the building.]

This magnificently arranged museum, which allows you to walk through the history of London from prehistoric time to the present, is one of London's real bargains. You could easily spend the rest of the day here. There are several theatrical exhibits including one on the excavations at the Rose Theatre site. The bookstore, as we mentioned before, is superlative. If time gets away from you, just call it a day and ask for directions to the **Barbican** or **St. Paul's tube station**.

9

London Wall

Part III

(1½ to 2 hours)

When you leave the museum take a left on the walkway marked **Nettleton Court**, which shortly turns into **Bastion High Walk**. More of the ancient city walls (the same ones you saw from inside the museum) will shortly appear on your left. Stop at the explanatory plaque. The street below and to the right is **London Wall** and somewhere between here and the next street ahead (**Wood Street**) was the now vanished Silver Street.

In late 1603 or early 1604 William Shakespeare moved into the home of Christopher Mountjoy, which was located on Silver Street near Cripplegate. It was a prudent move for several reasons. This was a far more fashionable district than Bankside, Will's fellow players and friends Heminge and Condell lived nearby, and it would be easy to slip out on an afternoon and check out the competition at the Fortune.

Mountjoy was a French Huguenot who made headdresses and ornaments for women. He also had a daughter who fell in love with one of his apprentices, a young man by the name of Stephen Belott. Shakespeare was apparently asked to assist in arranging the marriage. The details of the affair came to light in 1612 when Will was asked to give a deposition in a court case in which the now estranged young Belott was suing old Charles Mountjoy for non-payment of some promised parts of his daughter's dowry. This deposition, which was taken in Stratford, gives us our only clue to Shakespeare's everyday speech habits and also provides us with one of his six surviving signatures.

*Walk on now toward the hovering presence of a huge new office block called **Alban Court**.* In order to take advantage of air rights the building was built over the intersection of Wood Street and it is a remarkable piece of engineering—like a massive erector set. *Turn right as you reach a covered courtyard-like area at the end of Bastion High Walk. If you stand at the end of this terrace you can look down Wood Street and see the solitary steeple fragment of the church of St. Albans—a World War II bombing victim that was never rebuilt. To get back to street level, there's an escalator to your right or a ramp to your left. Either one will suffice. Once you have reached Wood Street walk past the funky modern building on your right with its external elevators and multicolored metal funnel pipes sticking out of the ground and head directly for the remnant of St. Albans. Turn left just beyond the steeple into **Love Lane**.*

In a short block you will see on your left a tiny open plot of green. This space preserves the foundation stones of the Wren church of St. Mary Aldermanbury. The bombed ruins of this church were labeled stone by stone and transported to the United States where, reconstructed, they stand today in Fulton, Missouri, barely two hours drive from the home of one of your authors (Jim De Young). It was at the dedication of the reassembled church that Sir Winston Churchill made his famous speech in which the term "Iron Curtain" was coined and where not too long ago former Soviet Premiere Gorbachev officially declared that the Cold War was over. *We stop here, though, because the square also contains a monument surmounted by a bust of William Shakespeare.*

Ironically, the memorial isn't for Will but for his fellow players and friends John Heminge and William Condell, who were church wardens of and buried in St. Mary Aldermanbury. Heminge (1556–1630) was a member of Lord Strange's Men for a time, a member of the Chamberlain's Men, and may have been the first actor to play Falstaff. Although he appears to have retired from acting around 1611, he continued on as business manager of the company. He is mentioned in Shakespeare's will and was a trustee in the Blackfriars gatehouse purchase. Like Shakespeare he appears to have ended his days a well-fixed and comfortable burgher.

Monument to Heminge & Condell, publishers of the first folio edition of Shakespeare

Condell (?–1627) seems to have joined the Chamberlain's Men about 1594 at the same time Shakespeare did, but did not become a shareholder until 1612. In 1623 Heminge and Condell gave the plays of William Shakespeare to the ages by compiling and overseeing the publication of the First Folio edition of his works. You can view a copy at the British Library, which is near Euston station. Without this labor of love many of the plays might have been lost forever. No truer friends had any man in terms of what they gave of their colleague to the rest of the world.

Follow the direction of Shakespeare's gaze out of the churchyard and walk south down **Aldermanbury Street**. *On your left is the Guildhall Library, which contains a nice bookstore and exhibit area. A left turn just past the library will deposit you into the new and spacious* **Guildhall Square**. The Guildhall is the ceremonial seat of government for the City of London. *You may wish to visit the medieval crypt or the Great Hall. The entrance is to your left.* Descriptions are available inside but one thing they may not tell you is that Richard Brinsley Sheridan composed the inscription on the monument to Lord Nelson in the Great Hall.

9

Guildhall

If you are standing in the courtyard with your back to the Guildhall, you should see across from you the Wren church of **St. Lawrence Jewry.** *Look at the weather vane atop the spire.* It is shaped like the gridiron on which St. Lawrence was roasted alive. A visit, not to the gridiron hopefully but to the church, is possible if you wish; *otherwise head for the small street at the back of the church and note as you pass that the Jacobean dramatist Thomas Middleton was baptized in the pre-Wren church and that Sir Thomas More preached there.*

As you exit the Guildhall Yard, you will almost immediately be out on **Gresham Street.** *Turn right on Gresham, go past* **Milk Street,** *and proceed one more block until you meet up with Wood Street once again. Turn left on Wood Street until the "T" junction at* **Cheapside.** *To your left you get a gorgeous view of the 222-foot spire of* **St. Mary-Le-Bow.** To be a true Cockney (or Londoner) you must have been born within the sound of the Bow bells that supposedly recalled the apprentice Dick Whittington to his hard duties in the city of London. The crypt of strong Norman arches (the first in the city built on "bows" of stones) still exists, although the church has been much changed inside. The spire is one of Christopher Wren's finest and also includes some bows of stone. It prompted an admirer in 1750 to say, "The steeple of Bow Church is as perfect as human imagination can contrive."

Now cross the street, jog ten yards to the left and enter **Bread Street.** *A house or two from the corner, on your right about where the fountain is in the subterranean court, stood the famous* **Mermaid Tavern** *where Ben Jonson held sway the first Friday of every month.* William Shakespeare was also a regular, for Jonson wrote in reference to him, "That such thy drought was and so great thy thirst, that all thy plays were drawn at the Mermaid first."

A man by the name of Fuller in 1662 recalled Jonson and Shakespeare in witty combat at the inn and described it thus:

> Master Jonson (like a Spanish galleon)
> built for higher in learning, solid but
> slow in his performance. Shakespeare,
> with the English man of war, lesser in
> bulk, but lighter in sailing . . . could
> take advantage of all winds by the
> quickness of his wit and invention.

Among the other wits, artists, and poets who frequented the Mermaid were Christopher Marlowe, Michael Drayton, John Donne, Inigo Jones, Thomas Campion, Beaumont and Fletcher, Sir Walter Raleigh, and much later on, in the 19th century, the poet John Keats who cemented its fame with the lines:

> Souls of poets dead and gone,
> What Elysium have you
> known,
> Happy field or mossy
> cavern,
> Choicer than the
> Mermaid Tavern.

Return to Cheapside and turn right. Pass St. Mary-Le-Bow and visit the interior if you wish. Cross to the other side of the street after you leave or pass the church and continue eastward on Cheapside (a corruption of the word "cheap" or "market") until it turns into **Poultry** *(which was the old chicken market). At Number 90 is a blue*

St. Mary-Le-Bow (entrance at left)

149

*plaque noting that Thomas à Becket, the ill-fated Archbishop of Canterbury, was born thereabouts. And finally you will reach the confusing and muddled intersection known as **Bank** that qualifies as the true center of the City of London. The **Mansion House** (home of the Lord Mayor of London) is on your right. A bit ahead and on your left, occupying the space between **Prince's Street** and **Threadneedle Street**, is the impressive and austere facade of Sir John Soane's most famous building, the **Bank of England.*** (Walk Three visits Soane's home, now an extraordinary museum.) Actually only the windowless perimeter is Soane's work; the seven-story interior is a 1925–39 rebuilding. The dramatist Richard Brinsley Sheridan once called the bank "The Old Lady of Threadneedle Street." A cartoonist picked up on it and the name has stuck ever since.

*Turn to your left up **Princess Street**, following the blank curtain wall of the Bank, and then right on **Lothbury** where Restoration theatre owner Thomas Killigrew was born. About one-third of the way down the street you will see on your left the spire of **St. Margaret, Lothbury.*** This church is built right over one of the lost rivers of London (the Wallbrook), which curves to run right under the Bank of England as well. The church escaped World War II destruction and the intimate interior is a Wren original, not a reconstruction. The furnishings come from several other now gone or destroyed churches and include a font and pulpit by Grinling Gibbons and a magnificent carved screen that features two-strand openwork balusters that are truly a marvel of grace and skill. *When you leave the church turn left and then right on **Bartholomew Lane**. About halfway along you will notice on your right an entrance to the Bank of England Museum where, if you are interested, you can get a fulsome history of the money and banking industry in Britain and even buy a bottle of Bank of England wine. If you have stopped, turn right again upon exiting; if not, just keep going up to **Threadneedle Street** where you turn right once again. Shortly you will be back at the busy Bank corner and, if anyone ever asks, you can brag that you have been all around the Bank of England.*

Now look for a tube station or subway access sign and head downstairs. Sniff the air. Jonathan Sutherland reports that "the smell of a freshly dug or opened grave is said to emanate from nowhere in this station." Perhaps it is just the odor of old money. *Once under the intersection find an exit sign marked Queen Victoria Street/ Walbrook, which should be Exit Eight. Emerge on **Walbrook**.* You are still in the bed of the stream that has come out from under the Bank of England and will now flow South down to the Thames. *A short distance down Walbrook on your left at the corner of **Bucklersbury** is the Wren **Church of St. Stephen Wallbrook**.* It is an odd building set on an oddly cramped site. A spire that seems a bit too small tops the square tower, but the interior is set around a remarkable dome, which is said to be an experiment for the later St. Paul's. Some people feel it is more beautiful than St. Paul's.

After years of restoration, the church is now open on Monday through Friday from 9 to 4. *Enter if you can.* The dome remains splendidly baroque while the free-form communion table at the center with its multicolored kneeling band and light beechwood benches brings you forcefully into the modern era.

Our theatre quest can also be satisfied here since the church is the last resting place of the architect and author Sir John Vanbrugh. Although perhaps best known as the architect of the great palace of the Dukes of Marlborough at Blenheim, Vanbrugh also designed the Queen's Theatre in the Haymarket (1705) and wrote several minor but still pleasant and witty 18th-century comedies including *The Relapse* (1696) and *The Provoked Wife* (1697).

Slightly to your right as you exit the church you should see a sign for Bucklersbury Street. Walk the short block down to **Queen Victoria Street***, then turn left and keep a sharp eye out for the remains of the Temple of Mithras, a Roman house of worship, found in 1954 during excavations for the large building behind it. It has been moved to its present location.*

Proceeding on down Queen Victoria Street you will arrive at another major intersection. On the right, in the pie-shaped wedge bounded by Queen Victoria Street and Watling Street, is the Wren church of **St. Mary Aldermary***.* It has a delightful ceiling of most un-Wren-like fan vaulting.

If you have visited the church, return to the right side of Queen Victoria Street and continue your stroll. If the hour is getting late or your feet are giving out, you may truncate the walk at the **Mansion House tube station** *coming up shortly.*

If you wish to continue, forge on past the tube station on Queen Victoria Street toward **Friday Street** *where you will see on your right the first church that Christopher Wren put his efforts to after the Great Fire of London.* **St. Nicholas Cole Abbey** (1667) is dramatically interesting because of its late 19th-century rector, Henry Clay Shuttleworth. Shuttleworth, who spoke out eloquently and at length on labor and housing conditions in late

St. Nicholas Cole Abbey

9

Victorian England, was one of George Bernard Shaw's models for the socialist vicar, James Mavor Morrell, in *Candida*.

*A little farther on is the well-known Peter's Hill view of **St. Paul's Cathedral**. To your left at that point is the access to the **Millennium Footbridge** now locally referred to as the "Wibbly Wobbly Bridge" because on the very day that it opened in 2000 it began to shake when people walked on it.* It took two years to repair, but now it is an attractive and heavily used access to both the Shakespeare's Globe theatre and the Tate Modern museum. There are lots of photo opportunities here.

*This is followed shortly on your right by the **College of Arms**.* William Shakespeare would have dealt with them when he was pursuing the granting of a Coat of Arms for his father in 1596. *Across from the College, on your left now, is another Wren church.* This elegant little jewel called **St. Benet** has been boxed in by modern sterile brick on two sides and a raised motorway on a third. It lies nestled, forlorn, and probably generally overlooked by most people who pass by. The old church would have been visible from the Globe theatre located just across the Thames and may have prompted the line in *Twelfth Night* act V scene 1 when the clown says, ". . . the triplex sir is a good tripping measure; or the bells of St. Benet, sir, may put you in mind: one, two, three."

As rebuilt by Wren, St. Benet has rich red and blue brick, striking white corner dressings, and large airy windows. Inigo Jones—the stage designer, architect, and father of English Classicism—was laid to rest in the old church in 1652, a scant 12 years before the Great Fire of London destroyed the building. Novelist Henry Fielding (1707–1754) was married in the present building. For theatrical trivia buffs the church

9

Millennium footbridge with St. Paul's Cathedral in background

St. Benet

also contains the tomb of John Charles Brooke, an officer of the College of Arms, who was one of the 16 people crushed to death when George III and his queen caused a riot during a visit to the Haymarket Theatre in 1794.

In order to continue now you must take the subway under **White Lion Hill**. *Follow a sign that points you toward* **Blackfriars** *and the* **Mermaid Theatre**. *Once back at street level you will see shortly on your right the church of* **St. Andrew by the Wardrobe**. We visited the other side of this church on Walk Two. You may remember that just up St. Andrew's Hill was the Blackfriar's Priory Gatehouse purchased by William Shakespeare in 1613. It is uncertain as to whether Shakespeare ever actually lived there though the church, in its Shakespeare memorial, claims him as a parishioner. No matter; it was a stone's throw from the Blackfriar's Theatre, which was the winter home of The Chamberlain's Men and certainly would have been convenient.

At the next stoplight intersection, a slight turn to the left will take you to **Puddle Dock and the Mermaid Theatre**. When it was opened on May 29, 1959, the bells of St. Paul's pealed a welcome to the first new theatre to be built within the confines of the City of London since the Puritans closed down the theatres in the 1640s. It was as much the brainchild of Bernard Miles (later Lord Miles) as the reconstructed Globe was of Sam Wanamaker. Miles persuaded the City of London companies to put up the money, and ran some very adventurous and successful seasons, with a repertoire that included revivals of infrequently seen classics: John Ford's *'Tis Pity She's a Whore*; little known works by the famous: Sean O'Casey's *The Bishop's Bonfire*; and unusual new plays, e.g., an adaptation of Frederick Rolfe's novel, *Hadrian VII*.

The Mermaid interior has been tinkered with since 1959, but was originally built within the shell of a bombed out Thameside

9

warehouse. It had an open proscenium stage, with seating for around 500 people in one sharply rising bank. At its opening Caroline Hawkins, the four-year-old daughter of actor Jack Hawkins, was rowed up the Thames dressed as a mermaid. She was carried into the theatre and presented on stage to the Lord Mayor of London, who took off her tail to symbolize that the Mermaid was here to stay. That remains to be seen as the still quite unfashionable location has caused the theatre to be dark a great deal in the past several years. A proposal to demolish the theatre was lodged in the year 2000, and its future remains uncertain.

With that fish story you may not to wish to stay around any longer either. There's not much to see at the theatre and the Blackfriars tube station is just a few steps away across the intersection in front of you.

9

WALK TEN

THE NOT-SO-BRIGHT LIGHTS OF SOHO

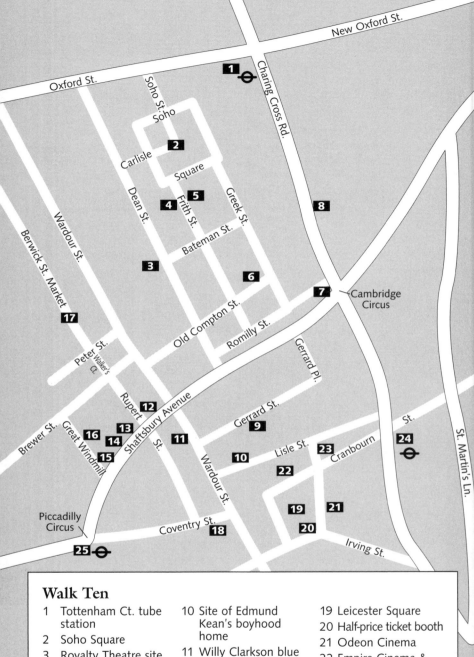

Walk Ten

1. Tottenham Ct. tube station
2. Soho Square
3. Royalty Theatre site
4. Macready House
5. Hazlitt's Hotel
6. Prince Edward Theatre
7. Palace Theatre
8. Phoenix Theatre
9. John Dryden residence
10. Site of Edmund Kean's boyhood home
11. Willy Clarkson blue plaque
12. Queen's Theatre
13. Gielgud Theatre
14. Apollo Theatre
15. Lyric Theatre
16. Windmill Theatre site
17. Berwick St. Market
18. Prince of Wales Theatre
19. Leicester Square
20. Half-price ticket booth
21. Odeon Cinema
22. Empire Cinema & Dance Hall
23. Daly's Theatre site
24. Leicester Square tube station
25. Piccadilly Circus tube station

⊖ Tube Station

STARTING POINT: Tottenham Court Road tube station (Central and Northern line).

APPROXIMATE TIME: One to one and one-quarter hours without a lunch stop.

*T*his walk covers some important theatres of the past and introduces you to several current West End theatres. It takes you on an optional tour past some alternative entertainment venues (sinful Soho is pretty ho-hum now, and you need have no fear of trekking around alone during the day) and visits a couple of street markets. Ultimately it deposits you in Leicester Square at the half-price theatre ticket booth. Time your start to get you to the square sometime after the 10 A.M. opening time. If it's a nice day, consider packing a lunch to eat in Soho Square.

Leave the **Tottenham Court Road tube station** through the exit labeled **Oxford Street South Side.** That is Exit Number 1. There's a McDonald's dead ahead of you as you reach the street. Once topside turn left and walk down to **Soho Street** (the first traffic signal), where you turn left again.

Walk down Soho Street. It is but a brief stroll to pleasant, tree-shaded **Soho Square.** If you're here around lunch time on a nice day this park will be overflowing with office workers taking their lunch and some of those rare English rays of sunshine. Find yourself a bench or plot of grass left or right of the entrance and sit a spell or have your lunch while you read the next few paragraphs.

According to Arthur Mee in his classic *London: The City and Westminster*, the name Soho comes from the hunting cry "So-ho" which was used by Charles II's illegitimate son, the unfortunate Duke of Monmouth, an early resident of the district, to try to rally his beleaguered forces at the Battle of Sedgemoor in 1685. The area was farmland in medieval times and belonged to an abbey. In 1536 Henry VIII acquired the land and promptly ceded portions to various supporters. Today's street names such as Monmouth, Leicester, Carlisle, and Newport recall some of those early owners and their palatial homes. Other streets in the area were named after 18th-century owners and builders like Wardour, Frith, Gerrard, and Shaftesbury.

The square that surrounds you was laid out in 1681 and has seen a rich dramatic and artistic history. Not enough of the buildings are

10

Mock Elizabethan hut in Soho Square

original to do a walkaround, but the scale remains congenial. As you sit and look about, you should be able to note the statues of Charles II done by Caius Cibber, father of the actor and producer Colley Cibber. On the east or left side of the square as you sit, the actor-manager George Colman the elder (1732–1794) lived for some eleven years. On the south side, in front of you, was the residence of Charles Kemble. Kemble was a minor actor and manager in a family of considerable renown. His elder brother Charles Philip Kemble (1757–1823) and his sister Sarah Siddons (1755–1831) were pre-eminent members of the London theatrical scene. Charles also had an attractive daughter, by the name of Fanny Kemble (1809–93), who lived at Number 29 Soho Square with him. She was equally at home in both tragedy and comedy and lived a varied and interesting life that is well told in a biography titled *Fanny Kemble* by Dorothy Marshall.

On the north side of the Square, somewhere behind you, the Soho Academy existed from 1726 to 1805. The school was famous for its Shakespeare performances and several of its pupils went on to become professional actors.

You can get up now and stroll toward the center of the square with its little mock Elizabethan hut. At the center turn right and exit the square via **Carlisle Street**. *At* **Dean Street** *turn left.* This is film country now and many production and distribution companies have their offices in the vicinity. *Walkers of the world unite and note high on the left above Number 28, the Quo Vadis restaurant, the blue plaque commemorating the former residence of Karl Marx.*

10

Another lost London theatre stood at Number 73 Dean Street (Royalty House), opposite the entrance of Bateman Street. From 1840 to 1953 this was the site of a tiny theatre known as the **Royalty**. The full story of this remarkable theatre can be read in Mander and Mitchenson's *Lost Theatres of London* and just a brief sample is given here.

Royalty Theatre site

The theatre was the brainchild of an actress by the name of Francis Maria Kelly. Miss Kelly had definite ideas about the training of young actors and actresses and decided that she needed her own theatre to do the job right. Her solution was to build her own theatre behind her house at Number 73 Dean Street. She began her planning for the theatre and accompanying school in 1834, retired from the stage to devote herself full time to the project in 1835, and completed the theatre in 1840, having sunk most of her wealth into its construction. The opening was disastrous, primarily because of a complicated scene-changing mechanism that had to be operated by a horse-powered treadmill. The chains, blocks, and tackles were so noisy that they made the actors inaudible. When it was operated the entire house shook and, according to one reviewer, gave the audience St. Vitus Dance. To top it off the ghost of a murdered 18th-century woman, whose skeleton had been discovered in the basement of the Queen Anne house that had occupied the site, kept walking down the stairs to the lobby, screaming, and then disappearing.

Miss Kelly finally disappeared from the scene in the mid-1840s having expended her fortune and her health in the luckless enterprise, but over the next 50 years some of the most important events in the English-speaking theatre occurred in the building. Charles Dickens acted here with his amateur company in Jonson's *Every Man in His Humor* in 1845. In 1875, the initial Gilbert and Sullivan collaboration, *Trial by Jury*, was performed here. Then in 1891, J. T. Grein and his Independent Stage Society took over the theatre and produced the first public performance in England of Henrik Ibsen's *Ghosts*. George Bernard Shaw's first major play *Widower's Houses* was given its initial production here in 1892 and one would hope with stronger performances than given by an apparently fetching but hopeless actress named Hope Booth. Shaw had reviewed her in a show at the Royalty earlier in the decade by noting that she was ". . . a young lady who cannot sing, dance, or speak, but whose appearance suggests that she might profitably spend three or four years in learning these arts, which are useful on the stage."

10

1892 also saw the first London production of Brandon Thomas' *Charlie's Aunt*. 1893 and 1894 respectively saw the premiers of Ibsen's *A Doll's House* and *The Wild Duck* as well as some of William Poel's experiments in Elizabethan staging. Shaw's *You Can Never Tell* opened there in 1899. There might be a legitimate argument for claiming that the modern theatre in Britain began quite close to where you are now standing.

After the turn of the century the fortunes of the theatre seemed once again hit and miss and it closed down just before World War II. Blitz damage forestalled attempts to reopen after the war and it was finally demolished in 1953, and the present office building, Royalty House, was built in 1955. Also laid to rest at that time was the busy ghost of Miss Fanny Kelly, whom Joe Mitchenson claimed to have seen in 1934.

After suitably lamenting the loss of the Royalty, turn to your left down **Bateman Street** *and travel the short block to the intersection of* **Frith Street**. *Turn left and walk up toward Number 64, which was the home of the tempestuous actor-manager William Charles Macready (1793–1873).* Macready was a notable tragedian, famous for "the Macready pause," and was one of the few real rivals to Edmund Kean. He is probably better remembered by American theatre buffs because of his famous rivalry with the American actor Edwin Forrest, which led in turn to the Astor Place riot in New York in 1849. Theatre historians have chronicled that event extensively, but you might want to get a quick popular sense of the affair by reading Richard Nelson's play *Two Shakespearean Actors*.

The building at Number 64 bears no memorial to Macready, but opposite at Number 6 is a plaque noting that William Hazlitt the eminent English man of letters and Shakespearean critic died there in 1830. It is now home to a hotel called appropriately **Hazlitt's**. We hope that current guests to this address do not often meet the same fate there as Mr. Hazlitt did. His remains are buried in the churchyard of St. Ann's Soho at the southern end of Dean Street.

Continue back down Frith Street crossing over Bateman Street now. Number 50 on the right is the present home of the Arts Theatre Club. Between Number 20 and Number 21 on the left are stage doors for the Prince Edward Theatre. Above the

Hazlitt's

10

doors is a plaque recording that the eight-year old piano prodigy Wolfgang Amadeus Mozart lived there in the spring of 1764 while he astonished all of London. For a bit of upbeat counterpoint you can also note that Ronnie Scott's famous jazz club is just about opposite to Mozart's digs. And then at Number 22 on the left (blue plaque) is the building in whose attic rooms James Logie Baird demonstrated television in 1926. In an event comparable to Mr. Bell's "Is that you Mr. Watson," Baird apparently borrowed a young crippled boy from downstairs to sit and become one of the first human beings to appear on a television screen.

*At **Old Compton Street** turn left to examine the frontage of the **Prince Edward Theatre.*** This theatre was built in the 1930s and spent a lot of time as a cabaret, a restaurant, and a cinema until it

Prince Edward Theatre

finally struck it rich with the musical *Evita*, which ran from 1978 to 1986. That was followed by *Chess*, which also had a long run. *Martin Guerre*, the blockbuster musical by the *Les Misérables* team of Boubil and Schonberg opened there in August of 1996 and was extensively rewritten and restaged in 1997 to no avail. It was followed by Hal Prince's acclaimed revival of *Showboat* in 1998. *Mama Mia!*, currently seems settled in for a long run. *Step into the unusual circular lobby if it is open.*

*Kitty corner across the road you may visit the **Three Grayhounds**, a watering hole for many Soho writers and artists who thrive on the cuisine and the convivialty of popular publican Roxy Beaujolais.* The mock Elizabethan frontage and décor are a product of the 1920s, but it still has a lovely cramped atmosphere. *Exit the pub and turn left on **Greek Street.** Shortly you'll reach **Romilly Street** where you will take*

10

161

The Three Greyhounds

another left. Jean Paul Marat, the French revolutionary, lived on this street in 1776. For theatre buffs the name may be familiar because of the Peter Weiss play of the sixties that won the longest title in the world contest going away. For the record the full title was *The Assassination and Persecution of Jean Paul Marat as Performed by the Inmates of the Asylum of Charendon Under the Direction of the Marquis de Sade.* That's *Marat/Sade* for short. *Romilly Street now leads out to the bustle of* **Cambridge Circus** *and the fanciful bulk of the* **Palace Theatre**, *now owned by Sir Andrew Lloyd Webber.*

This splendidly romantic looking theatre was built for Richard D'Oyly Carte and opened its doors in 1891 as the Royal English Opera House. It was renamed the Palace Theatre of Varieties in 1892. An early milestone event was the first appearance of the great ballerina Anna Pavlova in 1910. One wonders whether there was a problem with the performance as Jonathan Sutherland in his *Ghosts of London* reports that her shade still haunts the theatre. The theatre was a music hall and revue showcase for several years and then alternated between

10

The Palace Theatre

films and various musical extravaganzas. One of its early long runs was the 655 performances of the musical *No No Nanette* in 1925 and 1926. Musicals have been the staple since World War II; the 2,385 performance run of *The Sound of Music* from 1961–1967 was followed by Hal Prince's London production of *Cabaret,* starring Dame Judi Dench in her first musical, and Tim Rice and Andrew Lloyd-Webber's *Jesus Christ Superstar,* which opened in 1972. Even that run is just a footnote now as *Les Misérables* started its run in 1986 and is still going strong in the new millennium.

From the vantage point of Cambridge Circus you can see up **Charing Cross Road** *(to your left if you have your back to the Palace) and note another theatre marquee. That's the* **Phoenix Theatre.** The site had previously held a rather low-class music hall called the Alcazar so the addition of a sleek and sumptuous new legitimate theatre was a boon to the social standing of Upper Charing Cross Road. The current structure opened in 1930 with the premiere production of Noël Coward's *Private Lives.* It featured Coward and Gertrude Lawrence in the leads and a young fellow by the name of Laurence Olivier playing the boorish husband Victor Prynne. As noted by the Olivier biographer, John Cottrell, the future Lord was at the time engaged to be married to actress Jill Esmond and coming off a string of failures. He was not excited by the prospect of playing a simpering supporting role in a piece of nonsense. Coward persuaded him to take the part by offer-

ing him a good salary and an admonition, "Look young man, you'd better be in a success for a change." A success it was, and after three sell-out months in London, Coward transferred it to New York, where the handsome young Olivier caught the eye of Hollywood talent scouts. The climb to fame was on.

Upper Charing Cross Road between here and Tottenham Court Road is also still a concentration point for booksellers

The Phoenix Theatre

10

163

and, should you be in the market for play texts or books of any kind, this is a spot to be marked for return. Foyle's is the most historic of the stores, but you will also find Waterstone's, a large Borders, and a selection of discount and used outlets.

Walk back toward the covered marquee of the Palace Theatre. Find and walk down the left side of **Shaftesbury Avenue** *towards Piccadilly Circus and turn left into* **Gerrard Place**. *Travel one more short block and then turn right into* **Gerrard Street**. Welcome to London's Chinatown! While you take in the oriental ambiance, your imagination will have to supply the hall where Thomas Sheridan (1719–88), one of the founders of modern elocution and declamation and the father of playwright and politician Richard Brinsley Sheridan, gave his lectures. *At Number 43–44 (on your left) John Dryden (1631–1700) lived and died. A weather-beaten old blue plaque can now just be made out above the Loon Fung supermarket sign. A bit farther on at a location now obliterated was another residence of Charles Kemble and his enchanting daughter Fanny.*

Follow Gerrard Street until it deadends at **Wardour Street**. *Make a left turn there and then at the next turn pause and look down* **Lisle Street**. At number 9 (long since gone) on this rather grubby little backwater, was the boyhood home of the tempestuous actor Edmund Kean(1787-1833). His uncle, with whom he lived, would buckle a brass collar around the child's neck that read "This boy belongs at number 9 Lisle Street, please bring him home." Kean's early life of deprivation may indeed have given him special insights into the tragic roles that were his forte. He shot to fame in 1814 as Shylock at Drury Lane, and was at his best in villainous and tragic parts, such as Iago, Macbeth, and Richard III. A notorious womanizer and heavy drinker, he was once booed as Richard Crookback for being drunk. With typical bravado he roared back at the audience, "If you think I'm drunk, wait until you see Buckingham!" The ultimate compliment was paid by Samuel Taylor Coleridge, who said, "to see him act is like reading Shakespeare by flashes of lightning."

10

Reverse your course and retrace your steps back up Wardour Street. Just past Gerrard Street and on your left at Number 41–43 is an impressively decorated building currently housing the Wong Kei Chinese restaurant. A large clock hangs out over the street at the third floor and below that is a blue plaque honoring Mr. Willy Clarkson (1861–1934), a wigmaker and costumier, who lived and died there. His reputation was so strong that when he moved his shop from Wellington Street to these new premises two of the leading figures in the theatre of the day had a hand in the building construction. On either side of the current restaurant entry are two plaques. One notes that Sarah Bernhardt laid the building foundation stone in 1904; the opposite side records that Sir Henry Irving laid the coping stone in 1905. The carved head above the door also looks a good deal like the great Sarah. Devotion to wig-makers does not seem to run quite this deep among current performers. *Now continue to walk up Wardour Street until you reach the first traffic signal. This is Shaftsbury Avenue again. From the corner you can fully appreciate why it is now called the center of London's theatre district—the very heart of the West End. Four legitimate theatres are visible marching in a row down toward Piccadilly Circus. They are, in order, the* **Queen's**, *the* **Gielgud** *(formerly the Globe), the* **Apollo**, *and the* **Lyric**. *Turning left at the corner you can stroll down the left side of the street and take in each theatre as you come to it.*

The **Queen's Theatre** opened in 1907 as a match to the Gielgud a bit farther along. World War II bomb damage resulted in the modern facade

Building that holds Irving and Bernhardt plaques

you see today, but the interior retains its Edwardian flavor. This theatre almost seems to belong to Sir John Gielgud, and it is perhaps a bit ironic that it was the Globe that was renamed after him a few years ago. Some of the memorable moments that graced the Queen's stage under his aegis were his great 1930 production of *Hamlet*, and the 1937–38 classical season that featured *Richard II*, *The School for Scandal*, *Three Sisters*, and *The Merchant of Venice*. That quartette of

Shaftsbury Avenue's theatre district

10

productions had a cast of players that sounds today like a Who's Who of the 20th-century theatre. In that company were Peggy Ashcroft, Michael Redgrave, Alec Guinness, Anthony Quayle, George Devine, Glen Byam Shaw, Angela Baddeley, and Rachel Kempson. When the theatre reopened after reconstruction in 1959, its inaugural production was Gielgud's renowned Shakespearean program *The Ages of Man*. His final association with the theatre was his direction of a much acclaimed production of Noël Coward's *Private Lives* with Maggie Smith and Robert Stephens in 1974.

Next down the line is the **Gielgud Theatre**, *which opened as the Hicks Theatre in 1906, on the corner of Rupert Street and Shaftsbury Avenue.* It became the Globe in 1909 and the Gielgud in 1994. The producer/impresario Hugh "Binkie" Beaumont lived in an apartment atop the "Globe" for many years. It was reached by one of the smallest lifts in the world.

In keeping with the traditional image of the street, most of the successes at the theatre have been moderately long runs of fairly lightweight comedies or romances sprinkled here and there with an occasional classic or serious play. Its first real long run appears to have been an early (1923) Somerset Maugham piece called *Our Betters* which ran for over 500 performances. Other 500-performance shows were C.L. Anthony's *Call It a Day* in 1935, and *Robert's Wife* in 1938. Sir John brought his classic production of *The Importance of Being*

10

Gielgud Theatre

Earnest to its boards in 1939, when he played John Worthing, Peggy Ashcroft played Cecily, and Dame Edith Evans put a stamp for all time on the role of Lady Bracknell.

Luckier than its counterpart the Queen's, the Gielgud remained active throughout the war years and offered successful productions of *Thunder Rock*, *Dear Brutus*, and *The Petrified Forest*. One of the major critical landmarks of the post-war era was the 1949 production of Christopher Fry's *The Lady's Not for Burning* directed by and starring Mr. Gielgud. This production also featured a performance by a young Welsh actor by the name of Richard Burton. The fifties saw an *Evening with Bea Lillie* and Emlyn Williams in Dylan Thomas' *Growing Up*. The early sixties saw the opening of Paul Scofield in Thomas Bolt's *A Man for All Seasons* and long runs of Jean Kerr's *Mary Mary* and Peter Shaffer's *The Private Ear* and *The Public Eye*.

The **Apollo Theatre** *a bit farther along, opened its doors in 1901.* Its frontage is in French Renaissance style and features niches, pillars, and Neoclassic figures. With a fresh coat of paint in the early nineties it gleamed in the noon sun like polished ivory, but a patina of London soot has now dimmed its lustre. The interior has changed little since its opening aside from periodic redecoration. Built originally as a home for musicals, its roster for the early years includes few recognizable names. In recent years the fare has been mainly forgettable come-

10

Apollo
Theatre

dies, romances, and an occasional thriller. Some of the more recognizable titles have been *Idiot's Delight, Gaslight, Cradle Song, Private Lives, Butterflies Are Free, The Owl and the Pussycat, Lulu, Dial M for Murder,* and the revival of Anthony Shaffer's *Sleuth.*
The oldest theatre of the four is the cream and red brick **Lyric,** *which opened in 1888.* Perhaps the first major event of historical importance in the theatre's life occurred in 1893 when the great Italian actress, Eleanor Duse made her first London appearance in *La Dame aux Camélias.* During her stay she also appeared in Goldoni's *La Locandiera (The Mistress of the Inn)* and in Ibsen's *A Doll's House.* Another international star, Sarah Bernhardt, appeared here in 1898.
Musicals interspersed with classical seasons kept the theatre running throughout the first 30 years of the new century. In 1933, just after a major renovation, the theatre had a string of American successes including Alfred Lunt and Lynn Fontanne in Robert Sherwood's *Reunion in Vienna,* Sidney Kingsley's *Men in White,* and Kaufman and Ferber's *Theatre Royal.* The two major postwar hits were the 476-performance run of Terrence Rattigan's *The Winslow Boy* in 1946–47 and the John Clements-Kay Hammond revival of *The Beaux' Strategem* in 1948–49. Then it was time for the long-run champion to open. *The Little Hut* ran for 1,261 performances. Most of the more recent offerings have been in the popular or musical vein and have included shows such as *Cactus Flower, Plaza Suite, Habeus Corpus,* and *Five Guys Called Moe.* In 1997 it housed the transfer of the RSC's *Cyrano de Bergerac* starring Anthony Sher.
Continue down Shaftsbury Avenue to the next traffic light, where **Great Windmill Street** *angles off into the heart of seamy Soho. Look up that street to your right. The* **Windmill Theatre,** *an ancient, though for some not so honorable, Soho landmark, stands up there. It was dark and decrepit on our last walk through.*
If you wish to see a bit more of what is left of the gritty side of Soho and amble through a nice street market, take the following side trip up Great Windmill Street. If this is not your cup of tea, simply read the next paragraph on the Windmill Theatre from here and continue on down Shaftsbury Avenue until it arrives at **Piccadilly Circus.** *When you arrive at the Circus take a sharp left and head down* **Coventry Street** *toward the marquee of the Prince of Wales Theatre where we will stop briefly before proceeding on into* **Leicester Square** *and the termination of the walk.*
For those taking the side trip, walk up Great Windmill Street to the now darkened theatre. If you find nothing but construction chaos do not be surprised as redevelopment could descend on this area at any moment. Suffice it to say that the original site was supposed to have been on the location of a mill on a path that led up the slight hill from Piccadilly and the top of the Haymarket. Originally built in 1910 as a cinema, it was completely redesigned as a legitimate theatre in 1931. After some hit-and-miss productions and a brief return to films, a non-

10

stop variety and revue format was inaugurated. This developed into a burlesque style entertainment that featured comedy acts, dancing girls, and judicious nude tableaus. The proud claim during the Blitz was that "We Never Closed," and indeed the Windmill was the only theatre in London that did not miss a performance during all of World War II except for twelve compulsory closure days from September 4th to 16th of 1939. During the worst of the Blitz, the performers often slept nightly inside the theatre rather than risking travel on the streets during the bombings. The entertainment formulated at the Windmill was termed "Revaudeville" and breathed its last in 1964, but in its post-war years could claim to have launched the careers of then unknown comedians like Tony Hancock, Harry Secombe, and Peter Sellers. For a long time after that it was basically a strip club and as late as 1988 housed a night-club called Paramount City.

Across from the theatre is a quiet little pub called the Lyric. The sign has a theatre mask motif, there is a lovely tiled entryway, and the interior is full of prints and playbills from the Lyric theatre whose stage door is back across the street just to the right of the old entrance to the Windmill. Talk about actors having to use the back door. This one is about as back as it can get, particularly if you use as a contrast the elegant flower-bedecked Suffolk Street where the actors of the Theatre Royal Haymarket enter. (See Walk Seven.)

*Continue with the diversion to the top of Great Windmill Street. Turn right into **Brewer Street**. You are now in the heart of old seamy Soho and it still isn't exactly Mary Poppins Land. At **Rupert Street** take a left turn into the pedestrian path called **Walker's Court**. A short stroll through a gauntlet of pornography peddlers will take you out into the **Berwick Street Market**—a lively and cheap place to buy fruits, vegetables, and other items. Explore the market for a while and then turn around and go back through Walker's Court. This time cross Brewer Street, and go straight down Rupert Street. You will pass through a short flea market (mainly clothes and souvenirs) as you return to Shaftsbury Avenue. Cross it and continue on until you run into **Coventry Street** at the **Prince of***

Walker's Court

Prince of Wales Theatre

Wales Theatre. At this point everyone should be together again.

As Ronald Bergan notes in his lavishly illustrated *The Great Theatres of London*, "If a vote were to be taken on the best location for a theatre in the West End . . . the Prince of Wales would surely win." The initial theatre on the site was called the Prince's and opened in 1884. Located at the very crossroads of the entertainment district, it housed a veritable parade of the brightest starts of its era including Herbert Beerbohm-Tree, Lily Langtry "the Jersey Lily", Mrs. Patrick Campbell, Marie Tempest, Bea Lilly, and Gertrude Lawrence. Musical revue was the traditional occupant in the twenties and thirties. The old building was replaced in 1937 by the current Art Deco modern house. It seats a little over a thousand patrons and has quite spacious bars and front-of-house facilities. Aside from hosting the long running *Harvey* by Mary Chase, it has remained primarily a space for variety shows and musicals to the present day. The musical version of the hit film, *The Full Monty* was running in 2002.

*It is just a few steps more on Coventry Street to reach **Leicester Square** proper. Once there work your way into the grassy center near the Shakespeare statue.* The square is now more reputable than it was in the drug-dealing 1980s, but the local authorities are still trying to deal with public drunkenness, buskers, and tattoo artists. Though almost always crowded (you do need to watch your valuables closely in this area), the crowds during the daylight hours appear mainly to be young tourists chowing down on hamburgers and slices of pizza. *If you can find a bench sit a spell. On a pleasant day you might even hear the birds sing.*

Up until the 1600s this area was reserved for common grazing lands. Building started when the Earl of Leicester got permission to put his house approximately where the Empire Cinema is today. By the 1700s the square was built up completely and at various times contained the homes of fashionable and successful men from all walks of life, including Dr. John Hunter, a famous surgeon, the scientist, Sir Isaac Newton, and the artists Hogarth and Joshua Reynolds. Today their busts occupy

10

the corners of the garden square that was laid out in 1874 just as the area was developing into the music hall and cabaret center of the West End. The centerpiece of the square is, incongruously, that monument to William Shakespeare. His rather cloying statue peers benignly out at the chaos from under its thick coating of pigeon droppings and carries a somewhat bemused grin on its face.

Opposite the statue of Shakespeare, but looking away from him to the left, is a small bronze statue of Charlie Chaplin, in his costume as the little tramp, complete with cane. It is the work of John Doubleday, and was unveiled by Sir Ralph Richardson in April, 1981.

The juxtaposition of this island of grass and flowers with its sur-

Shakespeare statue in Leicester Square

rounding neon jungle is well worth some meditation. Today the entertainment is primarily chain restaurants, cinemas, street buskers, and pickpockets. There is concern about the overcrowding, disorder, and potential rectitude of it all. A century ago, as the music hall center of the West End, it probably had much the same atmosphere and called forth much the same kind of public reaction.

In their prime, the great Empire and Alhambra music halls of the turn of the century attracted some five to seven thousand people nightly into these environs. And then as now when large numbers of people congregated to eat, drink, and be merry there was also an accompanying cadre of street people ranging from musicians and panhandlers to pickpockets and worse.

But don't let that deter you from our real reason for ending at Leicester Square. London's own half-price theatre

10

Charlie Chaplin statue in Leicester Square

ticket booth, called TKTS just like the one in New York City, is now located in a nice little stone building at the bottom of the square. *If you have timed your walk right, you can join the hopefully small queue to pick up some of the best live entertainment bargains in the western world.* The booth is run by the Society of London Theatres, and offers half-price (plus a small service charge, which was two pounds 50 per ticket in 2002) current-day tickets to West End performances. Opening time was 10:00 A.M.–7:00 P.M. Monday through Saturday as of 2002. Don't worry if the queue seems long; it moves quite quickly if there are two windows open. You may pay with cash (that's English pounds) or credit cards, but not traveler's checks. You can buy only current-day tickets to the shows that are listed on the board and you cannot pick your seat or price as you might do at the box office.

No tickets, other than those hawked by the scalpers who hang around the queues, will be available for the latest musicals. Your best bet for seats to the really popular current shows is to order them through a legitimate ticket agency and pay the surcharge or better yet, go to or call the theatre's box office directly. The best half-price bargains in Leicester Square are to shows that have been running a while and are not now selling out, or shows that are in preview or have just opened and are not selling out. You'll also find a lot of tickets for long-running comedies and second-level musicals that continue to run on the basis of tourist group bookings. Be warned that the half-price tickets sold here generally are the top price tickets that people who pay full price aren't eager to buy. i.e. a lot of the tickets come from row 1 or row 2 or the side or rear of the stalls. Try to remember that if these were the best seats in the house, they would not be half price.

Half-Price Ticket Booth

In recent years several ticket agencies around the Leicester Square area have put up signs advertising half-price/bargain tickets and some even place the word "official" in their displays. They are not the official agency and any service fee they charge goes into their pockets and not into the Society of London Theatres' coffers to help support live theatre in London. Please use the real "official" booth.

Some day-of-performance tickets for every show at the National Theatre are sold each morning from their box office beginning at 10:00 A.M. Get there by 9:00 A.M. if you are interested in a popular show. Students and seniors are also eligible for specially rated day seats at the National Theatre and some other selected venues. Check current ticket brochures or *Time Out* for full details. For those of you on the true starvation budget, you may be able to get a cheaper seat overall by going to the theatre and buying one at list price in the Upper Circle or Gallery.

One final note on London Theatre tickets: There are at least 50 or more fringe/outlying theatres in London. The quality varies but an extraordinary amount of exciting theatre is going on outside of the West End. Fringe tickets are never sold at the half-price booth, but most of the theatres will take telephone orders. Your outlay will seldom reach ten pounds and may go as low as four pounds. Your best source for fringe programming is the weekly *Time Out* magazine. Buy one as soon as you hit town.

*Your tour of the "Not-So-Bright Lights of Soho" is now complete. Should you not be planning to get theatre tickets now, tube or bus transportation is close at hand (**Leicester Square** or **Piccadilly Circus** tube stations) to take you back to your lodgings. If you have decided to join the ticket queue or have some more time to read, a more detailed theatrical history of the Leicester Square area follows.*

On the east flank of the square is the 2,300-seat Odeon Cinema, which has been operating since 1937. It was on this site in 1854 that the Royal Panoptikon of Science and Art was constructed. This was an entertainment and display area designed to be a model of "Moorish grandeur." The external face was rounded off with two 100-foot minarets at each corner and the interior was finished in an ornate Saracenic style. The central core of the building was a nearly 100-foot domed rotunda with a giant fountain in the middle. Around and below were exhibits of machinery, manufactured goods, and displays devoted to the latest scientific discoveries. A gigantic organ dominated one corner of the dome.

The Exhibition Center fell on hard times by 1857 and was auctioned off. The huge organ was sent to St. Paul's Cathedral and the building was outfitted for circuses and equestrian spectacles. In line with its Moorish architecture it was renamed the Alhambra when it was reopened in 1858. It was refitted again in 1860 as the Alhambra Palace Music Hall. The old organ gallery was remodeled into a large

10

proscenium stage with 100 feet of fly space. The pit floor was furnished with tables, and with the gallery seating on the perimeters, the capacity was upwards of 3500 patrons. The early 1860s saw more new managements, a further refitting to increase the seating capacity to 4000 people, and another new name—the Alhambra Palace of Varieties. The programs were mainly music and dancing. Since some of the presentations did involve pantomimic action and some did stretch the bounds of contemporary propriety, the theatre also had a series of licensing problems. In 1871 they lost their music and dance license and got a drama license. The tables were removed from the pit and replaced by seats and the bars were moved into locations that were out of view of the stage. Another remodeling in 1882 added new galleries and seating in the balconies. This was completed just in time for a disastrous fire that gutted the entire building except for the exterior walls.

The Alhambra was rebuilt within a year. It retained the old front and the Moorish towers, but the interior was formed into a standard music hall with seating for about 4000. Programming leaned toward popular dance and acrobatics with a sprinkling of serious ballet including Diaghilev's *Ballet Russes de Monte Carlo*. Finally, after almost 60 years as one of the entertainment centers of London, the building was sold to the Odeon circuit of cinemas in 1936 and torn down to make way for a palace dedicated to the 20th-century equivalent of music hall—the motion picture.

*On the north side of the square you now see the **Empire Cinema and Dance Hall**.* This site has also been given over to entertainment since early in the 1800s when an old palatial home, Saville House, was reconstructed into an assortment of wine bars, dancing rooms, billiard parlors, revue stages, restaurants, etc. By 1848 this complex had a name, the Salle Valentino, and according to advertisements at the time some 2000 people could trip the light fantastic in the main dance hall and wander about through the small parlors that featured wrestlers, ventriloquists, fortune tellers, magic shows, etc.

In 1865 the Salle Valentino burned to the ground. It was rebuilt as the Royal London Panorama. At one point the operation featured an exhibition of the Charge of the Light Brigade painted on a huge 15,000-square-foot circular canvas. Remodelings occurred during the 1870s and 1880s ending in a standard proscenium theatre called the Empire in 1884. This was a 3500-seat house with a 32-foot proscenium stage. The bill of fare was varied but always musical. Contemporary ballets like *Giselle* and *Coppelia* were alternated with popular spectacles like a version of Jules Verne's *Around the World in 80 Days* complete with live elephants and a chorus of four hundred singers.

In 1887 the programming turned more toward the music hall as the managership moved to the famous Edward and Augustus Harris. The theatre became the Empire Theatre of Varieties. Like the

Alhambra, the Empire was a lively meeting place for all the high-spirited and hot-blooded gallants of the town. The galleries of both theatres had "promenades" where high class "ladies of the evening" circulated and vied for the attention of the rakes in the bars or the pit. The moral situation got so bad at the Empire in 1894 that the London County Council under pressure from an American social reformer, Mrs. Ormiston Chant, closed the theatre and demanded that the promenades be screened off from the auditorium.

Mander and Mitchenson report that young Winston Churchill and some of his fellow cadets from Sandhurst were attending the Empire not long after it had been

Empire Cinema & Dance Hall

reopened. They discovered that the new promenade barriers were nothing but flimsy fabric screens that could be easily punctured by a gentleman's walking stick. Hole poking was soon much too mild and it did not take long before the young men were tearing the screens out of their moorings. Churchill made one of his maiden speeches then and there against the council edicts and proceeded to lead the unruly mob out into the streets to parade up Piccadilly carrying the broken pieces of screening as banners.

After a major renovation in 1904 the presentations turned more to musical revues and then to musicals. The last show to run at the old Empire was George Gershwin's *Lady Be Good* with Fred and Adele Astaire. The wreckers moved in quickly and by 1928 the first Empire Cinema opened on the site. This was a 3500-seat movie palace with a fully equipped proscenium stage so that variety acts and music could also be accommodated. From 1949 to 1952 the Empire played a half-film and half-music dance revue program. It was closed in 1961 and remodeled into a large two-story dance hall with stage (now the

10

Empire Dance Hall) and into the smaller 1300-seat cinema that still bears the Empire name.

A final important lost London theatre that stood just off the north-east corner of the square between Cranbourn and Lisle streets was Daly's Theatre. It was called Daly's Theatre after the U.S. producer and impressario Augustus Daly and was built by George Edwardes the manager of the famous Gaiety Theatre for use by Daly's company. Daly had been bringing his American company to London each year from 1884 to 1891 and Edwardes sought to build the theatre and lease it to Daly at a profit, which he did for a few years. Daly's Theatre opened in 1893 and was the first theatre in London to be built on the cantilever principle, thus eliminating the posts that would normally have been necessary to hold up the balconies or circles. It had an Italian Renaissance frontage and a Rococo interior with seats for 1200 patrons. Daly opened the theatre with his production of *Taming of the Shrew*. Elenora Duse and Sarah Bernhardt both performed there in 1894. During the early part of the 20th century, the house was known primarily for musicals and operettas. Finally in 1937 Warner Brothers bought the site and remodeled it into a 1700-seat cinema.

Here's hoping that by now the ticket line is moving along and that your particular favorite is up on the board. Have a pleasant afternoon or evening at the theatre.

10

WALK ELEVEN

TAKE A STROLL IN RESIDENTIAL KENSINGTON AND HOLLAND PARK

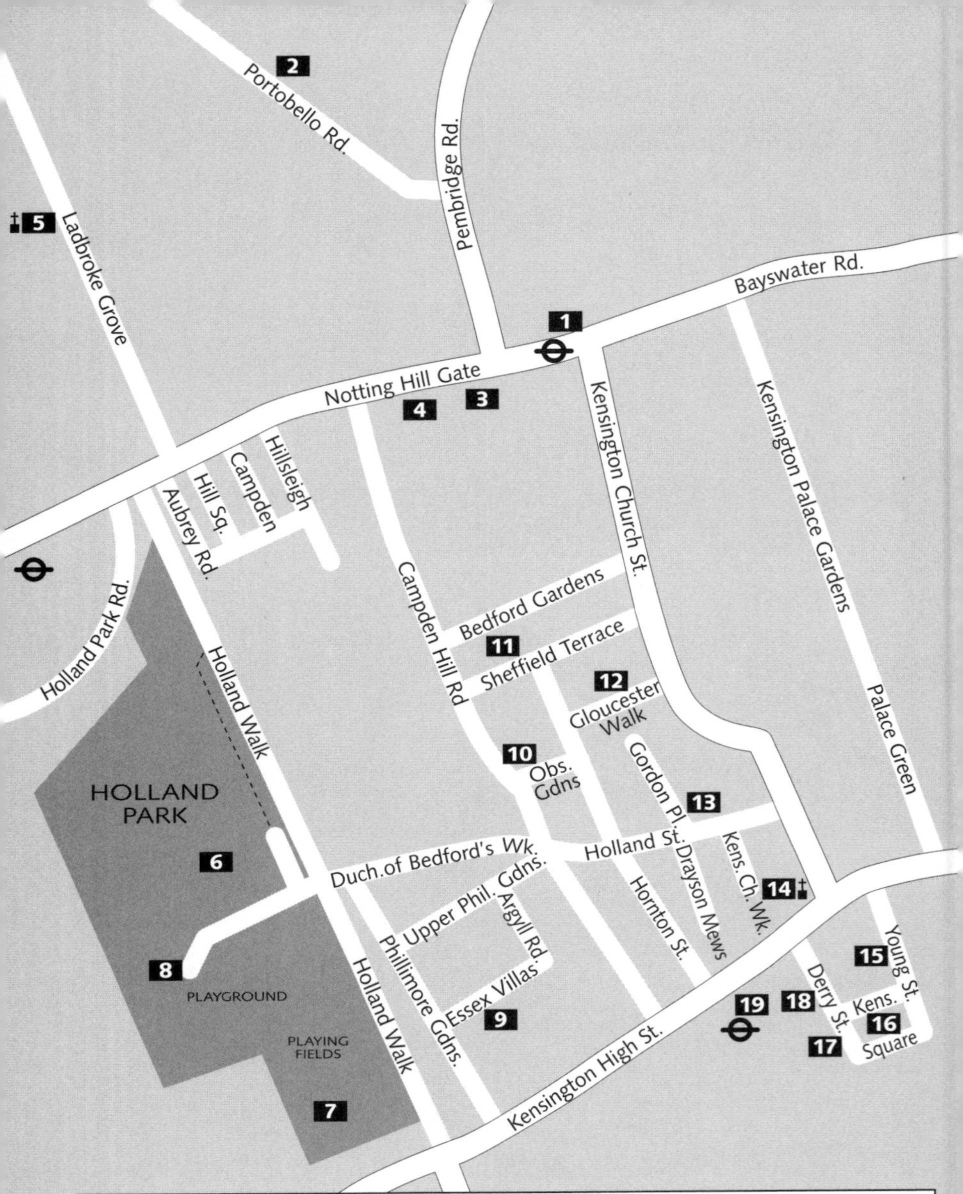

Walk Eleven

1. Notting Hill Gate station
2. Portobello Antique Market
3. Gate Cinema
4. Coronet Cinema
5. St. John's Ladbroke Grove
6. Holland House site
7. Commonwealth Institute
8. Public rest rooms
9. W.S. Gilbert house
10. Victorian flat block
11. Green Lodge—Agatha Christie house
12. J. M. Barrie and Jean Sibelius residences
13. The Elephant & the Castle
14. St. Mary Abbot's Church
15. Thackeray residence
16. Kensington Square
17. Mrs. Patrick Campbell house
18. Entrance to old Derry & Tom's roof garden
19. High Street Kensington tube station

⊖ Tube Station

STARTING POINT: Notting Hill Gate station (District, Circle, or Central line).

APPROXIMATE TIME: Two to three hours depending on how much time you spend in the park.

*T*oo *often the the major monuments, shopping streets, and entertainment centers trap the visitor to London. In this swirl of noise and business you can forget that real people live in London and if they live in Kensington they do it with a certain panache. This area has appealed to artists and literary people for over a hundred years. The walk doesn't have a lot of theatre references, but it takes you through an enchanting neighborhood park (Holland Park), an immaculately kept and architecturally fascinating residential neighborhood, a lovely church, and an oddity on top of a building.*

If you should choose a Saturday for this walk and are interested in antiques, Notting Hill Gate is close to the famous Portobello Road antique market. If interested in this side trip, take a right at **Pembridge Road** *after you exit the tube station. You will shortly pass the Prince Albert pub, home of the Gate Theatre. Keep going, watching for* **Portobello Road** *intersecting on your left. Turn into it and follow it or the crowds until the market comes into view.*

T*ake the tube to* **Notting Hill Gate**. *After clearing the exit gates, take the left turn to the street and mount the right-hand stairs (Notting Hill Gate South Side). You should emerge on the south side of the street and begin to stroll west (straight ahead) toward Holland Park Avenue. You will pass the Gate and Coronet cinemas and then shortly the street will turn from commercial to residential. You will pass* **Campden Hill Road** *and* **Hillsleigh Road** *on your way. Not too much farther will be* **Campden Hill Square**. *Turn left up the hill. On your right is a lovely wooded park that makes a private garden for the terrace houses that surround the square. If the wooded area is on your left and the houses on the right, you have gone one street too far.* This square was laid out in 1826 and many of the houses date from shortly after that time. The heavy iron fencing around the central park is original and the wrought

11

179

iron work and the door and window treatments on the houses are exquisitely varied.

The famous English painter J. M. W. Turner used to come to a friend's home on this hill because it was such a marvelous place from which to paint the sunset. *When you reach the top of the square, turn right. At Number 16, Charles Morgan, a novelist and critic, lived from 1894 to 1932. At Number 23 a blue plaque trumpets the residence of Sigfried Sassoon from 1925 to 1932, but sources indicate that the house was inhabited by the Davies family around the turn of the century.* There is nothing exciting about them, but their young children inspired J. M. Barrie to write his most famous work, *Peter Pan.*

*Continue on straight ahead until the street ends at **Aubrey Road**. Turn right and head back down the hill. Here you will see nicely kept houses of more modest proportion. They are one block off the square and no doubt intended for more middle class occupation. Nicely framed between the buildings ahead of you is the spire of St. John's Ladbroke Grove (1845). When you arrive back at Holland Park Avenue again, turn left and walk no more than about 20 yards farther. You are looking on your left for the entrance to narrow little **Holland Walk**. Take it and start up the hill. Make sure that you stay out of the bike path.* Initially brick walls hem in this walkway, but soon the right side will give way to the green of **Holland Park**. You can sense the difference almost immediately. Blackberry bushes crowd up to the fence, songbirds cry, and occasionally you'll hear from beyond the green leaves the sound of laughing children.

Look for the first opening in the fence (on your right) and take it into the park, where you can turn quickly left again and continue your stroll down a pleasant tree-shaded path.

*Keep your eyes to the right and soon another path will appear. About 20 paces more and the Tudor gables of what remains of **Holland House** will appear through the trees.* This

Spire of St. John's Ladbroke Grove

Holland Park

lovely old country home, built originally in 1607, was almost totally destroyed by bombs during World War II and today houses a youth hostel. There is, sadly, nothing much more to see, but the old house does have some theatrical connections.

The Holland Estate (roughly covering the area of the current park) was owned by the De Vere family, Earls of Oxford, until the time of James I. One owner, Edward De Vere (1550–1604), has had the distinction of being advanced by a contemporary relative as a possible author for Shakespeare's plays. His date of death above is just one of the inconveniences that needs to be worked around to justify the claim. The Jacobean house continued its theatrical connections on into the Commonwealth, when it reportedly was the site of bootleg performances after Cromwell and his men had closed the public theatres in and around the central city. Kensington at the time was a suburban country village. Joseph Addison, author of the tragedy *Cato*, and co-author with Richard Steele of the famous *Spectator*, lived in the house from 1716 to his death in 1719.

In the middle of the 18th century, the house was sold to Henry Fox, father of the great politician and orator, Charles James Fox. Fox became Baron Holland in 1763 and made Holland House into a center of political and literary activity. Theatrical figures, including Richard Brinsley Sheridan, John Philip Kemble, and Edmund Kean, were regular visitors.

11

Even today the arts continue to be associated with the park. The Orangery is often the scene of jazz concerts and poetry readings and there is an open-air theatre for opera and music.

Continue walking straight ahead past a school until you reach another major crossing path. There is an exit to the left leading to **The Duchess of Bedford's Walk** *that will take you out of the park. You may use it now if you wish.* **Otherwise, remember this spot. It is right at the doggie toilet and you must return to it in order to continue the walk after you make a foray deeper into the park.** *And if it is a pleasant day we urge you to do just that.* You will find lovely gardens (traditional English and Japanese), children's play areas, parading peacocks, modern sculptures in situ, and other surprises. Summer and winter the park is full of real Londoners of all ages and nationalities.

Park explorers should now take a right turn away from the exit, which will put you along the top of the playing fields. At the bottom of the fields is the curved roof of the **Commonwealth Institute**, *a museum and cultural center devoted to the countries of the British Commonwealth. Visit it if you have plenty of time. On the right you will pass the open-air theatre, where you can enjoy opera and/or music in the summer months.*

At the next intersection past the theatre, there'll be some tables and a snack bar to your right and off to the left an honest-to-goodness working drinking water fountain. Across from the fountain is a squat little building with a signboard on it. It contains a map of the whole park and even lists what flowers are in bloom and where. Here you can make a decision about what other parts of the park you wish to see. There's also a loo in the building. It's around to the side fronting on the children's play area. The men's room contains a scale and for 20 pence you can find out how many stone you weigh.

We will pause now while you make your own personal excursions in the park. *Pick up the text below when you return to the exit at the Duchess of Bedford's Walk that leads out of the park.*

You should now have taken your pastoral pleasure and returned to the exit. Upon leaving the park gate jog to the left a few yards, recross Holland Walk, and then enter the walled Duchess of Bedford Walk. About 20 yards on make a right turn into **Phillimore Gardens**. *You are thrust slam-bang quickly into posh, monumental, gleaming, Neoclassic Kensington. Walk on for three short blocks. Turn left at* **Essex Villas**. *At Number 8 on the right lived W. S. Gilbert (1836–1911), famed librettist and partner of Arthur Sullivan. Turn left at the end of Essex Villas up* **Argyll Road**. *Jog to the right on* **Upper Phillimore Gardens** *at the top of Argyll Road. You'll shortly arrive at the five-point intersection of* **Campden Hill Road.**

The obviously modern looking buildings to your right are the Kensington Town Hall and Library. You should turn left, cross the Duchess of Bedford's Walk again, and proceed up Campden Hill Road. As you

11

walk, a new development called the Philamores is on your left. At **Observatory Gardens** *you will want to feast your eyes across the road on a lovingly restored Victorian flat block.* Note in particular the ornate carvings, the mansard roof, and the wrought iron detailing. Corin Redgrave, of the famous Redgrave acting family used to live there. Another nearby theatrical resident was Kate Terry, the eldest of another great theatrical dynasty, who lived at Moray Lodge on Campden Hill after her marriage to Arthur Lewis and retirement from the stage. Her sister Ellen Terry was the most famous of her siblings, but Marion, Florence, and Fred also made their mark, as of course did Kate's grandson, Sir John Gielgud.

At or just behind Number 78 Campden Hill Road, *novelist and playwright John Galsworthy*

W. S. Gilbert residence

Restored Victorian flats

11

183

Left: John Galsworthy residence. Right: Agatha Christie residence

(1867–1933), lived for a while in 1903. At the next house, Number 80, you can also see a blue plaque identifying the former residence of novelist and critic Ford Maddox Ford (1873–1939). Continuing up Campden Hill Road you will soon come to **Sheffield Terrace**. *Look at each turning carefully as the sign for Sheffield Terrace will be low and behind you as you go up the hill. Turn right and go down to Number 58, Green Lodge. Note the carved unicorn and lion over the front door.* In it lived for many years (1934–1941 according to the new blue plaque) one of the world's most famous mystery writers, **Agatha Christie**. She gets a theatrical nod as the author of London's and the world's longest running play, *The Mousetrap*. It opened in 1952 and is still going strong into the new millennium. (See Walk Twelve, Part II for more information.)

Turn around and return to Campden Hill Road. Take a right, walk another block to **Bedford Gardens**, *then turn right again.* This street is a treasure of fascinating houses. Number 87–91 on the right have wrought iron balconies that seem right out of New Orleans. Number 54 on the left has a covered walkway from the street to the front door. Number 5 on the right was once the home of Richard Le Gallienne, a literary historian and poet. Theatre buffs may be more familiar with his daughter Eva Le Gallienne. She came to New York in 1915 and made a considerable reputation for herself as an actress and producer-director. She was instrumental in popularizing Ibsen in the United States during the 1930s and in the 1940s was a co-founder of the American Repertory Theatre. Number 4 on the left bears a blue plaque to the composer Frank Bridge, who lived there.

Follow Bedford Gardens through to **Kensington Church Street**, *turn right and go down the hill for two blocks to* **Gloucester Walk**. *Turn right.* **J. M. Barrie**, author of *Peter Pan* and *The Admirable Crichton*

lived on this street in 1892 and there is also a blue plaque honoring the composer Jean Sibelius, Number 15. This street also allows you to directly compare three different period architectural styles. On the right there are some Victorian Gothic flats and a modern block. On the left there are some traditional 18th-century stucco row houses.

Turn left when you reach the "T" intersection of **Hornton Street** *and follow it downhill until you reach the back of the public library. At* **Holland Street** *turn left. Don't be confused by the street number on the southeast corner house. Number 43 has been crossed out and 54 painted in above it. Walk up Holland Street and feast your eyes once again on residential London in all of its variety. On your right peek into* **Drayson Mews**. Prior to the age of automobile transport, mews used to be the stable areas for homes fronting on the larger streets. Some continue to be used for garage facilties today, but many have also been converted into quaint and secluded lodging spaces. *Next is a charming, gardened cul-de-sac called* **Gordon Place**. *Kitty corner from this jewel of a street is a pleasant neighborhood pub,* **The Elephant and the Castle**, *where you can sit outside on a bench under a cascade of flowers and enjoy a pint on a sunny afternoon or evening. The next tiny street is* **Kensington Church Walk**. *Take a right turn into it. It is quiet, elegant, and lined with specialty shops. At or around Number 10 the poet Ezra Pound lived.*

The lane opens out into a lovely hidden garden tucked in behind Sir George Gilbert Scott's **St. Mary Abbot's Church**. At 278 feet, its spire is the tallest in London. Buried somewhere in its churchyard are the Restoration theatre manager and actor, Thomas Killigrew (1612–1693); George Colman the elder (1732–1836), a playwright and theatre manager; and Mrs. Elizabeth Inchbald (1753–1821), actress and dramatist. Should the church be open, it is well worth a look, though its dark and

St. Mary Abbot's Church and garden

11

Top left: **William Thackeray residence**
Top right: **Mrs. Patrick Campbell residence**
Left: **Roof garden of Derry & Tom's**

gloomy Victorian atmosphere is a contrast to the uplifting lightness of many of Wren's church interiors.

If you move through the covered cloister that leads out from the east side of the church (push on the cloister door if it is not open), you will find yourself out into the traffic and the noise of **Kensington High Street***. Should the cloister be locked Kensington Church Walk will jog to the right and also gain you access to the high street.*

11

Cross the always-busy Kensington High Street toward Barker's department store. Turning left on the east side of the street proceed to the next corner, which is **Young Street** and turn right. Cross to the left side of the street so you can see clearly the pleasant house, number 16, where William Thackeray (1811–1863) lived and wrote Vanity Fair. Shortly you will reach once fashionable **Kensington Square**, which was laid out in 1685 for the courtiers who wished to live near the royal family at Kensington Palace. The French politician Tallyrand lived in the square for a while in the 1690s. John Stuart Mill, the philosopher and author of the treatise *On Liberty*, had a residence at Number 18. The artist Edward Burne-Jones lived at Number 41 from 1865–67. *Turn right and traverse one side of the square. Kitty corner to your left is number 33, the home for many years (1865–1940) of Mrs. Patrick Campbell, actress and friend of G. B. Shaw. A small gray plaque marks the house.* Shaw created the part of Liza Doolittle in *Pygmalion* for her and their long correspondence was published after Shaw's death. The letters were made into a dramatic work called *Dear Liar* by Jerome Kilty in 1960.

Turn right and you are now headed back toward Kensington High Street on **Derry Street**. *At Number 99 on the left is the entrance to one of London's little known oddities, the old roof gardens of the long defunct Derry and Tom's department store, which are sometimes still accessible during the day. Ask the security man if you can take a peek. Once on top of the building you can stroll through a set of landscaped gardens complete with trees, ponds, live ducks, and fountains.* It currently appears to be used mainly for private parties.

If gardens in the air are not your cup of tea, you can walk immediately back to the high street and turn left. The **High Street Kensington tube station** *(District and Circle lines) is to your left about 200 yards, just past Marks and Spencer. Your stroll through residential Kensington is finished.*

11

WALK TWELVE

COVENT
GARDEN
PROMENADE

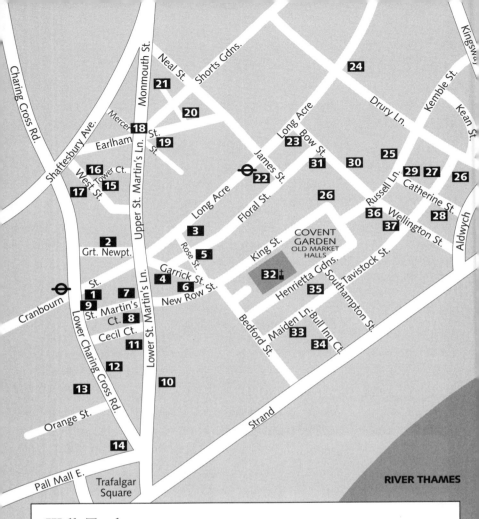

Walk Twelve

PART I

1 Leicester Square tube station
2 Arts Theatre
3 Stanford's Travel Books
4 Garrick Club
5 Lamb & Flag
6 Anne Frank tree
7 Albery Theatre
8 Salisbury Pub
9 Wyndham's Theatre
10 Coliseum Theatre
11 Duke of York's Theatre
12 Garrick Theatre
13 Irving statue
14 National Portrait Gallery

PART II

15 St. Martin's Theatre
16 New Ambassadors Theatre
17 The Ivy Restaurant
18 Seven Dials
19 Cambridge Theatre
20 Donmar Warehouse Theatre
21 Neal's Yard
22 Covent Garden tube station

PART III

23 Kemble's Head Pub
24 Prince of Wales Pub
25 Fortune Theatre
26 Aldwych Theatre stage door
27 Siddons Court
28 Duchess Theatre
29 Drury Lane Theatre
30 Globe Pub
31 Royal Opera House & Floral Hall
32 St. Paul's Covent Garden
33 Terriss plaque
34 Nell Gwynne Pub
35 Rules Restaurant
36 Theatre Museum
37 London Transport Museum
   Tube Station

STARTING POINT: Leicester Square underground station (Piccadilly or Northern lines).

APPROXIMATE TIME: The actual walking can be completed in two hours or so, but the stops could turn this into a full day of theatrical delight.

This long three part walk takes you to a number of important West End theatre venues (the Coliseum, Drury Lane, and Royal Opera House), passes by several book, print, and memorabilia shops, schedules stops at the National Portrait Gallery, Covent Garden Market, and the Actor's Church (St. Paul's Covent Garden), visits some atmospheric pubs, and finishes at the Theatre Museum. Begin this journey no earlier than 9:30 A.M. so the shops will be open and plan to spend the day. Avoid Mondays for Part III as the Theatre Museum is closed. As of publication the Royal Opera House runs auditorium tours three times a day. Eight spaces in the first tour are saved for sale on the day, but if your schedule is tight and seeing the backstage areas is a high priority it might be advisable to book a space by phone prior to the day you are taking the walk (020-7304-4000).

PART I
(Theatres, Books, Prints, and the National Portrait Gallery)

Leave the **Leicester Square tube station** via the **Charing Cross Road South** exit. Turn right a few paces, then right again to access **Cranbourn Street**. Walk to the next intersection. Look to your left to see **Great Newport Street** and a blue plaque honoring the painter Sir Joshua Reynolds. The black tile fronted building is now home to the Photographers Gallery. The exhibitions change frequently and are free.

From this vantage point you should also be able to see the marquee for the **Arts Theatre**. Cross the street to it. It was built in 1927 and was designed as a Club Theatre. Its stated purpose was to provide meal amenities, a congenial gathering place for people interested in theatre, and a small auditorium (339 seats) to stage new, challenging, or provocative plays that might not have sufficient drawing power to justify a larger West End theatre. In reality it was a bit of a charade to make it possible to offer plays that might run afoul of British

Arts Theatre

censorship laws. In 1968 the "club" distinction became unnecessary when the government finally abolished the requirement to submit play scripts to the Lord Chamberlain for approval.

In its "club" guise the Arts did play a significant role in modern English dramatic history. In 1955 the directorship of the Arts Theatre opened up. John Fernald had resigned to become head of RADA (Royal Academy of Dramatic Art) and George Devine rejected an offer to replace him because he preferred taking over the English Stage Company at the Royal Court Theatre. By default the job was offered to a young (age 24) university graduate who was working at the club as a play reader. His name was Peter Hall and his staging later that year of the English premiere of Samuel Beckett's *Waiting for Godot* made his reputation and propelled him onto the fast track that was to lead to the directorship of the Royal Shakespeare Theatre and the Royal National Theatre.

In 1966 Carol Jenner and her Unicorn Theatre for Children took over the premises. Jenner is gone now and the house currently runs productions by other managements. Eve Ensler's *Vagina Monologues* was settled in for a lengthy run at our last visit.

*Turn to your right (if you are facing the theatre) and walk toward the chaos of the six sided intersection ahead of you. To your left is **Upper St. Martin's Lane**. We will return to this spot and explore that area in Part Two of this walk. **Lower St. Martin's Lane** is to your right and John Gielgud maintained a flat at Number 7 in the 1930s. His friends knew it as Seven Upper. A little farther along the design team known as Motley had a studio.* Their third floor workspace was formerly the furniture workshop of Thomas Chippendale and had already known a number of well-off actors as customers in the 18th century. David Garrick was apparently one of those who shopped there. In the 1930s and early 1940s this was a popular gathering place for many West End actors including Gielgud. *In the distance down on lower St. Martin's Lane are the shining globe of the Coliseum Theatre and the spire of St.Martin-in-the Fields. We'll be walking by them shortly.*

Long Acre *is the street straight ahead of you. Cross St. Martin's Lane to reach Long Acre and walk up the right side of the street. Just before*

12

Garrick Club

*you get to Stanford's (an interesting map and travel bookstore), turn right down **Rose Street**. Take it through to **Floral Street**, then turn right again until Floral Street meets **Garrick Street**.*

From that vantage point look across the street and you'll see a rather dirty gray Italian Palazzo-style building built in 1860. It may not look inviting, but we guarantee that you would jump at the chance to get inside. You are staring at the **Garrick Club**, which was founded in 1831 and whose membership was originally limited to actors, dramatists, and other preeminent theatre people. That membership has broadened considerably in the 20th century to include publishers and other professionals, but it still includes a great many first rate theatre talents. The building was designed by F. Marrable and contains an excellent theatre library and an extraordinary collection of theatrical paintings and sculpture. Unfortunately, as it is a private club, you may not enter unless you are the guest of a member. If you have such a connection, use it.

*Turn left now and continue up Garrick Street. Keep a sharp eye out for an opening on the left. It's a continuation of **Rose Street** and nestled at the end is the delightful Georgian facade of the **Lamb and Flag** pub.* It was once associated with prize fighting and was called the Bucket of Blood. Today it is a popular hang out for theatre folks and tourists. John Dryden was mugged in the alley next to pub one night; the publican came to his rescue and dragged him inside to give him a reviving draught of fine English ale. You'll want to make a brief visit if it is open to explore its cramped nooks and crannies.

*Return to Garrick Street and turn left. At the next corner cross to the Garrick Club side of the street and approach the front door of the **Roundhouse Pub**. There's a brass plaque there noting that the young tree on the corner is dedicated to the memory of Anne Frank.* Anne's diary was adapted for the stage by Francis Goodrich and Albert Hackett and has been performed countless times on both amateur and professional stages around the world. The tree was planted by

12

The Albery

British actress Hannah Taylor and dedicated by Sir Ben Kingsley in 2001.

*Continue now into **New Row**. It is a delightful little street full of restaurants and shops of all kinds. Follow it and stop at your pleasure. Ultimately it will carry you right back to Lower St. Martin's Lane. You will emerge to see the **Albery Theatre** in front of you and a bit to the right.*

The Albery, built in 1903 by Charles Wyndham, was constructed on a vacant lot behind the 1899 Wyndham's theatre. Wyndham had already named the 1899 theatre after himself and didn't quite know what to call this one, so it became the "New Theatre" behind the old one. Or perhaps the name came from being directly across from New Row. In either case it took some 70 years before the now comfortably middle-aged New Theatre was finally given the name of Albery after Sir Bronson Albery, who was the stepson of Charles Wyndham. His second wife Mary Moore was the widow of the 19th-century playwright James Albery. Both the Wyndham and Albery families played major roles in the management of West End theatres for most of the last 100 years. The theatres retain a kind of symbiotic attachment to this day as both of their stage doors are on the Albery side with the Wyndham's actors having to cross an overhead bridge to gain entry to their dressing rooms.

Any pick of great plays or great seasons offered at this theatre would have to be personal, but most accounts do mention the great 1934 *Hamlet* of John Gielgud, the 1935 *Romeo and Juliet* in which Gielgud and Olivier alternated Romeo and Mercutio, and the 1944–48 Old

12

Vic Company seasons that featured Olivier, Edith Evans, and Ralph Richardson in a long series of classic performances. In the '80s the Albery was host to two well known controversial American imports, *Torch Song Trilogy* and *The Normal Heart*. A recent program lists Ostrovsky's *A Month in the Country* as the Albery's "biggest hit ever." Helen Mirren and John Hurt had people queuing around the block for tickets. In 1998 the theatre hosted a remarkable season from the Almeida Theatre Company that included Diana Rigg in a double bill of Racine's *Phedre* and *Britannicus* played in repertory. There was also Cate Blanchett in a revival of David Hare's *Plenty*.

*Just across the alley and to the left of the theatre is the **Salisbury pub**, a lovingly restored Victorian castle of mirrors, cut glass, and plush red upholstery.* The Salisbuy has often been called the Actor's Pub and is a popular meeting place for performers and spectators. *Cross the street and visit now if you wish or make a note to come back for lunch later as we will be returning past here to pick up Part II of the walk. Otherwise this is a must stop on any evening when you are seeing a play in the area.*

*If you are not stopping at the Salisbury now, cross the street and plunge straight ahead down **St. Martin's Court**, which runs between the Albery Theatre and the pub. On the left you will shortly pass Sheekey's Restaurant, a popular pre- or post-theatre eating spot. And don't forget to look off to your right for that overhead bridge that connects the backs of the Albery and Wyndam's.*

You will emerge onto Charing Cross Road. To your immediate right is the marquee of Wyndham's Theatre and just beyond that the Leicester Square tube station where we began our walk. Pause and consider **Wyndham's Theatre** for a moment.

The Salisbury Pub

12

Wyndham's Theatre

It was constructed, as we have mentioned previously, in 1899 by the 19th-century actor-manager Charles Wyndham and his leading lady (later to become his second wife) Mary Moore. Wyndham's career is fascinating. He was trained as a surgeon as well as an actor and while in America in the 1860s served with the Union Army in the Civil War. His ghost is still occasionally seen in the backstage areas and is identified as "a distinguished-looking gentleman with a mass of wavy, gray hair" by Jonathan Sutherland in his *Ghosts of London*. The original theatre site stretched all the way back to St. Martin's Lane and this theatre was built about four years before the Albery (New Theatre). Both buildings were designed by the same well-known theatre architect, W.G.R. Sprague. The lobby is rounded and quite pleasantly painted in a cool blue with faux marble pilasters.

From a historical perspective some of the important productions that have graced its stage have been the Joan Littlewood Stratford East transfers of Shelagh Delaney's *A Taste of Honey*, Brendan Behan's *The Hostage*, and the satiric musical *Oh, What a Lovely War!* In later years it has seen Vanessa Redgrave in *The Prime of Miss Jean Brodie* and Diana Rigg in *Abelard and Heloise* and *Medea*. Musicals have not been ignored, and both *The Boy Friend* and *Godspell* had runs here as well. In 1975 the National Theatre transfer of Harold Pinter's *No Man's Land* with John Gielgud and Ralph Richardson had a long run prior to its American tour. Some other distinguished productions have been the world premiere of Arthur Miller's *The Ride Down Mount Morgan* and the British premiere of Edward Albee's *Three Tall Women*. Yasmina Reza's *Art* ran here for five years beginning in 1996, completing over

12

Walk 12: Covent Garden Promenade

1500 performances before transferring to a smaller theatre.

If you are standing in front of the theatre and looking into the lobby turn to your right (away from the tube station) and walk one short block down Lower Charing Cross Road to **Cecil Court***. Turn left.* This pedestrian walkway is filled with book and print stores. *Take your time and browse where you will. At a minimum explore David Drummond's "Theatre Ephemera and Books." Cecil Court ends at* **St. Martin's Lane** *and a right turn will bring you into a favorable position from which to examine the imposing bulk of the* **Coliseum Theatre***.*

The Coliseum was designed by the extraordinary theatre architect, Frank Matcham, to the specifications of producer Sir Oswald Stoll, who had dreams of building a huge variety theatre in the Charing Cross area that was larger than Drury Lane in Covent Garden. It was opened in 1904 and remains to this day the largest theatre in the city, with a stated capacity of 2558 seats. It also has its resident ghosts. Of the three mentioned in *Ghosts of London,* our favorite is the young World War I officer who was killed in action on October 3rd, 1918, the night after he attended the theatre. He is seen moving down the circle to reoccupy his second row seat.

Cecil Court scene

The exterior style is Italian Renaissance. In addition to other amenities it originally possessed a large roof garden that was pulled down in 1951. The square tower is articulated with the roof by four pilasters and carved figures representing Art, Music, Science, and Architecture. Additional decoration proceeds skywards until at the pinnacle eight Cupids support a large illuminated globe that at one time used to revolve.

To read the accounts of this theatre in Mander and Mitchenson's *The Theatres of London* is to be continually amazed. There were lifts for the first time in Europe to take the audience to the upper parts of the building. There was a private elevator used solely to lift the King to the salon outside the Royal Box. (Of course the lift car got stuck.) There were restaurants and tearooms, facilities for sending and receiving messages and telegrams, and even a small post office and pillar box in the Main Entrance Hall. The huge stage had the first revolve in England—a massive table made up of three concentric rings capable

12

197

The Coliseum

of moving independently in both directions.

For all of its luxury the theatre failed as a variety house and was rechristened as a general house in 1906. By 1931 it was used mainly for revues, spectacles, and musicals. The late '40s saw it host a long string of big American musicals like *Kiss Me Kate, Annie Get Your Gun, Guys and Dolls, Can Can,* and *Pajama Game.* Hard times arrived by the '60s and the theatre was converted into a showplace for the early wide-screen cinema curiosity called Cinerama. After being designated as the new West End home of the Sadler's Wells Opera company in 1968, the theatre was closed for a complete redecoration. Later in that year it reopened. In 1974 the Sadler's Wells Company became the English National Opera and the theatre operates as their home to this day. The company's stated policy is to perform both new and classic operas in English. This is a large house and if you are an opera lover, tickets can be more available here and in a wider variety of price ranges than at the Royal Opera House.

*If you now continue to walk down the street toward the Coliseum, you'll find on your right the **Duke of York's** theatre.* This theatre began its life in 1892 as the Trafalgar Square. Three years later it took its present name. Like a number of other theatres in the area the Duke of York's has a resident ghost. She is named Violet Melotte, dresses all in black, and is said to be the wife of an early manager. Important or historic runs include *The Admirable Crichton* in 1902, *Peter Pan* in 1905, and *Misalliance, The Madras House,* and *Justice* in 1910 by Messrs. Shaw, Granville Barker, and Galsworthy respectively.

A renovation in 1979 restored the auditorium's pink, cream, and gold decor and cleared the stalls of supporting pillars. After reopening with Glenda Jackson's tour de force titled *Rose,* there was a strong production of O'Neill's *Strange Interlude* and a long run of the dance comedy *Stepping Out.* An American highlight of the 1980s was Al Pacino

12

starring in David Mamet's *American Buffalo*. In the mid-90s it became the temporary home of the Royal Court Theatre while its Sloane Square premises were being completely rebuilt. (The Royal Court Theatre Upstairs similarly found an interim base at the Ambassadors Theatre at the other end of Upper St. Martin's Lane.) A recent hit occupant has been Marie Jones' Olivier Award winner, *Stones in his Pockets*.

Continue your stroll down Lower St. Martin's Lane. Stop and visit the Coliseum lobby if you wish. Take the curve to your right and swing by the back of the Edith Cavell statue in the middle of the road and return up Lower Charing Cross Road until you reach the marquee of the **Garrick Theatre** *named of course after the great 18th-century actor David Garrick.*

Duke of York's Theatre

With its gold leaf nicely restored in 1986, the 700-seat Garrick probably looks as good as it did when it was built in 1889. Not that it didn't have some early problems. According to Mander and Mitchenson the early excavations hit an old river known to the Romans but misplaced by the Victorians. W. S. Gilbert of Gilbert and Sullivan fame was a major investor and was said to have remarked that he wasn't sure whether to continue with the building or rent out the fishing rights.

Over the years the theatre has thrived on a mixed diet of light comedy, farce, and an occasional drama. One early long run was achieved when the eleven-year hit *No Sex Please, We're British* transferred in from the Strand Theatre and went on to run four more years. The National Theatre's smash-hit production of *An Inspector Calls* by J.B. Priestley moved here in the mid-90s after a successful first transfer to the Aldwych, and settled into its third home for another long run that continued on into the new millennium. The house ghost is said to be that of Arthur Bourchier, one of the early managers. Bourchier had an apartment at the top of the theatre and a special set of stairs that led directly to the stage. It is called the "phantom staircase" and to this day he descends periodically and gently claps actors encouragingly on the back as they wait for their cues. In more recent years he has also been seen patrolling the upper circle.

12

Garrick Theatre

Turn away from the front of the Garrick now and locate a small gazebo. Cross to it. From there you should be able to find a large statue of Sir Henry Irving (1838–1905) almost hidden in the trees. Irving was England's greatest 19th-century actor/manager and, as was noted in Walk Five, the first English actor to be knighted in 1895. He was associated for years with the actress Ellen Terry at the Lyceum theatre and their Shakespeare productions are now legendary. Such was Irving's fame that the classic pillars of his beloved Lyceum Theatre were draped with black bands on the day of his death— October 13, 1905. This statue is one of the few open-air statues of theatre people in London. Two are of Shakespeare—one in Leicester Square (Walk Ten), and the other in the pocket park on the site of old St. Mary Aldermanbury (Walk Nine), a third is the bust of Augustus Harris outside the Drury Lane theatre (coming up later in this walk) and a fourth is the bust of Arthur Sullivan in the Embankment Gardens (Walk Four). One can barely count the Oscar Wilde memorial behind St. Martin-in-the-Fields (Walk Four).

*The building directly behind Irving's statue is the **National Portrait Gallery**.*

Statue of Henry Irving

12

Head for it by circling around to the left and go in. The gallery contains portraits of famous British citizens from Tudor times to the present. Admission is free, the loos are large and clean, and the atmosphere is pleasant and generally uncrowded. The organization is chronological; take the lift to the top floor and then simply walk down through the years. Costumiers and designers will have a field day here and the general theatre enthusiast should also find plenty to look at. While up on the top floor check out the lovely little café with a view out across Trafalgar Square and down Whitehall. There's another café in the basement. You will also want to browse in the Gallery's excellent book store. They have a particularly fine collection of costume materials and quality postcards, including the exquisite portrait of the young Ellen Terry by her first husband G.F. Watts.

This ends Part I of the Covent Garden walk. You could easily have used up a lot of time and no one will mind if you truncate your trip right now. *It's a short walk back to your left up* **Lower Charing Cross Road** *to the* **Leicester Square tube station** *or to your right, through Trafalgar Square to the* **Strand Station**.

National Portrait Gallery

12

From the National Portrait Gallery:

Left: William Shakespeare by John Taylor

Below: Sarah Siddons by Sir William Beechey

Bottom: Alan Bennett by Tom Wood

Photos on this page reprinted with permission of the National Portrait Gallery.

12

PART II
(Pub Grub and the Upper West End Theatres around Seven Dials)

If you are picking up Part II separately, *leave the* **Leicester Square** *tube station via the* **Charing Cross Road South** *exit. Turn right a few paces, then right again to access* **Cranbourn Street**. *This will lead you to the six-way intersection where we started Part I. Find* **Upper St. Martin's Lane** *and move up it toward* **West Street**.

For those pressing on directly from Part I, exit the National Portrait Gallery, take a few steps to your right, and use the Zebra crossing to reach the island on which the statue of Edith Cavell sits. From there cross into Lower St. Martin's Lane and head back past the Coliseum. Grab some lunch or refreshment at one of the restaurants along the way, or better yet stop at the **Salisbury**.

Keep walking back up St. Martin's Lane until you reach that six street intersection by the Arts Theatre where Part I started. Keep going as the street now officially becomes **Upper St. Martin's Lane**. *Look for* **West Street**. *Guild House, home to the offices of the British Actors Equity, is on the corner. Turn to the left on West Street and shortly you will reach the* **St. Martin's** *and the* **New Ambassadors** *(formerly the Ambassador) theatres, which between them have been home to the longest running play in London, or anywhere else for that matter.* Agatha Christie's *The Mousetrap* opened its run on November 25, 1952, at the Ambassador and then moved to the St. Martin's in 1974, where it is still running. It marked its 50th year in December, 2002 (that's almost 21,000 performances), and it is our guess that it will still be playing when you

St. Martin's Theatre

12

New
Ambassadors
Theatre

arrive. Miss Christie assigned the royalty rights for the play to her nine-year-old grandson and that young fellow is a very wealthy grand-father himself today.

Although owned separately, both theatres in front of you were designed by W. G. R. Sprague—the same architect who did the Wyndham's and Albery Theatres. The New Ambassadors (453 seats) was constructed first in 1913 and the St. Martin's (550 seats) followed in 1916. Now is certainly the time to get a ticket for *The Mousetrap* if you haven't had the pleasure sometime in the last half century.

Across the way from the the New Ambassadors stands the **Ivy Restaurant**, the long-favored haunt of leading actors, from the youthful star-dom of Noël Coward and John Gielgud right up to now. It remains a favorite for opening night parties, but if your name has not been up in lights somewhere in theatreland, it can be hard to secure a reservation, even for the wealthiest diners.

*Now enter **Tower Court**, which runs between the two theatres. Tower Court will curve a bit to the left and then take a sharp right just after the "Two Brewer's" sign and ultimately spill you out onto **Monmouth Street**. Look to your right for the gold decorated front of the*

12

The Ivy Restaurant

Dress Circle, *a shop at Number 57–59 Monmouth Street.* It claims to be the one and only "Showbiz Shop." You'll find books, posters, CDs, scores, and lots of other good stuff, most of it connected to the musical theatre.

When you exit the shop, turn right and continue up Monmouth Street until you reach the new column at once-infamous **Seven Dials.** This so-called circus was laid out in 1693 and was marked by an earlier column that had a sundial facing out onto each of the seven intersecting streets. By the 18th century the area had become one of London's worst slums. Hogarth portrayed its horrors in his engraving "Gin Lane" and Dickens described the environs in *Bleak House.* It's considerably more respectable now.

From the center of the circus you can examine the sleek, 1930 modern **Cambridge Theatre** *(1275 seats).* It has not worn well. Several remodelings have not managed to give the interior much warmth and geographically the venue has always seemed unfashionably detached from the West End. Its finest hours may have been during the 1970 National Theatre season when Maggie Smith starred in Ingmar Bergman's production of *Hedda Gabler* and Laurence Olivier played Shylock to the hilt in Jonathan Miller's production of *The Merchant of Venice.* The musicals *Fame* and *Grease* had moderately long runs in the 1990s.

Move now down **Earlham Street** *with the Cambridge Theatre at your right. Around Number 52 on the right side there are some bright red arches. The name Belco Centraal is painted above. Step into the first arch you reach, approach the large plate glass window, and look down. Shades of Arnold Wesker, you are looking right down on top of a restaurant kitchen.*

Seven Dials Circus

Cambridge Theatre

Almost directly across from your culinary visit is the sign for the **Donmar Warehouse** theatre. From 1961 to 1976 the space was used as a rehearsal hall. Then from 1977 to 1981 it became a studio theatre for the Royal Shakespeare Company. While their main season played at the Aldwych theatre, the Warehouse was intended to parallel their Stratford-Upon-Avon experimental house, The Other Place. The most famous transfer was the 1977 *Macbeth* with Ian McKellen and Judi Dench. A video of Trevor Nunn's legendary production can be purchased in the National Theatre and other good theatre bookshops.

When the RSC moved to the Barbican, the Pit fulfilled the experimental function. Ian Albery (another member of the Albery family) took over the theatre and formed a non-profit company to manage it. The name, by the way, derives from Ian's father Donald [Don] Albery and his friend the dancer Margot Fonteyn [Mar] and the fact that the building used to be a banana warehouse in the 19th century. Thus the Donmar Warehouse. With its 250 seats it continues to host an ever-changing pastiche of new plays, experimental revivals, productions of major touring Fringe

12

Donmar Warehouse Theatre

Neal's Yard

theatre companies, and general late-evening musical cabarets. Ronald Bergan's *Great Theatres of London* notes that the Donmar offers "genuine alternative theatre without solemnity" that seems to blend well with the mixed (age, class, and race) audiences that seem to frequent the newly revived Covent Garden entertainment area.

A few steps farther, on the Donmar Warehouse side of the street, is another diversion. There's an opening into **Thomas Neal's shopping arcade**. *Turn left and explore the flashily lit and gaudy new shops. Go out the opposite side, cross* **Shorts Gardens**, *enter the little alley, and find yourself in old* **Neal's Yard** *where there are delightful outdoor cafés and healthy whole food shops*. By the way all those Neals around here commemorate Thomas Neale who laid out the Seven Dials Circus in 1693.

If you've explored both areas, retrace your steps to Shorts Gardens and turn left until you reach **Neal Street**. *Turn right on Neal and walk on past the* **Crown and Anchor pub** *all the way up to* **Long Acre**. You will begin to notice an increase in foot traffic and trendy shops as we get closer to the Covent Garden area. It might be a good time to check your wallet or the closures on your bags. Pickpockets do work these crowds.

At Long Acre you should see the sign for the **Covent Garden tube station** *just across the street. You will be returning there up* **James Street** *after your visit to the* **Theatre Museum**, *which is the culmination point of Part III of this walk. Once again you could easily stop here and take the tube back to your residence leaving the rest of the walk to be picked up at another time.*

PART III
(Drury Lane, Royal Opera House,
St. Paul's–Covent Garden, and the Theatre Museum)

*I*f you are picking up Part III separately, turn left for a few steps upon exiting the **Covent Garden station**. You will shortly reach **Long Acre** where you turn right.

For those pressing on immediately from Part II, cross to the tube station side of the street when you reach Long Acre and turn left. At the intersection of Long Acre and **Bow Street** is the **Kemble's Head pub.** There's a sign outside that gives you a nice introduction to Covent Garden history. The interior of the pub is comfortably relaxing with lush green carpet and seat cushions, a dark bar, and chocolate brown walls. Two gas logs glow invitingly and the walls are decorated with theatrical prints.

The official namesake here is John Philip Kemble (1757–1823). The Kemble family and their residences have been mentioned before in these pages. It was an extraordinary mini-dynasty. John Philip had a sister, Sarah (1755–1831), who performed under her married name of Siddons. She

is generally considered to have been the superior performer. Charles Kemble (1775–1854), John Phillip's younger brother, was also an actor and he had a daughter, Fanny Kemble, who made a considerable name for herself both in Britain and the United States.

John Philip Kemble is perhaps best known as the man who consolidated the managerships of Drury Lane and Covent Garden in the early 1800s. When the Covent Garden theatre burned down in 1808, Kemble as manager put a fair amount of his own money into the recon-

Kemble's Head pub

struction. When it reopened in 1809 he attempted to raise admission prices in the pit. Performances were interrupted for over three months with shouts, catcalls, horns, bells, whistles, fistfights, and even the release of a live pig in the house. Kemble ultimately capitulated and reinstated the old pit entry fees. This fracas has gone down in theatre history as the famous "OP" or "Old Price Riots."

*After looking in at the pub continue on Long Acre one more block to **Drury Lane**. There's a pub called **The Prince of Wales** on the corner across the way. Before turning right you might want to cross the street and read the signboard on the pub that tells the story of how Drury Lane got its name.* It was originally the center of coach building activities in London, but in the 17th century it became more and more a theatrical and literary district. Samuel Pepys mentions in his diary walking down this street one morning and seeing Nelly Gwynn coming out of her lodgings. The critic and playwright, John Dryden, also lived on the north side of the street from 1682–1686. Further on down was the Old Queen's theatre where Henry Irving and Ellen Terry acted together for the very first time in a shortened version of *The Taming of the Shrew.*

*Return to the right side of Drury Lane and walk down past Number 55 until you see a small pocket park called **Drury Lane Gardens**.* It's on the former site of a burial ground dating back to 1877, but today has an enchanting playground and an outdoor basketball court. There is a fine explanatory sign just inside the park entrance.

*Exit the park and turn right to continue down Drury Lane. At the corner of **Russell Street** you can see the 1826 colonnade along the side of the Drury Lane Theatre. We'll be coming around in front of this theatre momentarily, but for now look on your right to get a fix on the marquee of the tiny 440 seat **Fortune Theatre**.* Named perhaps after its popular Elizabethan predecessor, which was located nowhere near here (see Walk Nine), this Fortune has the dis-

Fortune Theatre

12

tinction of being an amalgamation of the church and the stage. The building is shared with the Scottish National Church and religious areas are both over and under the present theatre. It was built in 1924 and mainly houses small cast shows. Its long run champion is the 1961 revue *Beyond the Fringe*. This show, besides starting a whole "satire" industry in London in the swinging '60s, launched the entertainment careers of four talented young Oxford grads—Peter Cook, Dudley Moore, Jonathan Miller, and Alan Bennett.

Kitty corner from where you are standing is a restaurant called Sarastro. It is a moderately pricey eatery, but with an interior that looks like a mad surrealistic prop storage area, it may be worth the cost to schedule a pre– or post–theatre repast there. At a minimum step in and ask about table availability just to get a peek.

Otherwise, cross Russell Street and keep going. Number 68 on your right is Brodie and Middleton—theatrical suppliers. If you are a tecnician or designer you may wish to step in if they are open. Then at **Tavistock Street** *turn right. Had you gone straight you would have run into* **Kean Street** *named after the actor Charles Kean (1811–1868).* Charles didn't have the raw talent of his more famous father Edmund Kean, but he was a competent, disciplined and hard working actor/manager whose productions according to the *Oxford*

SIDDONS COURT

39

Companion to the Theatre had a salutary influence on the Duke of Saxe Meinigen. *You also passed a* **Kemble Street** *a while back and now will shortly, not too far beyond the stage door of the Aldwych Theatre, find a building named Siddons Court, after the actress Sarah Siddons, who was the leading tragic actress of the British stage from 1782–1812. If this isn't a theatre area nothing is.*

When you reach **Catherine Street** *you'll see the marquee of The* **Duchess Theatre** *across to your left.* We covered this theatre in Walk Four, but to recap, The Duchess Theatre (747 seats) dates from 1929. Two of Emlyn Williams' best plays opened here and ran for over a year each. They were *Night Must Fall* (1935) and *The Corn is Green* (1938). T.S. Eliot's *Murder in the Cathedral* had its first West End production here in 1936 and Noël Coward's *Blithe Spirit* had already run a year at the Piccadilly Theatre before it transferred to the Duchess in 1942 where it continued through 1945 running up a total of 1997 performances.

In 1974 Kenneth Tynan's nude review *Oh Calcutta!* transferred into the theatre and for the next four years the house was filled with high class bodies and low class jokes. The Duchess also holds the West End record for shortest run ever. *The Intimate Review*, which premiered in 1930, did not even survive its opening night. The curtain was dropped and the audience dismissed before the conclusion of the show.

*Turn right at **Catherine Street** and head for the front of the **Drury Lane Theatre**.*

*Thirsty? On the way toward the theatre you'll see the **Nell of Old Drury** pub across the street to your left. There are some nice theatrical prints inside. One of the tables outside on the sidewalk may be as good a place as any to read a bit about the Drury Lane Theatre. If it looks full try the **Opera Tavern** three doors away, another favorite with actors.* To recount even the barest story of this venerable site would take, indeed has taken, volumes. For a far

Drury Lane Theatre

more thorough presentation than we can give you here, inquire at the box office about an interior tour. If you take a tour or attend a performance keep an eye out for one of the seemingly unending list of ghosts haunting the site. They are rumored to include King Charles

II, the actor Charles Kean, the clown Joe Grimaldi, the comedian Dan Leno, and a strange 18th-century courtier who was murdered and walled up in a passageway near the stage. Sutherland's *Ghosts of London* also reports that two actresses in recent years have felt invisible hands pushing them around the stage.

The first theatre on this site (Theatre Royal—Bridges Street) was built by Thomas Killigrew in 1663. He, you may remember if you have taken Walk Three, received one of the two Royal Patent dispensations to perform in London when Charles II returned to the English throne in 1660. It was a long narrow building (58 feet x 112 feet) with a capacity of around 700. The auditorium had an open pit,

Nell of Old Drury Pub

12

boxes, and galleries. Nell Gwynn was a performer here and Samuel Pepys attended. As W. MacQueen Pope says in *Ghosts and Greasepaint* the English seem to find eating and playgoing inseparable activities. As soon as the Drury Lane started operating, it employed a professional caterer and sometime procurer, Mistress Mary Meggs, who was familiarly known as Orange Moll. She controlled the girls who sold apples and oranges to everyone except those in the top gallery. Either the unruly group in the "Gods" didn't spend enough to make the climb worthwhile or it just didn't pay to provide them with additional missiles. Drury Lane number one escaped the Great Fire of London in 1666 but burned down anyway in 1672.

This was actually a good break for Killigrew. In 1671 his main competitor, William Davenent, had opened the larger, better equipped, and more elegant, Christopher Wren designed Dorset Garden Theatre. (See Walk Five) After the fire Killigrew went straight to Wren for his replacement. The Wren–designed second Drury Lane opened in 1674. This building held around 2000 people and you see prints of it often in theatre history textbooks. The auditorium had rings of boxes and rear galleries. The stage had a 17-foot apron and was 15 feet deep behind the proscenium. Christopher Rich remodeled the interior around 1695 to increase the seating. He shortened the forestage and added more boxes at the sides. Look for a nice model of it in the Theatre Museum.

Thomas Betterton was the leading actor at the second Drury Lane in its early years. In 1716 the building saw an assassination attempt on King George II and in 1735 the actor Thomas Hallam was murdered in the Green room by fellow thespian Charles Macklin in an argument over a wig. On a happier note, in 1745 Dr. Thomas Arne, music director of the theatre, composed a song in honor of George III. It was called "God Bless Our Noble King." The crowd rose to its feet when it was played and it started a tradition that continues to this day. Arne, who was a resident of the area, is buried in St. Paul's Covent Garden.

In 1747 the great actor David Garrick became manager of the Drury Lane. Many of his greatest triumphs occurred on its stage. The Adam brothers made more alterations to the interior in 1775 and finished them just in time to open the managership of Richard Brinsley Sheridan with his new play—*The School for Scandal.* John Philip Kemble took over the reins in 1788 but the Drury Lane's fortunes began to decline. The grand old place was finally razed in 1791 after an honorable life of almost 100 years.

12

The third Drury Lane was a monster of 3611 seats designed by Sir Henry Holland. It opened in 1794 with Sheridan back in the manager's position and John Philip Kemble and his sister Sarah Siddons as leading performers. Keeping a sad tradition alive, George III was shot in the building by a mad gunman in 1800.

Another of the great concerns for theatres at this time was fire. The third Drury Lane had an iron safety curtain installed and also had huge water tanks aloft to quench potential conflagrations. All this was to no avail and it burned to the ground in 1809. James Morwood's *Life and Works of Richard Brinsley Sheridan* cites a contemporary account of the fire that seems to capture the event well.

"The Thames appeared like a sheet of fire for the reflection of the flames, and the wind . . . carried the burning matter into the atmosphere, where it appeared for many miles around, like stars floating in the firmament. When the leaden cistern fell in, it produced a shock like an earthquake. . . . Sheridan went at 3 or 4 o'clock in the morning to the Piazza Coffee House, where he drank two or three bottles of wine. . . . To a friend who remarked at his Stoic tranquility, he famously replied, 'A man may surely be allowed to take a glass of wine *by his own fireside.*'"

Drury Lane Number Four, which opened in 1812, stands before you as the oldest operating theatre in London. It was designed by the architect Benjamin Wyatt and currently seats 2226 people. Lord Byron wrote a special prologue for the opening night. In its early years it saw some of the great successes by Edmund Kean. Gas lighting was added in 1817 to compete with Covent Garden. The classical portico was added in 1820 and the side colonnade on Russell Street was put in place in 1826. The pillars came from the demolition of part of John Nash's quadrant in Regent Street.

Charles Macready took over as manager in 1841. The theatre was refurbished and attained new eminence as the premiere hall for large-scale spectacles, operas, and melodramas. Utilizing its large elevator stage sections and giant treadmills there were boat races, horse races, and Ben Hur style chariot races. Scenic displays featured events like Piccadilly Circus at midnight in a blizzard, a full scale Zulu war, and Bank Holiday weekend at Hampstead Heath.

In 1915 cinema took over for a spell and the D.W. Griffith epics *"Birth of a Nation"* and *"Intolerance"* played there. A major interior remodeling occurred in 1921. The domed rotunda and the entrance staircases are now the only remaining features of the Wyatt's original Georgian design. The house continued as a venue for musicals and reviews and functioned throughout the World War II even though somewhat damaged by bombs. The postwar years saw a long string of American musicals including *Oklahoma, Carousel, South Pacific,* and *The King and I.* In 1958 *My Fair Lady* arrived and stayed for six years, a record surpassed recently by *Miss Saigon,* which chalked up over eight years. The National Theatre production of *My Fair Lady* has taken over recently. The six-year run of the 1958 production does not appear to be in jeopardy at this time.

It's now time to inspect the building a bit more closely. Enter the lobby and look around if only to see the Shakespeare statue, the historic plaques,

12

213

Drury Lane's Noël Coward statue

and the statue of Sir Noël Coward, which was unveiled by the Queen Mother in 1998. You may also wish to check for interior tour availability or tickets. Remember if you are on a budget that you can often get cheaper seats at the box office of a theatre than anywhere else. And if you are looking for seats to a sold out show, you may get lucky on a returned ticket just by checking at the box office.

Drury Lane's Shakespeare statue

When you leave the lobby to go outside again, turn right and walk toward the corner. The bust in the memorial on the wall is of **Augustus Harris,** *the manager of Drury Lane from 1879–1896. From the busy corner take a left for about 50 paces down* **Russell Street** *and then a right into* **Bow Street.** *You may notice the signs for the Theatre Museum across the way. Don't panic. We'll be back to this spot after we circle around and through Covent Garden.*

The corner of Bow and Russell has been at the center of London's artistic life for at least 200 years. Two of the capital's greatest theatres are in sight and as you look down Russell Street toward the old Covent Garden market build-

12

Memorial to Augustus Harris

ings, it should take little imagination to see instead of today's busy restaurants and shops the most important coffee houses of the 17th and 18th centuries. Will's Coffee House was right on the corner. John Dryden was its leading customer for 40 years. Samuel Pepys saw him there in 1664 ". . . with all the wits in town." Will's was also the favorite spot of the poet, Alexander Pope, who was introduced to the local wags by Covent Garden resident and playwright William Wycherly. *Opposite Will's was Button's Coffee House.* Joseph Addison was the reigning genius there. Also in this street were Tom's Coffee House (a hangout for Sam Johnson, Henry Fielding, Joshua Reynolds, Colley Cibber, Oliver Goldsmith, and David Garrick) and Davies' (Thomas Davies, prop.) where James Boswell met Dr. Johnson.

For now walk forward on Bow Street. John Rich (1682–1761), actor manager of Lincoln's Inn Theatre and builder of the first Covent Garden Theatre, lived nearby. The novelist Henry Fielding lived in the fourth house from Russell Street from 1707–54 and the actress Peg Woffington had lodgings in the sixth house from the corner for 40 years from 1720–1760. The actors Charles Macklin and David Garrick occasionally shared that residence with her. On your right, you'll shortly come to the cozy Globe Pub. Its walls are lined with celebrity pictures and some nice theatre prints.

Across the street and a bit kitty corner from the pub is the cast iron tracery of the **Floral Hall,** *which is now newly joined to the Royal Opera House. Somewhere between the Floral Hall and the Opera House lived the well-known Restoration playwright William Wycherley. And not far from where you're standing on the right side of the street was the infamous Cock tavern.* According to the stories, Wycherley's wife would allow him to go there only because it was close by and she could keep an eye on him. In 1663 at the Cock Tavern three courtiers got drunk, went out on the balcony, removed their clothes, and proceeded to harangue the public. The crowd below was not amused and the young men were arrested. Luckily for them Charles the II found their episode amusing and came forward to pay their fines.

Had that episode occurred 80 years later, the young ruffians would not have had far to go for their hearing. *A few more steps on is the Bow Street Police Station.* In 1748 this was the site of the Bow Street Police Court. The first magistrate of that court was area resident Henry Fielding. To assist in keeping control of what was one of the most raucous districts in town, Fielding created a corps of fit and speedy detectives who became known as the Bow Street Runners. The buttons of their uniforms were made of copper and thereby goes another name for the constabulary that has stuck through the years. Though not specifically theatrical, detective novel fans with an interest in the 18th-century ambiance of the Covent Garden area may wish to sample *Blind Justice* or *Murder in Grub Street* by Bruce Alexander. The books feature a blind Bow Street magistrate named Sir John Fielding

12

Floral Hall and Royal Opera House

and do a good job of capturing the sights, smells, sounds, and rhythms of London street life of the period.

Let's turn our attention now from police matters to the grand white portico of the **Royal Opera House** *or the Covent Garden Theatre. Theatregoers have been beating a steady path to this same plot of ground for more than 250 years.*

The first theatre on the site, dating from 1732, was an 1800-seat house known as the Theatre Royal Covent Garden. It was royal because it was in the direct line of succession for one of the two exclusive theatre patents awarded by Charles II. Covent Garden's patent came to manager John Rich via Sir Charles Davenant's Dukes Theatre at Dorset Garden (Walk Five). The other patent, as we just mentioned, resides with the Drury Lane Theatre and you actually can see it if you tour the building.

Interior Floral Hall

12

The architect for the first Theatre Royal was E. Shepherd. The ever cantankerous and litigious John Rich was the manager. At one point in his career he killed a fellow actor in a fight over a wig. A more joyful highlight of those early years is that the inaugural performance of Handel's oratorio *Messiah* took place there in 1744. Other historic productions were the first performances of Sheridan's *The Rivals*, and Oliver Goldsmith's *She Stoops to Conquer*. The first theatre was renovated in both 1784 and 1791. Then in 1807 it burned to the ground.

The second Covent Garden (1808) was modeled after the Temple of Minerva on the Acropolis and designed by the neoclassical architect Robert Smirke. Robert Flaxman contributed some grand exterior bas-reliefs. The interior and the stage epitomized the 19th century desire for scenic spectacle. The seating capacity was around 3000 and the proscenium opening was 43 feet wide and 38 feet high. The stage itself was 85 feet wide and 92 feet deep. Technical theatre history was made here as well. It was the first theatre to be lit by gaslight in 1817 and also the first building in which an early version of the follow spotlight was used in 1837. A pressured flame was focused on a block of lime that burned brightly at the single point of intense heat. This point of bright light was then focusable with a set of lenses. As you may have guessed, it was called a "limelight" and hence our phrase "in the limelight."

The first manager of the second theatre was John Philip Kemble, whom we mentioned a few pages ago as the man who got in trouble when he tried to raise prices to pay for the new building and set off the so called Old Price riots. All of the great actors of the 19th century played at the second Theatre Royal. Edmund Kean is perhaps best remembered for his final exit. He collapsed in March of 1833 while playing Othello to his son Charles' Iago. As he fell into his son's arms he is said to have cried out, "Oh God! I am dying...speak to them for me."

The actor William Charles Macready, well known for his new emphasis on historical costuming, became manager in 1837. He was followed by the remarkable Madame Vestris, who pioneered the development of the box set. You can see quite clearly how the invention of better lighting instruments from 1817 to 1850 seems to have led to more attention to costume and three-dimensional scenic detail. Once producers and audiences could see the stage more clearly, they seemed to demand more and better things to see.

Fire returned to the site again in 1856 leaving, as many contemporary prints showed, a smoking shell. The third and present Covent Garden, known then as the Royal Italian Opera House and now as the Royal Opera House, was opened in 1858. Sir James Barry, the architect, produced a Roman Renaissance building with a magnificent raised Corinthian portico. The statues on either side of the

12

facade and the Flaxman bas-reliefs from the previous building were reused.

The 19th-century building became increasingly inadequate to meet the demands of modern stagings of opera and ballet, so in the early 1990s a major redesign was projected to bring it into the 21st century. A controversial Lottery grant of £78 million enabled the work to begin, but not without a storm of controversy that encompassed architectural planning, aesthetic criteria, general administration, labor relations, and ticketing policies. In 1998 Placido Domingo weighed into the acrimonious debate about seat pricing, threatening not to return to its stage unless more cheap tickets were available than in the past. Resignations and dismissals continued to plague the project, but so much money and prestige had been committed that the operation continued to grind forward.

You may now visit the result and make your own assessment as to the worthiness of the renovation. Cross the street and enter the new lobby, which is open to the public daily. Only half of the old Floral Hall has actually been preserved, though it looks much larger because of the huge mirrored back wall. It was cut off at that point in order to allow for better scene changing facilities and storage for the stage. *At the box office you may inquire about booking a space for one of the regular daily backstage tours or getting tickets to a performance. Even if you cannot take a theatre tour, the public areas are open most days. Steps near the front lobby will access the Floral Hall and from there you can take the long escalator up to the Amphitheatre Bar and Restaurant. From that level outdoor galleries will let you gaze into the new costume shops, out over a pleasant expanse of the city, and down into Covent Garden itself.*

When you have reached this outdoor vantage point and before you actually plunge into the street level chaos below, some basic history might be helpful. The area below you was originally a garden belonging to the Convent of St. Peter at Westminster Abbey—hence Convent Garden and finally Covent Garden. The land was ceded to the Russell family by the crown in 1541 as a part of the widespread redistribution of religious holdings after the Reformation.

Francis Russell, the fourth Earl of Bedford, wanted to develop the estate further and in the 1630s work began under the architectural supervision of Inigo Jones, who was a consummate theatre artist as well as the King's favorite architect. Jones, you may recall, was responsible for bringing the concept of painted perspective scenery to England from Italy and designed splendid costumes and scenery for the Court Masques written by Ben Jonson in the early 1600s. His fascinating, but unbuilt, design for a 17th-century theatre is still waiting completion as a part of The Globe Theatre project on Bankside.

Jones also brought visions of neoclassic architecture and Italian town planning back from his continental visits and his design for Covent

12

Garden incorporated a large piazza, houses with open arcades, a stretch of the Duke of Bedford's own gardens, and a church.

The square, when completed, began to attract market traders and over the years became the central fruit, vegetable, and flower market in London. In the 1830s special cast iron market buildings were constructed. In 1974 growth, congestion, and transportation difficulties sounded the death knell for the Covent Garden that Londoners had known for two hundred years. The markets were relocated to suburban Nine Elms and the old buildings were redeveloped into the bustling shopping and entertainment mecca you see today. Covent Garden remains alive and very well. Refer to the bibliography if you wish to pursue the history of this remarkable area in more depth.

*After you have finished your explorations return to the front (Bow Street exit) of the theatre and turn left until you reach the small alley called **Floral Street**. Turn left again. While walking down the side of the theatre, watch for a plaque that marks the dividing line between the 1858 building and the new addition that provides improved backstage and technical spaces, rehearsal facilities, dressing rooms, and administrative offices.*

*When you reach the back of the Royal Opera House on **James Street**, you will plunge into the vibrant street life of today's Covent Garden; turn left toward the old market buildings; jog right as you near the piazza and look to your left for the classical portico of the church known as **St. Paul's Covent Garden**. Walk toward the building and position yourself where you can get a reasonably unobstructed view of the front. This may be a bit difficult as the buskers who perform there often attract large crowds.*

St. Paul's was designed as the architectural anchor for the piazza. The story is often told that the Duke of Bedford was a frugal man

St. Paul's Covent Garden

**St. Paul's
Covent Garden
from the back**

and not too keen about ecclesiastical ostentation. He emphasized to Inigo Jones, the architect, that he "wou'd not have it much better than a barn." To which Jones replied, "Well then, you shall have the handsomest barn in England."

The Tuscan portico you are looking at is clearly handsome and was obviously intended to be the entrance to the church. But the church authorities insisted that the altar be located at the east end of the sanctuary and thus the apparent front door is only a bit of theatrical magic. This is an amusing little irony as St. Paul's Covent Garden has become known as the Actors' Church. The theatre is a profession built on artifice and its members have long accustomed themselves to entering their hallowed performance ground by the back or stage door.

On May 9, 1662, Samuel Pepys recorded in his diary that he saw a Punch and Judy show under it. There is a stone on the left side under the portico commemorating the first mention of Punch and Judy in England. Pepys enjoyed it so much that he brought his wife back two weeks later. If you are lucky enough to be here in May, you may have a chance to see the remarkable puppeteer's service that is a part of the Maye Faire. During that time the entire interior garden of the church is full of Punch and Judy shows and booths where you can buy puppets, theatres, costumes, and other craft items.

Think also of this portico as a true stage set. *You are looking at the opening scene of George Bernard Shaw's* **Pygmalion** *and its musical namesake* **My Fair Lady***. Liza Doolittle is a Covent Garden flower girl and she meets her Henry Higgins underneath the portico of St. Paul's Covent Garden.* It remains today the central buskers' platform for Covent Garden and and throughout the year continues to provide a theatrical backdrop for the mimes, fire-eaters, jugglers, and street musicians who now frequent the piazza from morning till late at night.

After looking at the portico, walk forward and to your right around the block that contains the church. You should find yourself on **King Street** *and moving away from the market. Nicolas Rowe (1674–1718), a minor playwright and poet laureate of England, had lodgings on this street.*

12

David Garrick lived briefly at Number 27. Thomas Arne, the composer and main music director at the Drury Lane, was born on the street at Number 31. Number 35 was the original home of the Garrick Club.

When you reach **Bedford Street** *make a left and then shortly another left through the gates and into a path that will take you to the real entrance of St. Paul's. You'll find a delightful, flower filled garden/park.* Not one in a thousand of the hordes of tourists descending in a feeding frenzy on Covent Garden today will find this spot. And speaking of frenzy, if you want a deliciously creepy picture of Covent Garden as it was in the old vegetable market days, rent a copy of Alfred Hitchcock's classic film *Frenzy*. It takes place in and around the Covent Garden area.

Rest a bit on a bench if you wish; it's a lovely spot to have a sit or eat a sandwich. At your leisure enter the church, which is normally open from 8:30 to 4:30 Monday through Friday and for services on Sunday. Bear in mind that what you see inside is a reconstruction. The building burned in 1795 and was rebuilt to Inigo Jones' design. It was remodeled again in 1871. Wander to your heart's content. There is often a friendly parishioner around to answer questions. The church's long connection with the arts and actors is displayed throughout. Remember that both Drury Lane and the Royal Opera House have been in the parish since the 18th century.

Buried here are William Wycherly, Charles Macklin, and Thomas Arne, the composer of both "God Save the Queen" and "Rule Britannia," and more recently Dame Edith Evans (1888–1976) who is just next to the silver urn containing the ashes of the actress Ellen Terry. The church today is often the site for memorial services for members of the theatrical profession and handsome plaques commemorate a host of performers from Sir Noël Coward to Pantopuck the Puppetman (Mr. G.R. Philpott 1904–1978). Some of the plaques have verses on them. Vivien Leigh's carries a line from *Antony and Cleopatra*. "Now boast thee, death, in thy possession lies a lass unparallel'd."

Leave St. Paul's via your entry path. Upon reaching Bedford Street turn left. Stop briefly at the **Henrietta Street** *intersection.* Richard Brinsley Sheridan fought his third duel here with a certain Captain Matthew over a remark made by the Captain about Sheridan's beloved Miss Elizabeth Linley. The actress/manager/teacher Fanny Kelly (1790–1882) lived at Number 4 Henrietta Street while she pursued her performance career at the Drury Lane Theatre. We covered Ms. Kelly's later career in connection with the Royalty Theatre in Walk Ten. Elizabeth Sharland in her book *A Theatrical Feast* mentions the great critic Charles Lamb's infatuation with Kelly and quotes from her elegant decline of his marriage proposal. Sharland also notes that George Bernard Shaw was married to Charlotte Payne-Townshend in a registry office at Number 15 Henrietta Street in 1898. Shaw was so badly dressed at the occasion that some thought he was a witness

12

dragged in from the street or a beggar rather than the groom. A more complete account of this bizarre marriage ends the first volume of Michael Holroyd's massive four volume biography of Shaw.

Continue on Bedford Street one more block to **Maiden Lane** *and then turn left. You will shortly reach* **Exchange Court** *on the right. Just past that is the stage door of the Adelphi Theatre and about five yards farther is the plaque dedicated by Sir Donald Sinden in honor of the actor William Terriss, who was stabbed and killed here on December 16, 1897.* We mentioned this event in Walk Four when we were looking at the front of the Adelphi theatre. Terriss (1847–1897), a leading member of Henry Irving's company for some years, was stabbed in the back by the actor Richard Prince, a crazed small-part actor with an imagined grievance. According to Jonathan Sutherland in his *Ghosts of London* Terriss died in the arms of his mistress, Jessie Milward and one of his last utterances was that always prophetic line, "I'll be back!" His ghost has been seen at the Covent Garden tube station and in the theatre where lighting technicians have reported seeing a gray suited white gloved man bathed in a greenish light walking through rows of seats before disappearing into a wall. In 1928 an actress occupying Jessica Milward's former dressing room also reported a green light and the sense of being rocked back and forth while she was reclining on a chaise.

More than 50,000 Londoners lined the streets for Terriss' funeral, though Irving prophesied gloomily, and accurately, that nobody would be hanged for murdering an actor. The assailant was, however, declared insane and spent the remainder of his life in Broadmoor Prison. Terriss was known affectionately to the British public as "Breezy Bill," and also as "Number 1 Adelphi Terriss" because much of his best work was done when he was living at that address. Terriss, by the way, was well acquainted with George Bernard Shaw (they both lived at the Adelphi), and Shaw wrote the character of Dick Dudgeon in *The Devil's Disciple* for Terriss, who specialized in melodramatic portrayals. Ironically his murder occurred before the play could be produced.

Need an inexpensive pub nosh? Turn right at **Bull Inn Court** *and make your way down the gas lit passage to the tiny* **Nell Gwynne pub.** *Need a more commodious and expensive repast? On your right is the famous theatrical restaurant* **Rules,** *which with its 1798 opening date claims to be the oldest restaurant in London.* Sharland's *A Theatrical Feast* calls it "the unofficial 'green room' for the world of entertainment" in London. Loved by John Galsworthy, Charles Dickens, Henry Irving, Noël Coward, Graham Greene, Laurence Olivier, and Sir John Gielgud among many, it also was a favorite trysting spot for the Prince of Wales and his actress friend Lily Langtry. Their *tête-à-têtes* in a small room on the first floor were so regular that a special door was installed so that the Prince would not have to walk through the public rooms of the restaurant to get to his table.

12

You will shortly reach **Southhampton Street***. Turn left and head back toward the central piazza. On the left at Number 27 is a bas-relief plaque designating a residence of the great actor David Garrick from 1750–1772. Garrick is seen in profile flanked by the muses of drama.*

Nell Gwynne pub

On your right is The Jubilee Market, a crowded flea market where you might find a bargain or two, and directly ahead of you are the more upscale central market shops and restaurants.

There is theatre everywhere in the refurbished market halls, but only one spot that you must visit. In the South Hall (upstairs) is the tiny little **Benjamin Pollock Toy Shop***, an offshoot of the Pollock Toy Museum on Scala Street. They have a small collection of toy theatres, Punch and Judy parapheralia, and other theatre memorabilia.* If you are not familiar with the Toy Theatre movement, this visit might encourage you to visit the original Pollock's Toy Museum. (See the Unstrung Pearls section at the end of walks for more information.)

When you are finished in the market area, proceed to the side opposite St. Paul's church. The Royal Opera House complex is on your left and the London Transport Museum is on your right. (Their giftshop by the way has the largest and most complete selection of London Bus and Underground merchandise that you can find anywhere.) Dead ahead of you, beyond the barriers that keep the traffic out, is **Russell Street***. Walk toward it and you should have no trouble identifying on your right the entrance to the* **Theatre Museum***.* Enter and enjoy. The museum holds both permanent and seasonal exhibitions of all kinds of theatrical memorabilia, conducts workshops in all aspects of theatre work, has a regular lecture program, and stages readings and occasional productions. You need to make an appointment in advance to use the research facilities of the Study Room in the basement and spaces are normally limited to professional researchers and

12

Pollock's sign

writers in theatre history. *Two little hints: Make sure you look at all the famous handprints as you go down the entrance ramp and do hit the loos before you leave. The Shakespeare tiles are well worth seeing even if you don't need to use the facilities.*

The nearest Tube station to the Theatre Museum is the **Covent Garden station** on the Piccadilly Line. To find it from the Theatre Museum turn left as you exit and return to the market area via Russell Street then curve around to your right until you find James Street leading up out of the market. If you run into King Street or the church again, you've gone too far; turn around and go back. Move up James Street and shortly you'll reach Long Acre; the friendly blue and red circle of London Transport will be on your left. If this is your first visit to the dingy depths of the Covent Garden station be on the watch for the ghost of our murdered actor William Terriss who used the Covent Garden station as he traveled from his home in Putney to the Adelphi Theatre. He has been seen multiple times by the station staff over the years, always dressed in a gray suit with hat and white gloves. His identity was established in a séance.

Theatre Museum;
makeup demonstration at the Museum

WALK THIRTEEN

✤

THE OLD VIC
TO THE
NEW EYE AND
BEYOND

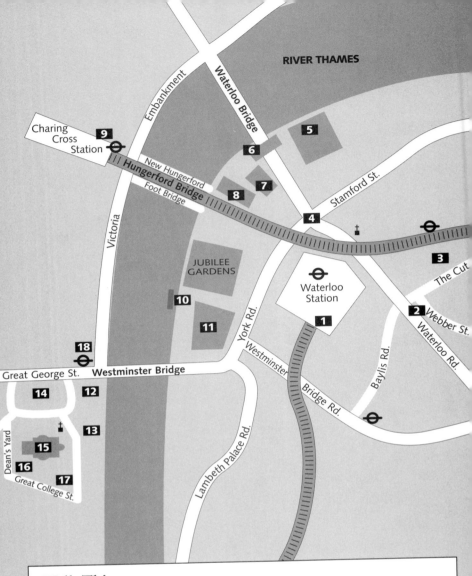

Walk Thirteen

1 Waterloo Station
2 Old Vic Theatre
3 Young Vic Theatre
4 IMAX Theatre
5 Royal National Theatre
6 National Film Theatre
7 Hayward Gallery
8 Royal Festival Hall
9 Embankment tube station
10 London Eye (Millennium Wheel)
11 Former London County Hall (aquarium, art gallery)
12 Clock Tower (Big Ben)
13 Houses of Parliament
14 Parliament Square
15 Westminster Abbey
16 Little Dean's Yard
17 Westminster School
18 Westminster tube station

⊖ Tube Station

STARTING POINT: Waterloo underground station (Bakerloo, Jubilee, or Northern line).

APPROXIMATE TIME: Two hours with modest stops; several hours if you decide to have a meal or enter some of the attractions along the way.

This walk begins at the spiritual home of the National Theatre (the Old Vic) and then takes you to the current National Theatre complex on the banks of the Thames. From there you move upriver with possible stops at the National Film Theatre, the Hayward Gallery, the Royal Festival Hall complex, and the London Eye. The culmination is a visit to Westminster Abbey and Poet's Corner—resting place of a veritable pantheon of English dramatists.

Your beginning point, **Waterloo Station**, is a major transportation hub and your arrival possibilities are infinitely variable. Once you do get there make your way to the main station concourse, which you then should leave by the **Waterloo Road** exit. This exit, identified with a tiny Number 2 on the overhead sign, is approximately opposite Track 4. Go down the escalator, turn right out of the station, and walk up to the first main stoplight intersection—**Baylis Road**. As you walk you will see ahead to the left the facade of the Old Vic at the beginning of the road named

Waterloo Station

13

227

The Cut. *To your right at the bargain bookstore is a nice example of a London street market. Check it out if you have the time or interest. Otherwise cross to the front of the theatre and move by it until you get to the corner of the building on Webber Street. Turn the corner and look for a plaque on the wall recording that the first stone was laid on September 14, 1816, by the Prince of Saxe–Coburg and HRH the Princess Charlotte of Wales.* She was the Prince Regent's only daughter and heir-presumptive to the throne, but by the time the new Royal Coburg Theatre opened its doors in 1818, she had died in childbirth. In 1833 it was renamed the Victoria Theatre after the 14-year-old Princess Victoria, who visited it that year with her mother, but never returned as Queen. This is hardly surprising, as the neighborhood soon became a byword for deprivation and depravity, and the standards of the theatre program declined accordingly, to what was described by one journalist in the 1840s as "the most degraded in London." Another said its productions were only "fit for an audience of felons." *You might wish to stay here for a moment in the relative quiet of the side street while you read the rest of the history of this noble building.*

Emma Cons, whose motivation was more moral than theatrical, began its transformation in 1880. She and some wealthy philanthropic backers set out to combat the evils of alcohol by reopening it as the Royal Victoria Coffee and Music Hall. Since it was not licensed to present plays, its repertoire consisted of variety acts, musical concerts, and later opera, interspersed with lectures and temperance meetings. When Miss Cons died in 1912, she passed on the management of the Victoria Hall to her niece, Lilian Baylis, who had been her assistant since 1898.

Emma Cons plaque

Lilan Baylis, by Miss Cecil Leslie

Reprinted with permission of the National Portrait Gallery

13

228

Miss Baylis immediately obtained a theatre license from the Lord Chamberlain, and the first Shakespearean productions were presented in the spring of 1914. The Victorian Hall had staggered from one financial crisis to another since 1880, but the outbreak of World War I was to prove its salvation. While the commercial managements in the West End turned to light escapist fare, Miss Baylis offered a season of combined opera and Shakespeare, from October 1914 to the end of April 1915. She produced 16 operas and 16 plays in less than 30 weeks.

Over the next decade and a half, under the direction of men like Ben Greet, Robert Atkins, and Harcourt Williams, and with the drawing power of actresses like Sybil Thorndike and Edith Evans, what had now become know simply as the "Old Vic" built up a loyal following. It was John Gielgud's arrival in 1929 to lead the company that brought additional audiences flocking over the Thames to see him in several parts, most notably as Richard II and Hamlet. The following year Ralph Richardson joined him, and soon anyone with ambitions to be taken seriously as a classical actor wanted to make their mark here. The roll-call in the '30s included Peggy Ashcroft, Laurence Olivier, Alec Guinness, Michael Redgrave, Flora Robson, and Charles Laughton.

Like her predecessor Miss Cons, Lillian Baylis was both religious and frugal. Her primary prayer was, "Please God, send me a good actor, but send him cheap," according to Elizabeth Sharland in *A Theatrical Feast*. As the good lady literally lived at the theatre, she cooked her meals on a gas ring just off stage and rehearsals were often accompanied by the aroma of frying sausages. To an actor trying to survive on the meagre company stipend, this must have been an additional trial. In spite of the penny pinching, Sharland asserts that "Lillian Baylis did more single-handedly for the British theatre than any other woman in history."

On her death in 1937, Tyrone Guthrie took over the reins of the company, and when the theatre was bombed in 1941 he kept the Old Vic flag flying in the provinces. In 1943 Ralph Richardson and Laurence Olivier were released from the Navy to become co-directors of the Old Vic Company at the New Theatre (now the Albery) and those productions have gone down into theatrical legend.

The renovated building was reopened in 1950, and in an ambitious five-year plan Michael Benthall presented the entire Shakespeare canon. In 1962, the Old Vic seemed the natural choice as the temporary home of the newly formed National Theatre under its first director Laurence Olivier. Once again the Waterloo Road became the first stop for all theatre lovers. When the National moved into its purpose-built South Bank quarters in 1974, the fortunes of the Old Vic began another period of uncertainty, until the Toronto based impresario, Ed Mirvish, bought it, pumped millions into refurbishment,

13

The Old Vic

and began to support several different companies. In 1997 the Peter Hall Company launched an ambitious repertoire of classics and new plays, but at the end of that year the Mirvish family decided to get out from under their continuing losses and return to Canada. So in 1998, one of the most famous landmarks in the 20th-century history of British drama went dark. As of the year 2000 the theatre was owned by the Old Vic Theatre Trust and was hosting periodic commercial productions again. (Just as this edition was going to press, it was announced that the American actor Kevin Spacey will become the new artistic director for the Old Vic. Detailed plans were unavailable, but Spacey has said that he plans to appear in at least two productions a year and has no qualms about using his movie star status to get "bums on seats.") *Step back around to the front of the theatre now and enter the lobby if it is open. Pay particular attention to the graceful staircase that winds upward to the circles.* Hopefully the theatre will not be dark when you pass this way as then you may have an opportunity to visit the interior of this architectural masterpiece.

*Upon leaving the lobby turn right and this time cross **Webber Street**. On your right is the former Old Vic Annexe.* It was dedicated in 1958, but now serves as the **National Theatre's Studio.** Scripts that the National has taken an interest in are given readings here and authors are given a chance to work on the text.

*Now walk farther along **The Cut** for 200 yards, until you reach the **Young Vic** on the left-hand side of the road.* In 1946 a company for

13

children called the Young Vic was formed as an off-shoot of the Old Vic Centre, which was an Old Vic–operated acting school headed by Michel St. Denis. The new company was directed by George Devine, who later went on to a major career as the director of the English Stage Company at the Royal Court Theatre. London performances were often given as matinees at the Old Vic and the troupe also did extensive regional touring. Financial problems sank the first Young Vic in 1951.

Young Vic

Almost twenty years later the director Frank Dunlop was able to get a new company going. And more importantly, with a grant from the National Theatre and another from the Arts Council, he was able to get the theatre built. The Young Vic was and is nothing fancy. It was constructed in less than a year out of concrete blocks on an old bomb-site.

The main auditorium holds about 450 people on red-painted bleacher seats that surround a long thrust style playing area on three sides. There is also a small black box studio theatre that will accommodate about 100 patrons. The goal was to have an open and informal space that offered an alternative to the more formal proscenium style theatres of the west end and would therefore appeal to younger audiences. This junior branch was opened by Dame Sybil Thorndike on August 12, 1970, to double as a young people's theatre and a studio for the National Theatre Company. In the early '70s this was one of the livliest theatres in London with performances ranging from a smash revival of John Osborne's *Look Back in Anger* to a visit from the rock group The Who. In 1974 it became independent of the National Theatre, but continued its eclectic production philosophy of old standards, new plays, visiting fringe groups, and foreign companies (e.g., Peter Brook's Paris production of *Ubu Roi*). It now hosts a mixture of its own productions and some from the Royal Shakespeare Company. There has also been talk of a new building on the site.

Turn around and retrace your steps back along **The Cut**. Unfortunately, you can no longer pay a visit to R. Cooke's traditional London eatery. A few years ago you could get a heaping plate of eels

13

231

13 Scenes from the National Theatre: exterior, bookshop, and restaurant

Royal Festival Hall

and mash or a homemade meat pie in an atmosphere that easily rekindled juicy memories of "Sweeney Todd." *When you return to* **Waterloo Road** *at the Old Vic Corner, turn right and walk past* **Waterloo Station** *until you reach the large roundabout at the far end. You will eventually pass on your right the Church of St. John the Evangelist and then the London IMAX Theatre. Just past the IMAX theatre is the underpass access to the east side of* **Waterloo Bridge**. **Do not attempt to stay on the surface here as the pavement (sidewalk) quickly disappears and you will find yourself literally in an oncoming traffic lane.**

Descend to the underpass and follow the signs to **Waterloo Bridge**. *As you come up the ramp onto the bridge, you will see the flytower of the* **National Theatre** *complex immediately on your right. Shortly there will also be a set of steps leading down to the building access.* This high vantage point, and indeed the entire bridge, is an excellent place for photos. It's also a good place to read a bit about the history of the National Theatre. (If it is too chilly or raining, proceed down the stairs and find some cover in the cozy lobby of the theatre before you read the following.)

What you see before you is the result of a process that started as far back as the 19th century when English arts advocates began to feel that Britain ought to have a government sponsored theatre that could stand alongside the long established National Theatres in most of the rest of Europe. Inside the almost £20 million pound complex, which was opened in 1976–77, are four well equipped and varied auditoriums plus dressing rooms, rehearsal facilities, and technical shops. The largest theatre is the open staged Olivier, which has over 1100 seats and a huge stage with full fly capacity above and a massive elevator and revolve system on the floor and below. The second theatre is the adjustable proscenim Lyttelton, which seats 890 patrons. It is

13

named after Oliver Lyttelton (Lord Chandos), who was the National Theatre's first chairman. An extra theatre called the Loft, which seated around 100 patrons, was carved out of the portions of the Lyttelton lobby in 2001, but will apparently be abandoned after the 2002 season. Finally there is the 300–400 seat Cottesloe, which is named after Lord Cottesloe, who was the chairman of the South Bank Theatre Board. This is a fully flexible space, ringed by narrow balconies on three sides, that can be set up for proscenium viewing, theatre in the round, or even productions. This facility was originally conceived as a venue for experimental work and chamber theatre projects, but it has proved to be a superlative home for traditional and classical work as well. Denys Lasdun, the architect, originally said that there was in his mind also another theatre. This was to be the building itself. It has wide streets, little cul de sacs, squares, terraces, galleries, and a panoramic backcloth of a bend in the Thames known as the "King's Reach" which stretches from St. Paul's to Somerset House. This idea was perhaps most fully developed in the late fall of 2000 when one could watch a film projected on the exterior flytower of the Lyttelton.

The foyers of the National, where the attractions include exhibitions, a particularly good theatre bookshop, and bars and restaurants where you can enjoy a coffee, snack, or full meal, are open from 10:00 A.M. to 11:00 P.M. And as Lasdun said, "A great attempt has been made to keep it small inside. People say what a big building it is, but it's not a building at all, it's a piece of the city. The spaces are relatively small, so you can get into a huddle with just a few people and not feel lost in it. The scale is very important. It is a human building in which people are part of the architecture—it won't make sense without people in it or on it all the time." Before the evening performances there is free music in the Lyttelton foyer on the ground floor, and frequent platform performances in the three auditoria—talks, interviews or discussions at modest prices. Your very first stop after you enter the building should be the box office where you may obtain brochures on the current schedule, pricing, discounts, etc., book a backstage tour, check on tickets for future performances, or secure seats for the day's performances. (The day seat allocation goes quickly for popular shows, so join the queue early if you are angling to see a sell out.)

The history of the opening of the building was in sharp contrast to its smooth running today. A less resilient director than Sir Peter Hall, who succeeded Olivier, would have had a nervous breakdown from the succession of building delays, union obstructionism, and political and press attacks that attended that long drawn out saga in the mid-1970s. In desperation the Company started giving open-air performances on the Lilian Baylis Terrace overlooking the river, to herald their arrival on the South Bank. At the first acoustic test on the Lyttelton Stage Albert Finney could not resist the temptation to

13

frighten the assembled gathering by mutely mouthing his lines, and only when their faces went white did he break the silence with his normal voice. (For one version of the full story of this troubled period read *Peter Hall's Diaries 1972–80* or ask the folks at the bookstore to recommend additional titles that cover the whole of the history of the National Theatre.)

The first three directors each made a massive contribution towards the creation and maintenance of the National as the best as well as the most important theatre in the land. Sir Laurence Olivier launched it into orbit at the Old Vic, Sir Peter Hall brought it safely into its berth at the South Bank, and Richard Eyre consolidated its reputation with an astonishing success rate (recognized by the award of his knighthood at the end of his term there). In 1998 he handed over to Trevor Nunn, a man whose track record at the RSC (Royal Shakespeare Company) and elsewhere was impeccable. Nicolas Hytner has been tapped to take over the reins in 2003. In an interview that appeared in the *Chicago Tribune*, he outlined his vision as follows. "One of my goals is to get playwrights of my generation to work on the grand scale that the National offers. And I want to see if we can spend our money a little differently, so that things can perhaps get done a little faster and quicker and not so expensively. Because we must find a way of getting really cheap tickets out to a different and broader audience." It would appear that the National will continue to rest in a very safe pair of hands.

If your walk began early, you could end your visit by having a coffee or lunching at the National, but if you prefer to push on there are several other possibilities for refreshment of mind and body on the route. Turn left out of the Theatre and you will have the option of paying homage to the electronic arts. Right under Waterloo Bridge is the **National Film Theatre** *(established in 1953 and at this site since 1958).* Memberships can be purchased and the four screening rooms are generally busy seven days a week. The buffet and bar are open to the public. *Behind the National Film Theatre and buried even more firmly under the Waterloo Bridge approach lies the* **Museum of the Moving Image** *(1988).* Unfortunately this colorful, interactive history of film and television museum, encased in a quixotic glass and chrome building that managed to make a virtue out of its less than promising location, is closed and may not reopen. *A final browse might also be saved for the used book tables set up right under the vaulted arch of the bridge.*

If modern art calls you more strongly than the silver screen, take the stairs just a few paces after you emerge from under the **Waterloo Bridge**. *They will lead you to the* **Hayward Gallery**, *which houses some of the most stimulating art exhibitions to be found in the metropolis.* The building itself, opened in 1968, is a classic example of the controversial poured concrete "brutalism" style of the '60s. You may wish to

13

compare it to the Royal National Theatre, which shares some of the same exterior features.

Return to the Thames walk and continue your journey upstream. *You will shortly see small and medium-sized concert halls, the **Purcell Room** and **Queen Elizabeth Hall**, followed by the 3000 seat **Royal Festival Hall**, which is usually just as lively during the day as the National Theatre. The RFH has bars and restaurants on several floors, with live music at lunchtimes, busy record and book shops, and events that range from music in the large concert hall to literary debates and discussion in the small Voice Box upstairs.*

In terms of London's aesthetic history, the Royal Festival Hall marks the beginning of the development of the South Bank as an arts enclave. It was designed as the centerpiece of the Festival of Britain in 1951 and has remained the linchpin of what is known as the South Bank Centre (comprised of all the concert halls, the National Theatre complex, the museums, and the galleries). In the 1980s a board was set up to coordinate the development of the river frontage and the commercial and residential environment between the river and Waterloo station. Work continues to this day to improve the access, livability, and vitality of the area.

To end this walk now, go to the back of the Festival Hall and follow the signs to Waterloo tube station. For a more attractive conclusion locate the stairs to the new Hungerford pedestrian bridge on the upstream side of the RFH and cross the Thames along the railroad tracks. Descending the stairs on the other side will bring you to the Embankment station (Northern, Bakerloo, Circle, and District lines).

The London Eye

13

Westminster Bridge and the Houses of Parliament

*But if there is still spring in your step, continue along the South Bank toward Westminster Bridge where the extraordinary pleasure of one of London's newest attractions awaits you. The **London Eye** is one of the hottest tickets in town and although you can try to queue up and take your chances, the better plan is to see about making a booking while you are there. The London Aquarium and an art gallery in the former London County Council Hall are also in the vicinity.*

At this point you can climb the stairs to Westminster Bridge. It might be difficult to imagine the "calm so deep" mentioned by Wordsworth in his poem "Composed upon Westminster Bridge" in 1802, but the views do remain splendid and reflective of his words.

> "Earth has not any thing to shew more fair:
> Dull would he be of soul who could pass by
> A sight so touching in its majesty."

Finish crossing the bridge toward The Clock Tower (containing the bell called Big Ben), The Houses of Parliament and Westminster Hall. If Parliament is sitting, you could queue at the St. Stephen's entrance to watch the daily drama in either house. You could also check on tours of the complex.

*If politics are not to your fancy, continue immediately across Parliament Square, past **St. Margaret's Westminster**, where Nicholas Udall, author of the first extant English comedy Ralph Roister Doister, is buried, to Westminster Abbey. The Abbey is a working church as well as one of London's major tourist attractions and access is always subject to scheduled services. Should this be your first trip to the building,*

13

arranging for one of the guided or audio tours might be advisable. This is the setting for the Memorial Services of some of Britain's greatest actors—Sir Henry Irving, Sir Ralph Richardson, Lord Olivier, Dame Peggy Ashcroft—as well as luminaries from other walks of life. The south transcept of the Abbey has long been known as Poet's Corner and there you will find memorials to a galaxy of literary and dramatic figures including John Dryden, William Shakespeare, Ben Jonson (he's buried in the nave but has a medallion here), David Garrick, Henry Irving, Charles Dickens, Noël Coward, and Sir Laurence Olivier (whose ashes were interred here in 1991). The area is now so full of plaques and busts that in 1997 Oscar Wilde was commemorated by a stained glass window, unveiled by Sir John Gielgud at a ceremony attended by many leading actors and writers.

*If you exit the Abbey from the front door you can turn left on **Dean's Yard** until you locate the entrance to **Little Dean's Yard**. Beyond that, though not accessible to the public, are the precincts of Westminster School.* Nicholas Udall, the school master and writer of *Ralph Roister Doister,* was one of its early headmasters and the school has a long and noble tradition of drama. Ben Jonson, John Dryden, and Christopher Wren were graduates. Every other year the Queen's Scholars perform a Plautus or Terence comedy in Latin as required by Queen Elizabeth I at the refounding of the school in 1560.

When you have completed your exploration of the Abbey and its environs you can return to Westminster Bridge, where you will find the Westminster tube station (District, Circle, and Jubilee lines) at the foot of the Big Ben clocktower. Bus lines from the area can also take you back up Whitehall to Trafalgar Square and the West End.

Westminster Abbey

13

❀

UNSTRUNG
PEARLS

❀

No matter how you string individual pearls there are always a few that will not fit conveniently on any strand. They are either too modest, too specialized, or simply too far off a planned route to allow for easy inclusion. Other jewels are just so large or important that they seem to call for an unencumbered visit of their own. Here then, in a rough order of importance, is a final list of not-to-be missed theatrical pearls in London.

1. THE VICTORIA AND ALBERT MUSEUM: Exhibition Road and Cromwell Gardens SW 7 (South Kensington tube station). Take the tunnel that starts right in the tube station and follow the signs. This is the national museum of fine design and applied art and any theatre lover with a technical or design interest will glory in the decorative objects, the furniture collections, the fabrics, and especially the costume court.

2. THE NATIONAL GALLERY: Trafalgar Square and **THE TATE BRITAIN:** Milbank are the city's two world-class classical art galleries. They are not specifically theatrical, but they are two of London's general jewels and all visitors with any kind of arts sensitivity should have them high on their priority list. This is not meant to mitigate the importance of the many other galleries that vie for your attention in the city.

3. SAMUEL FRENCH'S THEATRE BOOKSHOP: 52 Fitzroy Street W1 (Warren Street tube) It was for many years, when it was located in an enchanting old building just off Covent Garden, London's preeminent theatre bookstore. It now has several competitors, but is still top notch. A visit here makes a nice pairing with Number 4 Pollock's Toy Museum. They are quite close together.

4. POLLOCK'S TOY MUSEUM: 1 Scala Street W1 (Goodge Street tube, Northern line) Scala Street is literally just behind the tube exit. Turn right out of the station, then right on Goodge street, then right again on Whitfield, and you will see it on the corner of Scala Street. For devotees of Punch and Judy and the charming 19th-century Toy Theatre movement, this little museum is a treasure and a must. Open 10–5 every day except Sunday. Admission charge three pounds as of 2002.

5. THE ROYAL COURT THEATRE: SW1 (Sloan Square tube). An argument might be made that this is the fourth most important theatre in London after The Globe, the Drury Lane, and Covent Garden. Its reputation as the place where new playwrights are either discovered or confirmed remains as strong today as it was when Shaw, Pinero, Barker, Osborne, et al. were first produced. Visit it. They have a great bookstall.

6. THE BANQUETING HOUSE: Whitehall SW1 (Charing Cross tube) Inigo Jones designed the hall, Rubens painted the ceiling, and Charles the First lost his head over the whole affair. This is a general tourist destination, but as a theatre buff you are obligated to go if only to imagine the sumptuous Court Masques that were staged there by Inigo Jones and Ben Jonson.

7. DULWICH PICTURE GALLERY: Gallery Road SE21. If you like your art galleries modest in size, high in quality, and exquisitely designed, this Sir John Soane building will be to your liking. Edward Alleyn, the great Elizabethan actor, was the founder of Dulwich College. Some of his personal collection of paintings and those of a colleague, Richard Cartwright, formed the original nucleus of the gallery's holdings. Here, among the Rembrandts, Tiepolos, Rubenses, and Van Dykes, you will find portraits of Alleyn, his wife, Richard Burbage, and Nathan Field, an actor whose name appeared in a cast list in the First Folio. Edward Alleyn's first wife was the stepdaughter of the theatre owner/producer Philip Henslowe. Henslowe's diaries were found amongst Alleyn's papers and are now located in the Dulwich College archives. Travel to the gallery by taking a train to West Dulwich from Victoria Station. Turn right out of the station, then take a left at the first crossing (Gallery Road). It is about a ten minute walk. At our last visit the Gallery was open 10–5 T–F.

8. GEORGE BERNARD SHAW'S HOME AT AYOT ST. LAWRENCE: If you feel the need to see a bit of country and still keep a theatre purpose in mind, a visit to Shaw's Corner might be just the ticket. It was Shaw's home for over 40 years and is now a lovely National Trust Museum. Take a train to Welwyn Gardens from Kings Cross station and then a taxi. Hours are limited so check them before setting out.

9. BRITISH LIBRARY: Euston Road NW1 Underground Euston (Northern or Victoria Line) Serious scholars know that this library holds one of the greatest research collections in the world, but it is also worth a visit by the more casual theatre buff. A life size statue of Shakespeare by the sculptor Roubiliac is near the front entrance. It used to stand in David Garrick's Temple to Shakespeare at his country home just outside of London. The main gallery always displays some of the library's most significant holdings. These include national treasures such as Magna Carta and literary materials such as documents by or relating to Shakespeare. A second gallery is available for periodic exhibits on people or themes. A recent exhibit featured materials on the life and work of Oscar Wilde. There is an excellent book and gift shop as well.

10. OUTLYING OR FRINGE THEATRE VENUES: Consider searching out places such as the Almeida Theatre, Hampstead Theatre, Lyric Theatre Hammersmith, Kings Head Theatre, Orange Tree Theatre, Riverside Studio Theatre, Sadler's Wells Theatre, Southwark Playhouse, and the Theatre Royal Stratford East to add to your historical understanding and your viewing pleasure. A future edition may be able to find a way to include these venues and some of the others that are doing exciting and memorable creative work in the Greater London area.

****

Those are the final pearls. Walk in peace and above all care for this beautiful city. London, like Shakespeare, is for all time and all peoples, but it's truly special for those who hold a love of the art of live theatre in their hearts.

SELECTED BIBLIOGRAPHY

Adcock, A. St. John. *Famous Houses and Literary Shrines of London*. New York: Barnes and Noble, 1993.

Andrews, Richard. *The London Theatre Guide*. London: Metro Publications, 2002.

Arnold, Wendy. *The Historic Hotels of London*. London: Owl Books, 1987.

Ash, Russell. *The Londoner's Almanac*. London: Century Publishing, 1985.

Bergan, Ronald. *The Great Theatres of London*. San Francisco: Chronicle Books, 1988.

Berry, Patricia Dee. *Theatrical London*. London: Allan Sutton Ltd., 1995.

Borer, Mary Cathcart. *Covent Garden*. London: Abelard-Schuman Ltd., 1967

Bowsher, Julian. *The Rose Theatre: An Archaeological Discovery*. London: The Museum of London, 1998.

Brockett,Oscar. *History of the Theatre*. New York: Alleyn and Bacon, 1995.

Chambers, Michael. *London The Secret City*. London: Ocean Books, n.d.

Clunn, Harold P. *The Face of London*. London: Simpkin Marshall Ltd., 1982.

Connell, Charles. *They Gave Us Shakespeare*. Stocksfield: The Oriel Press, 1982.

Cook, Judith. *The Golden Age of the English Theatre*. London: Simon and Schuster Ltd., 1995.

Cottrell, John. *Laurence Olivier*. London: Hodder and Stoughton Coronet Edition, 1977.

Day, Barry. *This Wooden "O": Shakespeare's Globe Restored*. London: Oberon Books, 1996.

Donaldson, Frances. *The Actor Managers*. London: Weidenfeld and Nicolson, 1970.

Edwards, Christopher ed. *The London Theatre Guide 1576–1642*. London: The Burlington Press Ltd., 1979.

Fairfield, Sheila. *The Streets of London*. London: Macmillan Publishers Ltd., 1984.

Fay, Stephen. *Power Play: The Life and Times of Peter Hall*. London: Hodder and Stoughton, 1995.

French, Ylva. *London Blue Guide*. London: A & C Black, 1998.

Gardner, Douglas. *The Covent Garden Guide*. London: Ernest Benn Ltd., 1980.

Glinert, Ed. *A Literary Guide to London*. London: Penguin Books, 2000.

Goodwin, John ed. *Peter Hall's Diaries*. New York: Harper and Row, 1984.

Gray, Robert. *A History of London*. New York: Taplinger Publishing Company, 1978.

Halliday, F. E. *Shakespeare*. New York: Thomas Yoseloff, 1961.

Hartnoll, Phyllis ed. *The Oxford Companion to the Theatre*. Oxford: Oxford University Press, 1983.

Jackson, Peter. *Walks in Old London*. New York: Barnes and Noble, 1995.

Jenner, Michael. *London Heritage*. London: Michael Joseph Ltd., 1988.

Jones, Edward and Woodward, Christopher. *A Guide to the Architecture of London*. New York: Thames and Hudson, 1992.

Kempson, Rachel, Lady Redgrave. *Life Among the Redgraves*. New York, E.P. Dutton, 1986.

Kendall, Alan. *David Garrick: A Biography*. London: Harrap Ltd., 1985.

Kiernan, Pauline. *Staging Shakespeare at the New Globe*. London: Macmillan Press, Ltd. 1999.

Kimball, George. *The Pocket Guide to London Theatre*. Topsfield, MA: Salen House Publishers, 1987.

MacGregor-Hastie, Roy. *Nell Gwyn*. London: Robert Hale, 1987.

Mac Queen-Pope, Walter. *Ghosts and Greasepaint*. London: R. Hale, 1951.

Mander, Raymond and Mitchenson, Joe. *The Theatres of London*. London: New English Library, 1975.

Mander, Raymond and Mitchenson, Joe. *The Lost Theatres of London*. Rupert Hart-Davis, 1968.

Marowitz, Charles ed. *The Encore Reader*. London: Methuen and Company Ltd., 1965.

Mee, Arthur. *London: The City and Westminster*. London: Hodder and Stoughton, 1975.

Morton, Brian. *Americans in London*. New York: William Morrow, 1986.

Morwood, James. *The Life and Works of Richard Brinsley Sheridan*. Edinburgh: Scottish Academic Press Ltd., 1985.

Nicholson, Robert. *London Guide*. London: Robert Nicholson Publications, Ltd., 1990.

Ousby, Ian. *Blue Guide Literary Britain and Ireland*. London: A.C. Black Limited, 1985.

Rasmusen, Steen Eiler. *London the Unique City*. Cambridge, MA.: The MIT Press, (revised edition) 1982.

Richards, Timothy M. and Curt, James Stevens. *City of London Pubs*. Newton Abbot: David and Charles Ltd., 1973.

Rigg, Diana (compiler). *No Turn Unstoned*. New York: Doubleday and Company, Inc., 1983.

Roberts, Howard and Godfrey, Walter H. eds. *London County Council Survey of London: Bankside*. Vol. XXII. London: London County Council, 1950.

Rodgers, Malcolm. *Blue Guide Museums and Galleries of London*. London: Ernest Benn Ltd., 1983.

Room, Adrian. *Dictionary of Britain*. London: Oxford University Press, 1986.

Rosenthal, Harold. *Covent Garden: Memories and Traditions*. London: Michael Joseph Ltd, 1976.

Rossiter, Stuwart ed. *Blue Guide London*. London: Ernest Benn Ltd., 1998.

Rossi, Alfred ed. *Astonish Us in the Morning: Tyrone Guthrie Remembered*. London: Hutchinson and Company, 1977.

Rumbelow, Donald. *The Triple Tree: Newgate, Tyburn, and Old Bailey*. London: Phaidon Press Ltd., 1984.

Sampson, Anthony. *The Changing Anatomy of Britain*. New York: Random House, 1982.

Sanderson, Michael. *From Irving to Olivier*. London: Athlone Press, 1984.

Scimone, G.M.S and Olding, Simon (eds.) *London's Museums and Collections*, 3rd edition. London: Canal Publishing Company, 1998.

Sharland, Elizabeth. *A Theatrical Feast*. Somerset: Barbican Press, 2002.

Smith, Irwin. *Shakespeare's Blackfriars Theatre*, 1964.

Speaight, Robert. *Shakespeare: The Man and His Achievement*. London: J.M. Dent and Sons, Ltd., 1977.

Sutherland, Jonathan. *Ghosts of London*. Derby: Breedon Books Publishing Company, Ltd., 2002.

Thorne, Robert. *Covent Garden Market*. London: The Architectural Press, 1980.

Tunstall, Brian. *The Pictorial History of Southwark Cathedral*. London: Pitkin Pictorials Ltd., 1967.

Williams, George C. *Guide to Literary London*. London, B.T. Batsford Ltd., 1973.

Wilson, Jean. *The Archaeology of Shakespeare*. London, Alan Sutton Publishing, Ltd., 1997.

Wittich, John. *Discovering London's Inns and Taverns*. London: Shire Publications Ltd., 1996.

Wylie-Harris, William. *American Links with the City of London*. London: W.H. Wylie-Harris, 1977.

INDEX

Abelard and Heloise, 196
Absurd Person Singular
  (Ayckbourn), 99
Accused (Archer), 121–122
Actor's Pub. *See*
  Salisbury Pub
Actors' Church. *See* St.
  Paul's Covent
  Garden
Adam Street, 64
Adam, James, 62
Adam, Robert, 62, 64
Adam, William, 62
Adams, John Quincy, 127
Addison, Joseph, 181, 215
Adelaide Street, 61
Adelphi Court, 63
Adelphi Terrace, 52, 62,
  64, 65
Adelphi Theatre, 52,
  65–66, 222
Adelphi, The, 62
Adelphia Terrace, 52, 62,
  64, 65
Admirable Crichton, The
  (Barrie), 63–64, 198
Admiral's Men, 135
Admiralty Arch, 52, 53
Aesthetic Movement,
  99–100
Agas map, 15
Ages of Man, The, 166
Alban Court, 146
Albany, 101
Albany Court, 101
Albany Courtyard, 96, 101
Albee, Edward, 196
Albemarle Club, 105
Albery Theatre, 190,
  194–195, 229
Albery, Bronson, 194
Albery, Ian, 206
Albery, James, 194
Aldermanbury Street, 147
Aldgate, 128–129, 131
Aldwych Street, 71
Aldwych Theatre, 73, 74,
  101, 190. 210
Alexander, George, 113
Alhambra (music hall), 171
Alhambra Palace Music
  Hall. *See* Odeon
  Cinema
Alhambra Palace of
  Varieties. *See*
  Odeon Cinema
All Hallows by the Tower,
  124, 125, 126–127
Alleyn, Edward
  church for, 7, 130,
    143–144
  Finsbury Fields, 142
  Fortune Theatre, 130,
    141
  home of, 7

ownership by, 15
Allies statue, 96, 104–105
Almack House, 115
Almack's Assembly Rooms,
  115
Almeida Theatre Company,
  195
Almeida Theatre, the, 74,
  243
Ambassadors Theatre, 199
American Bar, 69
American Buffalo (Mamet),
  199
American Repertory
  Theatre, 184
Amphitheatre Bar/
  Restaurant, 218
Anchor Inn, 2, 3, 10
Anchor Terrace, 16
Androcles and the Lion
  (Shaw), 114
Angel Court, 108, 113
Angel of Christian Charity.
  See Eros, statue of
Anne Frank tree, 190,
  193–194
Annie Get Your Gun, 198
Anthony and Cleopatra
  (Shakespeare), 114
Anthony, C.L., 166
antiques. *See* Portobello
  Road antique market
Apollo Club, 80
Apollo Theatre, 68, 156,
  165, 167–168
Archaeology of Shakespeare,
  The (Wilson), 38,
  142
Archer, Jeremy, 121–122
Arches, The, 58
Architecture. *See also*
  Observatory Gardens
  art deco, 69
  modern, 35
  neoclassic, 46, 218
  Victorian, 178, 183,
    185, 195
Argyll Road, 182
Arlington Street, 109
Arms and the Man (Shaw),
  55–56
Arne, Thomas, 212, 221
Around the World in Eighty
  Days (Verne), 174
Arsenic and Old Lace, 73
Art (Reza), 196–197
Art and Architecture of
  London, The
  (Saunders), 101
Art Deco, 69
Art Nouveau Pub, 25
Arts Theatre, 190,
  191–192
Arts Theatre Club, 160
Ashcroft, Peggy, 238

Assassination and Persecu-
  tion of Jean Paul
  Marat... (Weiss), 162
Astaire, Fred/Adele, 175
Astor Place riot, 160
Astor, Nancy, 115
Athenaeum Club, 108, 116
Atkins, Robert, 229
Aubrey Road, 180
Auntie Mame, 66
Avenue, The. *See*
  Playhouse, The
Ayckbourn, Alan, 99

Bacon, Francis, 26, 58,
  103–104
Baird, James Logie, 161
Ball, Emma, 135
Bank intersection, 150
Bank of England, 46, 138,
  150
Bank of England Museum,
  150
Bank tube station, 138,
  150
Bankside area, 3, 218
Bankside Power Station.
  See Tate Modern
  Art Gallery
Bankside. *See* New Globe
  Walk
Banqueting House, The,
  242
Barbican Arts Complex. *See*
  Barbican Centre
Barbican Centre, 87, 136,
  138, 143, 145
Barbican Centre entrance,
  142, 143
Barbican Estate, 142
Barbican tube station, 138,
  145
Bard, the. *See* Shakespeare,
  William
Barker, Harley Granville,
  62
Barnum, P. T., 102
Barrie, James
  home of, 28, 63–64,
    106, 178, 184–185
  works of, 180, 184–185
Barry, E. M., 61
Barry, Elizabeth, 49
Barry, James, 217
Bart, Lionel, 66
Bartholomew Fair
  (Jonson), 15
Bartholomew Lane, 150
Basevi, George, 104
Bastion High Walk, 146
Bateman Street, 160
Baylis Road, 227
Baylis, Lilian, 228–229
Bear baiting, 11
Bear Gardens, 10, 15, 16

248

Bear Gardens Museum, 16
Beau Geste, 68–69
Beaumont, Francis, 7, 9,
    11, 149
Beaumont, Hugh "Binkie,"
    166
Beaux Stratagem, The
    (Farquhar), 54
Beaux' Strategem, The
    (Hammond), 168
Becket, Thomas, 150, 192
Beckett, Samuel, 99
Bedford Gardens, 184
Bedford Street, 221
Bedford, Duke of,
    219–220
Bedford, Earl of, 218
Beech Street, 143
Beechey, William, 202
Beerbohm-Tree, Herbert,
    101, 118–120
Beeson, William, 89
Beggar's Opera, The
    (Gay), 32, 49
Behan, Brendan, 196
Belgravia, 99
Bell Inn, 24, 34
Bell Yard, 34
Belle Sauvage Inn, 24, 33
Belott, Stephen, 146
Benbow House, 15
Benjamin Pollock Toy
    Shop, 223
Bennet Street, 111
Bennett, Alan, 202, 210
Benthall, Michael, 229
Bergan, Ronald, 170, 207
Berkeley Square, 96, 105
Berkeley Street, 105
Bernhardt, Sarah, 66, 118,
    164, 168, 176
Berry Brothers & Rudd,
    108, 111
Berry, Patricia Dee, 118
Berwick Street Market,
    156, 169
Bethlehem Hospital. *See*
    Old Bedlam
Bethnal Green Museum of
    Childhood, 136
Betterton, Thomas, 49, 88,
    212
Betty, William, 63
Beyond the Fringe, 210
Big Ben, 53, 226, 237
Bishop of Ely, 28, 30
Bishop of Ely's Banqueting
    House, 28–29
Bishop of Winchester, 7, 8,
    9, 35. *See also*
    Winchester Palace
Bishop's Bonfire (O'Casey),
    153
Bishopsgate, 4, 125, 131
Blackfriars Gatehouse, 36
Blackfriars Lane, 38
Blackfriars Monastery, 24,
    36–37

Blackfriars Priory, 38
Blackfriars Priory Gate-
    house, 36
Blackfriars Pub, 24, 38
Blackfriars Theatre, The,
    36, 86–87, 153
Blackfriars tube station, 15,
    24, 38, 138, 154
Blackfriars, precincts of, 34
Blake, William, 140–141
Blanchett, Cate, 195
Bleak House (Dickens), 45,
    205
Blithe Spirit (Coward), 72,
    210
Blitz (Bart), 66
Blitz, the, 34, 54, 65, 160,
    169
Bloomsbury, 103
Bolt Court, 76, 86
Boodles, 108, 111
Booth, Hope, 159
Borough High Street, 17,
    18
Borough tube station, 2,
    18
Boswell, James, 91, 215
Boubil, 161
Boucicault, Dion, 101
Bourchier, Arthur, 199
Bouverie Street, 86
Bow Street, 208, 214
Bow Street Police Court,
    215
Bow Street Police Station,
    215
Bow Street Runners. *See*
    Bow Street Police
    Station
Bowsher, Julian, 16
Boy Friend, The (Wilson),
    59, 196
Boydell, John, 116
Boys' companies, 37
Bracegirdle, Anne, 49, 77
Bradley, William, 133
Braham, John, 112
Branagh, Kenneth, 99
Brayne, John, 132–133
Bread Street, 148
Brecht, Bertolt, 32
Brewer Street, 169
Brick Court, 81
Bridewell Palace, 89
Bridewell Prison, 76, 92
Bridewell Theatre, 76,
    89–90
Bridge, Frank, 184
Briers, Richard, 99
Britannicus (Racine), 195
British Academy of Film
    and Television Arts
    (BAFTA), 100
British Actors Equity, 203
British Broadcasting
    Company (BBC),
    71, 74, 99

British Library, 135, 147,
    242–243
British Library of Political
    and Economic
    Science, 48
British Museum, 36, 103
Broad Street, 130–131
Brodie and Middleton, 210
Brodribb, John Henry. *See*
    Irving, Henry
Brooke, John Charles, 153
Brooks Club, 108,
    110–111
Brummel, Beau, 110
Brushfield Street, 131
Bucket of Blood. *See* Lamb
    and Flag Pub
Buckingham Arcade, 61
Buckingham Palace, 52, 53,
    111
Buckingham Street, 61
Bucklersbury, 150
Buckstone, John Baldwin,
    122
Bull Inn Court, 222
Bunhill Fields Cemetery,
    138, 140–141
Bunhill Row, 141
Bunyan, John, 140, 143
Burbage House, 124, 134
Burbage, Cuthbert, 4, 37,
    135
Burbage, James, 4, 37,
    86–87, 132–133,
    134
Burbage, Richard, 4, 37,
    81, 132, 135
Burbages' Theatre
    company. *See*
    King's Men
Burgess, Anthony, 92
Burke, Edmund, 111
Burkhardt, Robert, 27
Burlington Arcade, 96,
    102, 103
Burlington Beadles, 103
Burlington Gardens, 101,
    103
Burlington House, 96, 102
Burney, Charles, 64
Burney, Fanny, 64
Burton, Richard, 67, 167
Bury, John, 66
Bush House, 52, 74
Business of Murder, The,
    106
Butley (Gray), 99
Butterflies Are Free, 168
Button's Coffee House,
    215
Byron, George, 101, 213
Byward Street, 126

Cabaret (Prince), 163
Cabaret entertainment,
    161, 171, 207
Cactus Flower, 168
Cade, Jack, 20

Caesar and Cleopatra (Shaw), 114
Call It a Day (Anthony), 166
Callas, Maria, 109
Cambridge Circus, 162
Cambridge Theatre, 190, 205
Campbell, George, 60
Campbell, Mrs. Patrick, 187. *See also* Kilty, Jerome
Campden Hill, 183
Campden Hill Road, 182
Campden Hill Square, 179–180
Campion, Thomas, 85, 149
Can Can, 198
Canada House, 52, 54
Candida (Shaw), 152
Cannon Street, 10, 20
Cannon Street railway bridge, 10
Cannon Street tube station, 15
Canterbury Tales (Chaucer), 19
Cardinal Cap Alley, 14
Cardinal's Wharf, 2, 14
Carey Street, 48, 49
Carlisle Street, 158
Carmen, 118
Carousel, 213
Carte, Richard D'Oyly
Coutts Bank, 60
memorial to, 57, 70
Palace Theatre, 162
production of Savoy Operas, 64
Savoy Theatre, 67–68
Carter Lane, 34, 38
Carter, Hubert, 119
Carting Lane, 66
Catharine of Aragon, 28–29
Cathedral Street, 8
Catherine Street, 72, 210
Cato (Addison), 181
Cavell, Edith, 199, 203
Cawarden, Thomas, 37
Cecil Court, 197
Cecil Street, 65
Central Criminal Courts, 24, 32,33,78-79. *See also* The Old Bailey
Chairman, the, 59
Chamberlain's Men, The, 135, 142, 147, 153. *See also* King's Men
Chambers, William, 101, 126
Chancery Lane, 43, 49, 58
Chancery Lane tube station, 24, 25, 40, 41, 50
Changeling, The (Webster), 130, 145
Changing of the guard, 53

Chaplin, Charlie, 109, 171
Chapman, Robin, 92
Charing Cross Railroad Station, 55
Charing Cross Road, 47, 163
Charing Cross Station/ Hotel, 52, 55, 59
Charles II
Child's Bank, 80
Nell Gwynn and, 55, 116
son of, 157
statues of, 158
theatre patents by, 88, 89, 216
Charles II Street, 117
Charlie Girl, 66
Charlie's Aunt (Thomas), 160
Charlotte, Princess of Wales, 228
Charterhouse Street, 28, 30
Chaste Maid in Cheapside, A (Middleton), 11
Chatham House, 115
Chaucer, Geoffery, 7, 19, 29, 129
Cheapside, 148
Chekhov, Anton, 99
Chess, 161
Chicago, 66
Child's Bank, 79–80
Children of the Chapels' Royale, 37
Children of the King's, 87
Chimes at Midnight (Welles), 77–78
Chinatown, 164
Chippendale, Thomas, 192
Christ Church Spitalfields, 124, 131
Christie's Auction House, 108, 115
Christie, Agatha, 119, 178, 184, 203
Christoferus (Chapman), 92
Chu Chin Chow, 119
Church Entry, 38
Churchill, Winston, 104–105, 146–147, 175
Cibber, Caius, 158
Cibber, Colley, 53, 110, 215
Cibber, Theophilus, 120
Cinerama, 198
Cittie of York pub, 24, 25–26
City of London, 8
City of London Festival, 127
City of London Information Center, 24, 34
City Road, 140
Clarence House, 111
Clark, Brian, 69

Clarkson, Willy, 156, 164–165
Claypole, Noah, 5
Cleveland, Duchess of, 116
Clifford Street, 104
Clink Prison, 9
Clink Prison Museum, 9–10
Clink Street, 8, 9
Clive, Colin, 68
Clock Tower, 53, 226, 237
Coaching inns, 18, 19
Coal Hole Tavern, 66–67
Cock Tavern, 215
Cockney, 148
Cockpit public house, 24, 36
Coleridge, Samuel Taylor, 164
Coliseum Theatre, 190, 192, 197–198
College of Arms, 138, 152
Collier, Jeremy, 26–27
Colman, George, 158, 185
Comedy of Errors (Shakespeare), 27
Commonwealth Institute, 178, 182
Commonwealth period, 48, 89, 181
Complete Works of William Shakespeare Abridged, The, 99
Condell, William, 146, 147
Congreve, William, 49, 77, 85, 118
Cons, Emma, 228
Conti, Tom, 69
Convent of St. Peter at Westminster Abbey. *See* Covent Garden
Cook, Judith, 133
Cook, Peter, 210
Cooney, Ray, 99
Copeland, Alexander, 101
Coppelia, 174
Copper, Gladys, 114
Copyrights, 92–93
Corn is Green, The (Williams), 72, 210
Coronet Cinema, 178, 179
Corsican Brothers, The (Boucicault), 101
Costuming, theatre, 217, 218, 241
Cottrell, John, 163
Country Wife, The (Wycherley), 92
Court Masques, 48, 218, 242
Coutts Bank, 52, 59–60, 63
Covent Garden, 49, 60, 208
Covent Garden Market, 191, 214–215
Covent Garden Theatre, 70, 208-209, 217-

219. *See also* Royal
Opera House
Covent Garden tube
station, 190, 207,
222, 224
Coventry Street, 168
Coward, Noël
as actor, 63, 73, 114,
204, 222
memorial to, 214, 221
works of
Blithe Spirit, 72, 210
Private Lives, 163
Cowley, Richard, 135
Cradle Song, 168
Cranbourn Street, 191,
203
Craven Street, 55
Crimean War Memorial,
108, 117
Criminal Courts Building,
33
Cripplegate, 142
Criterion Theatre, 96,
98–99
Cromwell, Oliver, 48, 61,
80, 144, 181
Crowder's Well Pub, 145
Crown and Anchor Pub,
207
Crown jewels, 125
Crown Office Row, 82
Crown Passage, 108, 112
Crutched Friars, 128–129
Cursitor Street, 50
Curtain Playhouse, The
(Linnell), 133
Curtain Road, 132, 133
Curtain Theatre, 4, 135
Curtain, The, 4, 124, 133
Cut, The, 228, 230
Cyrano de Bergerac, 168

Daly's Theatre, 156, 176
Daly, Augustus, 176
Dance, George, 32, 129,
130, 134
Daubeny, Peter, 74
Davenant, Charles, 120,
216
Davenant, William, 48, 88,
89, 212
David Copperfield
(Dickens), 56
Davies Bear Garden/
Amphitheatre, 15
Davies family, 180
Davies' Coffee House, 215
Davis, Moll, 116
Day, Barry, 11
de Lacey, Henry. *See*
Lincoln, Earl of
De Morgan, William, 99
De Vere, Edward, 181
Dead Man in Deptford, A
(Burgess), 92
Dean Street, 158
Dean's Yard, 238

Dear Brutus, 167
Dear Liar (Kilty), 187
Defoe, Daniel, 140, 143
Dekker, Thomas, 91
Delaney, Shelagh, 196
Dench, Judi, 101, 163
Derry and Toms
Department Store,
179, 186, 187
Derry Street, 187
Devil Tavern, 80
Devine, George, 192, 231
Devonshire Row, 130
Diaghilev's Ballet Russes de
Monte Carlo, 174
Dial M for Murder, 168
Diamond trade, 28
Dickens, Charles
as actor, 159, 222
home of, 18, 28
Old Curiosity Shop, 47
St. James House, 99,
112
works of
Bleak House, 45, 205
David Copperfield,
56
Edwin Drood, 42
Martin Chuzzlewit,
82
Oliver Twist, 5
Pickwick Papers, 20,
28, 91
*Uncommercial
Traveller, The,* 127
Docklands, 85
Doll's House, A (Ibsen),
160
Domesday Book, 49
Domingo, Placido, 218
Donmar Warehouse
Theatre, 190,
206–207
Donne, John, 45–46, 149
Dorset Garden Theatre, 48,
76, 88, 89, 93, 212
Dorset Rise, 88
Dorset Stairs, 88
Doubleday, John, 171
Dover Street, 105
Dowding, Lord, 78
Dowland, John, 36
Drake, Sir Francis, 8
Drayson Mews, 185
Drayton, Michael, 149
Dress Circle shop, 205
Drury Lane, 209
Drury Lane company, 70,
88
Drury Lane Gardens, 209
Drury Lane Theatre
Duke's Company and,
216
first, 212
fourth, 213–214
management of, 120,
208
patent for, 216

second, 48–49, 212
third, 101, 212
view of, 73, 190, 209
Dryden, John, 80, 87, 156,
164, 193, 209, 215
du Maurier, Gerald, 114
Duchess of Bedford's Walk,
182
Duchess of Malfi, The
(Webster), 32, 132
Duchess Theatre, 52, 72,
190, 210
Dufferin Street, 141
Duke of York's Theatre,
190, 198, 199
Duke's Company, 88
Dukes Theatre, 216
Dulwich Picture Gallery,
242
Dunlop, Frank, 231
Duse, Eleanora, 73, 168,
176

Earlham Street, 205
Eccles, Christine, 16
Edward I, 61
Edward III, 35
Edward VII, 71
Edwardes, George, 176
Edwards, George, 73
Edwin Drood (Dickens), 42
Egyptian Hall. *See* Pic-
cadilly Arcade
Egyptian House, 102
Eisenhower, Dwight, 115
Eleanor crosses, 61
Eleanor of Castile, 61
Elephant and the Castle,
The, 185
Elevator (lift), use of
theatre, 197, 213,
233
Eliot, T. S., 72, 210
Elizabeth I, 28, 30, 35, 60,
83, 85, 134
Elizabeth II, 3
Elizabethan clowns/jesters,
34
Elizabethan era, 4
Elizabethan theatre
books for, 17
figures of, 7, 55, 85, 92,
132, 135
model for, 19–20, 141
Stationers' Hall and,
92–93
Elliot, Michael, 105–106
Elsinore, 71
Ely Court, 30
Ely Palace, 29
Ely Place, 28, 30
Ely, Bishop of, 58
Embankment Gardens, 52,
56, 59, 61
Embankment Place, 52
Embankment tube station,
52, 56, 226

Emerson Street. *See* New Globe Walk
Empire Cinema/Dance Hall, 156, 170, 171, 174–176
Empire Theatre of Varieties. *See* Empire Cinema/Dance Hall
English National Opera, 198
English Parliament, 37
English Stage Company, 192, 231
Ensler, Eve, 192
Eros, statue of, 97
Essex Villas, 182
Evans, Edith, 114, 221
Evening with Bea Lillie, An, 167
Evergreen (Rogers & Hart), 65–66
Every Man in His Humor (Jonson), 159
Evita, 161
Exchange Court, 222
Executions, 4, 32–33
Exeter Hall, 69
Eyre, Richard, 235

Falstaff, John, 3
Fanny Kemble (Marshall), 158
Fanny's First Play (Shaw), 63
Farquhar, George, 54
Farrant, Richard, 37
Farringdon Street, 91
Faustus, 34
Fenchurch Street station, 124, 128
Fernald, John, 192
Festival of Britain, 114, 236
Fetter Lane, 85
Fielding, Henry, 32, 82, 120, 152, 215
Financial Times, The, 16
Finney, Albert, 234–235
Finsbury Fields, 131, 142
Fire, danger of, 89, 127, 152, 213
Five Guys Called Moe, 168
Flaxman, Robert, 217
Fleet Lane, 33
Fleet Prison, 76, 91–92
Fleet River, 31, 33, 91
Fleet Street, 50, 79, 84, 86, 91
Fletcher, John, 7, 9, 11, 149
Fletcher, Yvonne, 115
Floral Hall, 215
Floral Street, 193, 219
Fontanne, Lynn, 168
Fonteyn, Margot, 206
Foote, Samuel, 121
Ford, Ford Maddox, 184
Ford, John, 153

Forrest, Edwin, 160
Fortnum & Mason, 96, 100
Fortune Street, 141
Fortune Theatre, 16, 130, 138, 139, 141–142
Fortune Theatre (Drury Lane), 190, 209–210
Fountain Club, 69–70
Fountain Court, 81
Fountain Tavern, 69–70
Fox, Charles James, 111
Fox, Henry, 181
Franklin, Benjamin, 55
Frayn, Michael, 69
French Without Tears (Rattigan), 99
Frenzy (Hitchcock), 221
Friday Street, 151
Frith Street, 160
Frohman, Charles, 74
Fry, Christopher, 167
Fulwood Place, 26
Furnival Street, 50
Furnival's Inn, 24, 28

Gaiety Girls, The, 73
Gaiety Theatre, 71, 72–73
Gallati, Mario, 109
Galsworthy, John, 63–64, 183–184, 222
Garden Court, 82
Gardens, roof, 187, 197
Garrick Club, 190, 193, 221
Garrick Street, 193
Garrick Theatre, 73, 199
Garrick, David
chest of, 85
Drury Lane, 212
Hogarth paintings, 46
home of, 192, 221, 223
social life of, 64, 111, 215
Gas lighting, 58
Gaslight, 168
Gate Cinema, 178, 179
Gate Theatre. *See* Prince Albert Pub
Gaunt, John of, 29
Gay, John, 32, 49
Geffrye Museum, 47, 136
General Tom Thumb, 102
George I, 116
George III, 153, 212
George Inn Yard, 2, 19
George Inn, the, 3
George IV Pub, 48
George Pub, 79
George V, 44, 118
Gerrard Place/Street, 164
Gershwin, George, 175
Ghosts
at tube station, 222, 224
in bank, 60
in church, 127, 130
in music hall, 71

in theatre, 114, 120, 122, 159, 160, 162, 196, 197, 198, 199, 211, 222
Ghosts (Ibsen), 159
Ghosts and Greasepaint (MacQueen-Pope), 119, 212
Ghosts of London (Sutherland), 114, 144, 162, 196, 197, 211, 222
Gibbons, Grinling, 150
Gibbs, James, 54, 71, 78
Gielgud Theatre, 156, 165–167
Gielgud, John
as actor, 196
Coutts Bank and, 60
Criterion Theatre, 99
family of, 183
Haymarket Theatre, 121
home of, 192
Lyceum Theatre, 71
social life of, 204, 222
Gilbert and Sullivan, 56, 57
Gilbert Bridge, 143
Gilbert Monument, 52, 56
Gilbert, William S., 56, 182, 199. *See also* Gilbert and Sullivan
Giselle, 174
Gladstone, William, 78, 101
Glass Menagerie, The (Williams), 121
Glinert, Ed, 77
Globe Pub, 190, 215
Globe Theatre. *See also* Shakespeare's Globe Theatre
archaeology and, 16, 17
construction of, 4
model of, 4, 141
second site of, 4
site of, 2, 9, 10, 15, 16, 36, 37, 133
Globe, the. *See* Gielgud Theatre
Gloucester Walk, 184
Godliman Street, 34
Godspell, 196
Golden Age of the English Theatre, The (Cook), 133
Golden Hinde, 8
Golden Lion Pub, 108, 115
Goldfish, The, 63
Goldoni, 168
Goldsmith Building, 83
Goldsmith, Oliver
grave of, 76, 83
home of, 27, 81
social life of, 91, 215
works of, 83, 217
Gondoliers, The (Gilbert & Sullivan), 68
Goodrich, Francis, 193

Gorbachev, Mikhail, 147
Gorboduc (Norton &
    Sackville), 83, 90
Gordon Place, 185
Gough Square, 85
Gower, John, 7
Gracechurch Street, 4
Grafton Street, 105
Gray's Inn, 26
Gray's Inn Gardens, 24, 26
Gray's Inn Hall, 24, 27, 41
Gray's Inn Road, 25, 28
Gray's Inn Square, 24, 26
Gray, Dorian, 114
Gray, Simon, 99
Great Catherine (Shaw), 63
Great Eastern Hotel, 130
Great Eastern Street, 132
Great Fire of London
    destruction by, 35, 89,
        127, 152
    memorial for, 2, 3
    reconstruction after, 35,
        91, 151
    wind change of, 28, 29,
        31
Great Newport Street, 191
*Great Theatres of London,
    The* (Bergan), 170,
    207
Great Windmill Street, 168
Greek Street, 161
Green Lodge, 178, 184.
    See also Christie,
    Agatha
Green Park, 109
Green Park tube station,
    96, 106, 108
Green Room Club, 64
Greene, Graham, 101, 222
Greene, Robert, 131
Greet, Ben, 229
Grein, J. T., 159
Gresham Street, 148
Griffin marker, 13, 124,
    131, 132
Growing Up (Thomas),
    167
Guild House, 203
Guildhall, 138, 147–148
Guildhall School of Music
    and Drama, 87–88,
    143
Guildhall Yard, 148
Guinness, Alec, 56, 229
Guthrie, Tyrone, 44, 229
Guys and Dolls, 198
Gwynn, Nell, 46, 55, 80,
    116, 209, 212

Habeus Corpus, 168
Hackett, Albert, 193
Hadrian VII (Rolfe), 153
Hal, Prince, 3
Half-price ticket booth,
    156, 171–172
Hall, Peter, 99, 192, 234
Hallam, Thomas, 212

Hambling, Maggi, 61
Hamlet (Shakespeare), 34,
    44, 71, 135
Hammersmith, 56, 125,
    243
Hammerstein, Oscar, 7
Hammond, John
    Clements-Kay, 168
Hampstead Heath, 213
Hampton, Christopher,
    106
Hancock, Tony, 169
Handel, George Freidrich,
    217
Hardwicke, Cedric, 62,
    114
Harris, Arthur, 78
Harris, Augustus, 60, 200,
    214
Harris, Edward, 174–175
Harris, Richard, 67
Hart Street, 128
Harvard Chapel, 7
Harvard, John, 18
Hatchard's Bookshop, 96,
    100
Hatton Gardens, 28, 30
Hatton, Christopher, 28,
    30
Hawkins, Caroline, 154
Hawkins, Jack, 154
Hawksmoor, Nicolas, 131
Hawthorne, Nathaniel, 42
Hay Hill, 105
Haydon, Benjamin, 102
Hayes, Helen, 121
Haymarket Theatre, 65,
    108, 117, 119,
    120–121, 153
Haymarket, The, 106, 109,
    118, 120–122, 151,
    168
Hayward Gallery, 226,
    235–236
Hazlitt's, 160
Hazlitt, William, 31, 43,
    86, 160
Heartbeat London (Elliot),
    105–106
Hedda Gabler (Ibsen), 205
Heminge, John, 4, 146,
    147
Heminge-Condell
    monument, 138, 147
Henning, John, 117
Henrietta Street, 221
Henry IV, 29, 48, 77
Henry V (Shakespeare), 11
Henry VI (Shakespeare),
    20, 82
Henry VIII, 28–29, 37,
    44, 89, 157
Henry VIII
    (Shakespeare), 7
Henslowe, Philip, 7, 9, 15,
    16
Henslowe, Richard, 141,
    142

Her Majesty's Theatre,
    108, 118, 119
Hess, Myra, 54
Hewitt Street, 133
Hiccocks, Johannes, 83
Hicks Theatre. *See* Gielgud
    Theatre
High Holborn, 27, 50
High Street, 18
High Street Kensington
    tube station, 178,
    187
Hillsleigh Road, 179
Histrio Mastix (Prynne), 34
Hitchcock, Alfred, 221
HMS Belfast, 5
Hodge the cat, 86. *See also*
    Johnson, Samuel
Hog Lane. *See* Curtain
    Road
Hogarth, William, 46, 91,
    170, 205
Hogshead, the, 91
Holborn, 25, 28, 41, 43
Holborn Circus, 28, 31
Holborn tube station, 74
Holborn Viaduct, 31, 50,
    91
Holland Estate, 181
Holland House, 178,
    180–181
Holland Park, 178, 179,
    180–182
Holland Park Avenue, 179,
    180
Holland Street, 185
Holland Walk, 180
Holland, Henry, 101, 212
Holy Cross, 128
Holywell Lane, 132
Holywell Priory Land, 133
*Honorable History of Friar
    Bacon and Friar
    Bungay, The*
    (Greene), 131
Hope Theatre, 15
Hornton Street, 185
Hostage, The (Behan), 196
Hostel, youth, 35, 181
Houndsditch, 129
Housekeepers of the
    Chamberlain's Men,
    4, 9. *See also* King's
    Men
Houses of Parliament, 53,
    226, 237
Howard Hotel, 77
Hoxton Fields, 135
Hume, David, 111
Hungerford pedestrian
    bridge, 236
Hunter, John, 170
Hurt, John, 195
Huxley, Aldous, 101
Hytner, Nicolas, 235

Ibsen, Henrik, 159, 160
Idiot's Delight, 168

If I Were A King, 113
Importance of Being Earnest, The (Wilde), 102, 114
Inchbald, Elizabeth, 185
Independent Stage Society, 159
Inn of Chancery, 41. *See also* Staple Inn
Inner Temple, 26, 86
Inner Temple Hall, 76, 82–83
Inner Temple Lane, 83, 84
Inns of Court, the, 20, 25, 27, 38, 80
Inspector Calls, An, 99
Institute of Directors, 108, 116–117
Intimate Review, The, 72, 210
Iolanthe (Gilbert & Sullivan), 68
Ireland Yard, 36, 37
Irish Republican Army (IRA), 33, 130
Irving, Henry
   as actor/manager, 66, 70–71, 118, 209, 222
   Coutts Bank and, 60
   homes of, 96, 105, 106
   memorial service for, 238
   social life of, 164
   statue of, 190, 200
Ivy Restaurant, 190, 204
Ivy, The, 109

Jackson, Glenda, 198
Jacobean theatre, 7, 17, 181
James I, 9, 35, 37, 84
James II, 80
James Street, 207, 219, 224
Jenner, Carol, 192
Jesus Christ Superstar, 71
Jewry Street, 128
Joan Littlewood Stratford East, 196
John Adam Street, 62, 65
John Carpenter Street, 87, 88
John Harvard Public Library, 18
John Lobb, Bootmaker, 111–112
John of Gaunt, 29
John Wesley Highwalk, 145
Johnson's Court, 76, 85
Johnson, Samuel, 10, 64, 85, 91, 215
Jolly, George, 89
Jones, Glyn, 90
Jones, Henry Arthur, 101
Jones, Inigo
   burial of, 152

designed by, 45, 46, 218, 220, 242
   scenery by, 48
   social life of, 149
Jones, Marie, 199
Jonson, Ben
   as a mason, 44
   family of, 130, 144
   home of, 55
   imprisonment for, 18, 32
   social life of, 80, 135, 148–149
   works by, 15, 159, 218
Journey's End (Sheriff), 68–69
Jubilee Market, 223
Justice (Galsworthy), 63–64, 198

Kean Street, 210
Kean, Charles, 60, 65, 210
Kean, Edmund, 60, 67, 85, 110–111, 156, 164, 181, 213, 217
Keats, John, 149
Keep the Home Fires Burning, 73
Kelly, Fanny, 160, 164, 221
Kemble Street, 210
Kemble's Head Pub, 190, 208
Kemble, Charles, 158, 164, 208
Kemble, Fanny, 158, 208
Kemble, John Philip, 181, 208, 212, 217
Kemble, Phillip, 60, 158
Kemble, Sarah. *See* Siddons, Sarah
Kempe, William, 4
Kensington Church Street, 184
Kensington Church Walk, 185
Kensington High Street, 186
Kensington Palace, 186
Kensington Square, 178, 186–187
Kensington Town Hall/ Library, 182
Kerr, Jean, 167
Kew Gardens, 49
Killigrew, Thomas, 48, 88, 89, 120, 150, 185, 211
Kilty, Jerome, 187
King and I, The, 213
King Charles I, 61, 242
King Charles II
   Child's Bank, 80
   Nell Gwynn and, 55, 116
   son of, 157
   statues of, 158
   theatre patents by, 88, 89, 216

King Edward I, 61
King Edward III, 35
King Edward VII, 71
King George I, 116
King George III, 153, 212
King George V, 44, 118
King Henry IV, 29, 48, 77
King Henry VIII, 28–29, 37, 44, 89, 157
King James I, 9, 35, 37, 84
King James II, 80
King Lear (Shakespeare), 18
King Lear (Tate), 18
King Street, 112, 220
King William III, 49, 80
King William Street, 3
King's Master of Revels. *See* Cawarden, Thomas
King's Men, 9, 35, 36, 37–38, 48
King's Revels, 89
King's Wardrobe, 35
Kingsland Road, 134
Kingsley, Ben, 194
Kingsley, Sidney, *168*
Kingston, Gertrude, 63
Kingsway, 52, 71, 73–74
Kirk, Michael, 58
Kiss Me Kate, 198
Knightsbridge, 99
Kronborg Castle, 71
Kyd, Thomas, 92

La Dame aux Camélias, 168
La Locandiera (Goldoni), 168
Lady Be Good (Gershwin), 175
Lady Elizabeth's Men, 87
Lady Windermere's Fan (Wilde), 114
Lady's Not for Burning, The (Fry), 167
Lake Havasu (Arizona), 4
Lakeside Terrace, 143
Lamb & Flag Pub, 190, 193
Lamb, Charles, 31, 43, 82, 221
Lancaster Place, 70
Landseer, Edward, 53
Langtry, Lillie, 99, 222
Lanman, Henry, 133
Lasdun, Denys, 234
Laughton, Charles, 229
Law Courts Buildings, 40, 49
Lawrence, Gertrude, 163
Le Caprice, 109
Le Gallienne, Eva, 184
Le Gallienne, Richard, 184
Leather Lane, 28
Leicester Square, 156, 170–171

Leicester Square tube
    station, 156, 173,
    190, 191, 201, 203
Leicester, Earl of, 170
Leigh, Mike, 69
Leigh, Vivien, 69, 109,
    114–115, 221
Les Misérables, 161
Lewis, Arthur, 183
Libel, 56
Liberty area
    Elizabethan theatre, 8
    land as, 28, 37
Licensing Act of 1737, 82,
    120
*Life and Works of Richard
    Brinsley Sheridan*
    (Morwood), 213
Lighting, theatre, 67–68,
    213, 217
Lillo, George, 135
Lilly, Bea, 66
Lillywhite's, 98
Lincoln's Inn, 26, 34, 41,
    44
Lincoln's Inn Chapel, 40,
    44
Lincoln's Inn Fields, 40, 46
Lincoln's Inn Fields
    Theatre, 40, 48, 49
Lincoln's Inn Gate House,
    40, 44
Lincoln's Inn New Hall/
    Library, 46
Lincoln's Inn Old Hall, 40,
    45
Lincoln's Inn Old Square,
    40, 45
Lincoln, Earl of, 44–45
Lind, Jenny, 69
Line, Anne, 29
Linnell, Rosemary, 133
Lion King, The (John &
    Taymoor), 71
Lisle Street, 164
Lisle's Tennis Court, 48
Little Adelphi, 62–63
Little Dean's Yard, 226,
    238
Little Hut, The, 168
Little Theatre, 62–63
Little Theatre in the Hay.
    See Haymarket
    Theatre
Liverpool Street station,
    124, 125, 130, 136
Lloyd's Avenue, 128
Lock & Company, Hatters,
    108, 111
Locke, John, 103–104
London Aquarium, 237
London Assurance
    (Boucicault), 101
London Bridge, 3, 4, 5, 20
London Bridge tube
    station, 2, 17, 20

London County Council
    Hall (former), 226,
    237
London Cross, 61
London Eye, 226,
    236–237
London Inns of Court, 26
London Merchant, The
    (Lillo), 135–136
London Shakespeare
    League, 134–135
London Silver Vaults, 40,
    43
London Transport
    Museum, 190, 223
London tube station
    architecture, 15
London wall, 145, 146
London Wall Street, 146
London Zoo, 53
*London: The City and
    Westminster* (Mee),
    116, 157
Long Acre, 192–193, 207
Lord Admiral's Men, 16
Lord Chamberlain, 120,
    192, 229
Lord Chamberlain's Men,
    133
Lord Mayor of London, 79
Lord Strange's Men, 135,
    147
*Lost Theatres of London,
    The* (Mander &
    Mitchenson), 55–56,
    63, 159
Lothbury street, 150
Love for Love (Congreve),
    49, 85
Love Lane, 146
Lower Regent Street, 97,
    99, 117
Lower St. Martin's Lane,
    192
Lower Thames Street, 3
Lucy, Thomas, 144
Lud Gate, 85, 91, 92
Ludgate Circus, 92
Ludgate Hill, 33, 92, 93
Lulu, 168
Lunt, Alfred, 114, 168
Lyceum Theatre, 52, 60,
    70, 200
Lynn, Vera, 105
Lyric Pub, 169
Lyric Theatre, 156, 165,
    168
Lysistrata, 63
Lyttelton Stage, 234
Lyttelton, Oliver, 234

Macbeth (Shakespeare), 32
MacGregor-Hastie, Roy,
    116
Macklin, Charles, 212, 215,
    221
Macready House, 156, 160
Macready, Charles, 213

Macready, William, 18,
    160, 217
Madame Tussaud, 70
Madras House, The, 198
Magna Carta, 49
Magpie & Stump, 24, 33
Magpie Alley, 86, 87
Maid Lane. *See* Park Street
Maid's Tragedy, A
    (Beaumont &
    Fletcher), 7, 11
Maiden Lane, 66
Mall, the, 53
Mama Mia!, 161
Mamet, David, 199
Man For All Seasons, A,
    126, 167
Mander, 55, 63, 65, 159,
    160
Manningham, John, 81
Mansion House, 138, 150
Mansion House tube
    station, 76, 138, 151
Marat, Jean Paul, 162
Marco Pierre White
    restaurant. *See*
    Criterion Theatre
Marconi, Guglielmo, 71
Marlowe, Christopher, 32,
    92, 132, 133, 149
Marrable, F., 193
Marshall, Dorothy, 158
Marshalsea Prison, 18
Marshalsea Road, 17–18
Marston, Edward, 34
Marston, John, 83
Martin Chuzzlewit
    (Dickens), 82
Martin Guerre, 161
Martyrs, 29
Marx, Karl, 158
Mary Mary (Kerr), 167
Mary, Queen of Scots, 60
Massinger, Philip, 7, 9, 85
Matcham, Frank, 197
Maugham, Somerset, 166
Maye Faire, 220
Mayfair district, 97, 105
Mayfair Intercontinental
    Hotel, 96, 106
Mayfair Theatre, 96, 106
Medea, 196
Medici Galleries, 96, 105
Mee, Arthur, 116, 157
Meggs, Mary "Orange
    Moll," 212
Melba, Nellie, 69
Mellon, Harriot, 60
Melotte, Violet, 198
Memorial services, 100
Men in White (Kingsley),
    168
Merchant of Venice, 21,
    165, 205
Meridien Hotel, 96, 99
Mermaid Tavern, 138, 148
Mermaid Theatre, 138,
    153–154

Merrie England, 68
Merry Devils, The (Marston), 34
Merry Wives of Windsor, The (Shakespeare), 144
Messiah (Handel), 217
Mews, 185
Middle Temple, 26, 80
Middle Temple Garden, 82
Middle Temple Hall, 76, 81
Middle Temple Lane, 80
Middleton, Thomas, 11, 27, 148
Midsummer Night's Dream, A (Shakespeare), 43, 68
Mikado, The (Gilbert & Sullivan), 68
Miles, Bernard, 153
Milk Street, 148
Mill, John Stuart, 187
Millennium footbridge, 15, 152
Millennium Wheel. See London Eye
Miller, Arthur, 196
Miller, Gilbert, 114
Miller, Jonathan, 210
Milton, John, 144
Mirren, Helen, 195
Mirvish, Ed, 229–230
Misalliance, 198
Miss Saigon, 213
Mitchenson, 55, 63, 65, 159, 160
Mitre Tavern, 24, 30
Monmouth Street, 204–205
Month in the Country, A, 195
Monument Street, 3
Monument tube station, 2, 3, 17, 20
Moore, Dudley, 210
Moore, Mary, 99, 194, 196
Moorgate, 131, 142
More, Thomas, 37, 45, 49, 126, 143, 145, 148
Morgan, Charles, 180
Morgan, J. P., 87–88
Morley, Robert, 109
Morley, Thomas, 143
Mortimer, John, 83–84
Morwood, James, 213
Motley, 192
Mountjoy, Christopher, 146
Mousetrap, The (Christie), 73, 119, 184, 203
Mozart, Wolfgang Amadeus, 161
Murder in the Cathedral (Eliot), 72, 210
Murdoch, Iris, 99
Museums
 Bank of England, 46, 138, 150

Bear Gardens, 16
Bethnal Green Museum of Childhood, 136
British, 36, 103
Clink Prison, 9–10
Geffrye, 47, 136
HMS Belfast, 5
London Transport, 190, 223
Museum of London, 32, 138, 145
Museum of Mankind (former), 96, 103
Museum of the Moving Image, 235
National Gallery, 52, 54, 77, 241
National Portrait Gallery, 47, 200–201
Pollock Toy, 223, 241–242
Public Record Office, 40, 49
Sir John Soane's, 40, 41, 46, 47
Tate Britain, 116, 241
Theatre, 69, 190, 207, 212, 223–224
Victoria and Albert, 54, 241
Music hall, 58–59, 65, 71
My Fair Lady (Shaw), 220. See also Pygmalion
Mysteries, The, 71

Nash, John, 59, 116, 117–118, 121
Nash, Thomas, 91
National Film Theatre, 226, 235
National Gallery, 52, 54, 77, 241
National Portrait Gallery, 47, 190, 200–201
National Theatre, 70, 71, 74, 173, 196, 232–235
National Theatre Company, 231
National Theatre's Studio, 230
Neagle, Anna, 66
Neal Street, 207
Neal's Yard, 190, 207
Neale, Thomas, 207
Nell Gwynn (MacGregor-Hastie), 116
Nell Gwynne Pub, 190, 222
Nell Gwynne's Cellar, 112
Nell of Old Drury Pub, 211
Nelson's Column, 52, 53
Nelson, Richard, 160
Nettleton Court, 146
New Adelphi Terrace, 52, 64

New Ambassadors Theatre, 190, 203–204
New Bond Street, 104
New Bridge Street, 92
New Globe Walk, 10–11, 15, 35, 133
New Inn Yard, 132
New Row, 194
New South Wales House, 65
New Theatre. See Albery Theatre
New Way to Pay Old Debts, A (Massinger), 7, 85
New Zealand House, 118
Newcastle, 33
Newgate, 31, 32
Newgate Prison, 32–33
Newton, Isaac, 170
Nicholas Nickleby, 74
Night Must Fall (Williams), 72, 210
Nine Elms, 219. See also Covent Gardens
No Man's Land (Pinter), 196
No No Nanette, 163
No Sex Please, We're British, 73, 199
Noises Off (Frayn), 69
Norfolk House, 115
Norfolk, Duke of, 60
Normal Heart, The, 195
Norman Conquest, 49
Northumberland Street, 55
Norton Folgate, 131
Norton, Thomas, 83
Notting Hill Gate tube station, 178, 179
Novello, Ivor, 73
Number 23 Old Buildings, 40, 44
Nunne, Trevor, 235

O'Neill, Eugene, 198
Observatory Gardens, 183
Octoroon, The (Boucicault), 101
Oddbins' Wine shop, 31
Odeon Cinema, 156, 173–174
Oh Calcutta! (Tynan), 72, 210
Oh, What a Lovely War!, 196
Oklahoma, 213
Old Bailey, 24, 32, 33, 78–79
Old Bailey Street, 33
Old Bedlam, 130
Old Blue Last Pub, 133
Old Boar's Head Tavern, 3
Old Compton Street, 161
Old Curiosity Shop, 40, 47
Old Derry & Tom's roof garden, 178, 186, 187
Old Gaiety Theatre, 52

Old Hall, 45
Old King Lud Pub. *See*
  Hogshead, the
Old King's Theatre, 56
Old Lady of Threadneedle
  Street, The. *See* Bank
  of England
Old Price Riots, 209, 217
Old Queen's Theatre, 209
Old Spring Gardens Area,
  52, 54
Old Street, 134
Old Street tube station,
  124, 136, 138, 139
Old Vic Annexe. *See*
  National Theatre's
  Studio
Old Vic Centre, 231
Old Vic Company, 44, 54,
  195, 229–230
Old Vic Corner, 233
Old Vic Theatre, 67, 70,
  226, 227–230
Old Vic Theatre Trust, 230
Olde Bell, 91
Oliver Twist (Dickens), 5
Olivier Award, 199
Olivier, Laurence
  as actor, 68, 163
  memorial service for,
    238
  memorial to, 114
  Old Vic Theatre, 44,
    54, 195, m 229
  social life of, 222
Olympic, The, 72
OP. *See* Old Price Riots
Opera Tavern, 211
Opera, English, 118
Orangery, The. *See* Holland
  Park
Orrel, John, 17
Othello (Shakespeare), 48
Other Place, The, 206. *See*
  also Royal Shake-
  speare Company
Otway, Thomas, 78
Our Betters (Maugham),
  166
Owl and the Pussycat, The,
  168
Oxford Companion to the
  Theatre, 135, 210
Oxford Street, 157

Pacino, Al, 198–199
Page, Mary, 141
Pajama Game, 198
Palace Theatre, 156,
  162–163
Palace Theatre of Varieties.
  See Palace Theatre
Pall Mall, 116
Pantopuck the Puppetman.
  See Philpott, G.R.
Paramount City. *See* Wind-
  mill Theatre
Park Street, 10, 15, 222

Parliament Square, 226,
  238
Passion Play, 28
Patents, theatre, 48, 88,
  89, 120, 121, 211,
  216
Patience (Gilbert &
  Sullivan), 68, 99–100
Pavlova, Anna, 162
Peer Gynt (Richardson), 44
Pembridge Road, 179
Peninsular House, 108,
  116
Penn, William, Jr., 92
Penn, William, Sr., 127
Pepys Street, 127
Pepys, Samuel
  Child's Bank, 80
  diary of, 15, 87, 209,
    211–212, 220
  Great Fire of London,
    127–128
  home of, 61, 90
  social life of, 215
Peter Hall Company, 230
Peter Hall's Diaries 1972-
  1980 (Hall), 235
Peter Pan (Barrie), 28,
  63–64, 180, 198
Petrified Forest, The, 167
Phantom of the Opera, The
  (Webber), 120
Phedre (Racine), 195
Philamore Gardens, 183
Philanthropist, The
  (Hampton), 106
Phillimore Gardens, 182
Phillips, Augustine, 4
Philpott, G.R., 221
Phoenix Theatre, 156, 163
Photographers Gallery, 191
Piccadilly Arcade, 96, 102
Piccadilly Circus, 96, 97,
  168
Piccadilly Circus tube
  station, 96, 156, 173
Piccadilly Theatre, 72
Pickering Place, 111
Pickford's Wharf, 8, 9
Pickwick Papers (Dickens),
  20, 28, 91
Pilgrim's Progress, A
  (Bunyan), 140
Pilgrims, 9, 32
Pinch, Ruth, 82
Pinero, Arthur Wing, 114
Pinter, Harold, 196
Pirandello, Luigi, 106
Plantagenet, Richard. *See*
  York, Duke of
Players Club, 59
Players Theatre, 52, 58
Playhouse Yard, 24, 37
Playhouse, The, 52, 55–56,
  59
Plaza Suite, 168
Plunder (Travers), 74
Poel, William, 160

Poet Laureate. *See* Cibber,
  Colley
Poet's Corner. *See*
  Westminster Abbey
Pollock Toy Museum, 223,
  241–242
Pool of London, 5
Poole, Henry, 38
Pope, Alexander, 215
Pope, Thomas, 4
Port of London Authority,
  125
Portobello Road, 179
Portobello Road antique
  market, 178, 179
Portsmouth Street, 46
Portugal Street, 48
Poultry Street, 149
Pound, Ezra, 185
Priestley, J. B., 101, 199
Prime of Miss Jean Brodie,
  The, 196
Primrose Street, 131
Prince Albert, 31
Prince Albert Pub, 179
Prince Albert, statue of, 31
Prince Charles, 35, 58
Prince Charles' Men, 89,
  133
Prince Edward Theatre,
  156, 160–161
Prince Henry's room, 84
Prince of Wales Pub, 190,
  209. *See also* Princess
  of Wales Pub
Prince of Wales Theatre,
  156, 168, 169–170
Prince Philip, 65
Prince's Men, 87
Prince's Theatre. *See* Prince
  of Wales Theatre
Prince, Hal, 161, 163
Princess of Wales Pub, 58
Princess Street, 150
Prisoner of Zenda, The, 113
Private Ear, The
  (Shaffer), 167
Private Lives (Coward),
  163
Prostitution, 11, 66–67
Provoked Wife, The
  (Vanbrugh), 151
Prynne, William, 34
Public Eye, The
  (Shaffer), 167
Public Records Office, 40,
  49
Puddle Dock, 153
Pump Court, 82
Punch and Judy, 220, 223,
  242
Punch Tavern, 91
Purcell Room, 236
Puritans, 34, 153
Pygmalion (Shaw), 187,
  220

Quayle, Anthony, 166

Queen Alexandra, 71
Queen Anne's company, 133
Queen Elizabeth Hall, 236
Queen Mary, 118
Queen Mother, 111, 214
Queen Victoria, 31, 71, 112, 228
Queen Victoria Street, 38, 151
Queen Victoria's Honors List, 71
Queen's Chapel of the Savoy, 52, 70
Queen's Men, 89
Queen's Revels, 87
Queen's Scholars, 238. See also Westminster School
Queen's Theatre, 118, 151, 156, 165–166
Queens Head Yard, 18
Queensbury, Marquess, 69, 105
Quin, James, 49
Quinney, Richard, 34–35

Rains, Claude, 114
Rake's Progress paintings (Hogarth), 91
Raleigh, Walter, 26, 149
Ralph Roister Doister (Udall), 237
Rangoon Street, 128
Rape of Lucrece, The (Shakespeare), 93
Rattigan, Terrence, 99, 109, 168
Recruiting Officer, The (Farquhar), 54
Red Cross Way, 17
Red Lion Pub, 108, 112
redevelopment (London)
    Aldwych/Kingsway, 71
    Anchor Terrace, 16
    Bankside area, 3
    Blackfriars Pub, 38
    Dickensian warehouse district, 8
    Great Windmill Street (Soho), 168
Redgrave, Corin, 183
Redgrave, Michael, 229
Redgrave, Vanessa, 196
Reform Club, 108, 116
Reformation, 218
Relapse, The (Vanbrugh), 151
Republic of Texas, 111
Restoration theatre, 27, 41, 48, 54–55, 116, 127, 150
restrooms, public, 178, 182, 201, 224
Reunion in Vienna (Sherwood), 168
Revenge (Kyd), 92

Reynolds, Joshua, 64, 102, 111, 170, 191, 215
Reza, Yasmina, 196
Rice, Tim, 163
Rich, Christopher, 49, 60, 212
Rich, John, 215, 216, 217
Rich, William, 92
Richard II (Shakespeare), 18, 29–30
Richard III (Shakespeare), 28, 81, 110
Richardson, Ralph, 44, 54, 106, 171, 196, 229
Ride Down Mount Morgan, The (Miller), 196
Rigg, Diana, 195, 196
Ring (Wagner), 118
Ritz Hotel, 108, 109
Ritz, Cesar, 69
Rivals, The (Sheridan), 217
Riverside House, 10
Robert Street, 62, 63. See also Adam, Robert
Robert's Wife (Anthony), 166
Robinson, John, 64
Robson, Flora, 229
Roche, John, 29
Rogers and Hart, 65–66
Rolfe, Frederick, 153
Roman roads, 18
Romeo and Juliet (Shakespeare), 133
Romilly Street, 161–162
Roosevelt, Franklin, 104–105
Ropewalk, The, 101
Rose (Jackson), 198
Rose Alley, 16
Rose Street, 193
Rose Theatre, 2, 3, 15, 16, 145
Rose Theatre, The (Eccles), 16
Rose Theatre, The: An Archaeological Discovery (Bowsher), 16
Rosseter, Philip, 85, 87
Roundhouse Pub, 193
Rowe, Nicolas, 220
Rowlandson, Thomas, 62
Royal Academy, 25, 38, 96, 102
Royal Academy Courtyard, 102
Royal Academy of Dramatic Arts (RADA), 119, 192
Royal Air Force Church, 78
Royal Automobile Club, 108, 116
Royal Coburg Theatre. See Victoria Theatre
Royal College of Surgeons, 46
Royal Court Theatre, 192, 199, 231, 242

Royal Court Theatre Upstairs, 199
Royal Courts of Justice, 76, 78–79
Royal English Opera House. See Palace Theatre
Royal Festival Hall, 70, 226–227, 233, 236
Royal Italian Opera House. See Covent Garden Theatre, 217
Royal London Panorama. See Empire Cinema/ Dance Hall
Royal National Theatre, 74, 105, 192, 226
Royal Opera Arcade, 108, 118
Royal Opera House, 190, 198, 215, 216. See also Covent Garden Theatre
Royal Panopticon of Science and Art. See Odeon Cinema
Royal Shakespeare Company (RSC), 74, 206. See also Barbican Arts Complex
Royal Shakespeare Theatre, 192
Royal Society for the Encouragement of Arts, Manufactures, and Commerce, 65
Royal Strand Theatre, 77
Royal Victoria Coffee and Music Hall. See Victoria Theatre
Royalty Theatre, 156, 159–160
Rubens, Peter Paul, 242
Rules restaurant, 190, 222
Rumbelow, Donald, 33
Rumpole and the children of the Devil (Mortimer), 84
Rumpole of the Bailey (Mortimer), 83–84
Run for Your Wife (Cooney), 99
Rupert Street, 169
Russell family, 218
Russell Street, 209, 214, 223
Russell, Francis, 218
Rutland House, 48
Rylance, Mark, 81

Sackville, Thomas, 90
Sackville, William, 83
Sadler's Wells, 58
Sadler's Wells Opera company. See English National Opera
Salad Days, 66

Salisbury Court Theatre, 77, 87, 89
Salisbury Pub, 190, 195, 203
Salisbury Square, 89Street, 65
Salle Valentino. *See* Empire Cinema/Dance Hall
Salome, 114
Samuel French's Theatre Bookshop, 241
Sarastro restaurant, 210
Sassoon, Sigfried, 180
Saunders, Ann, 101
Savile Row, 104
Saville House, 174
Savoy Buildings, 69
Savoy Court, 67
Savoy Hotel, 20, 57, 60, 67, 69
Savoy Operas, 57, 60, 68, 99-100. *See also* Gilbert and Sullivan
Savoy Palace, 67, 70
Savoy Theatre, 52, 57, 60, 64, 67–69
Saxe Meinigen, Duke of, 210
Scenery, theatre
  box set for, 217
  changeable/drop, 48
  elevator for, 143
  historical accuracy in, 72
  mechanized, 66, 159
  painted perspective for, 218
  revolve system for, 197, 213, 233
  spotlight for, 217
Schonberg, 161
School for Scandal (Sheridan), 50, 212
Scofield, Paul, 167
Scottish National Church, 210. *See also* Fortune Theatre
Seacoal Lane, 33
Seaman's Memorial, 126
Secombe, Harry, 169
Second Blackfriars Theatre, 38
Second Mrs. Tanqueray, The (Pinero), 114
Sedgemoor, Battle of, 157
Seething Lane, 127
Seething Lane Gardens, 124, 127
Sellers, Peter, 169
Serle Street, 49
Seven Dials, 191, 203, 205
Seven Dials Circus, 190, 205
Seven Stars, The, 49
Seven Upper. *See* Gielgud, John
Severed Head, A (Murdoch), 99
Shadwell, Thomas, 87

Shaffer, Anthony, 168
Shaffer, Peter
Shaftsbury Avenue, 97
Shaftsbury, Lord, 97–98
Shakespeare Gallery of London, 116
Shakespeare window, 6
Shakespeare's Blackfriars Playhouse (Smith), 38
Shakespeare's Globe Theatre
  Exhibition Centre/tour for, 2, 11
  reconstruction of, 3, 7, 12, 16, 20
  seating/tickets for, 11, 13
  view of, 14
Shakespeare's Globe Theatre Company, 81
Shakespeare's Globe Theatre. *See* Globe Theatre
Shakespeare, Edmund, 5, 7
Shakespeare, Judith, 35
Shakespeare, Susannah, 36
Shakespeare, William, 3, 4, 32
  anecdote about, 81, 148–149
  correspondence with, 35
  homes of, 36, 132, 146, 153
  memorial to, 36, 171, 200, 214
  painting of, 202
  playhouses of, 37
  plays of
    Anthony and Cleopatra, 114
    Comedy of Errors, 27
    Hamlet, 34, 44, 71, 135
    Henry V, 11
    Henry VI, 20, 82
    Henry VIII, 7
    King Lear, 18
    Macbeth, 32
    Merry Wives of Windsor, The, 144
    Midsummer Night's Dream, A, 43, 68
    Othello, 48
    Rape of Lucrece, The, 93
    Richard II, 18, 29–30
    Richard III, 28, 81, 110
    Romeo and Juliet, 133
    Taming of the Shrew, The, 209
    Twelfth Night, 12, 68, 81, 152, 212
    Two Gentlemen of Verona, 11

    Two Noble Kinsmen, 7
    Venus and Adonis, 43, 93
    Winter's Tale, The, 11, 68
Shakespeare statue/window, 6, 7
  will/testament of, 49
Shakespearean Recess, 46
Sharland, Elizabeth, 67, 221, 222, 229
Shaw, George Bernard
  home of, 242
  marriage of, 221–222
  works of
    Androcles and the Lion, 114
    Arms and the Man, 55–56
    Caesar and Cleopatra, 114
    Fanny's First Play, 63
    Great Catherine, 63
    Pygmalion, 187, 220
    Widower's Houses, 159
    You Can Never Tell, 160
She Stoops to Conquer (Goldsmith), 83, 217
Sheekey's Restaurant, 195
Sheffield Street, 48
Sheffield Terrace, 184
Shenandoah Shakespeare Company, 38
Shepherd, E., 217
Sher, Anthony, *168*
Sheridan House, 96, 104
Sheridan, Richard Brinsley
  Coutts Bank, 60
  home of, 104
  social life of, 111, 181, 221
  wit of, 64, 147, 150
  works by, 212
Sheridan, Thomas, 164
Sheriff's, R.C., 68
Sherlock Holmes Pub, 55
Sherwood, Robert, 168
Ship Pub, 128, 129
Shoe Lane, 91
Shoreditch, 4, 16, 37
Shoreditch High Street, 4, 132
Short View of the Profaneness and Immorality of the English Stage (Collier), 26–27
Shorts Gardens, 207
Showboat (Prince), 161
Shubert brothers, 74
Shuttleworth, Henry Clay, 151–152
Sibelius, Jean, 185

Sicilian Adventurer, The (Tate), 18
Siddons Court, 190, 210
Siddons, Sarah, 78, 158, 202, 208, 212
Siege of Rhodes, The, 48
Sikes, Bill, 5
Silk Street, 143
Silver Mousetrap, The. See Woodhouse and Son, Ltd., A.
Simpsons-in-the-Strand, 69
Sinden, Donald, 66, 101, 122
Six Characters in Search of an Author (Pirandello), 106
Sleuth (Shaffer), 168
Sly, William, 135
Smirke, Robert, 54, 217
Smith, Adam, 103–104
Smith, Irwin, 38
Smith, John, 32
Smith, Maggie, 166, 205
Soane Museum, Sir John, 40, 41, 46, 47
Soane, John, 150, 242
Society of Actuaries Hall, 40, 41
Society of London Theatres, 172–173
Society of West End Theatres, 114
Soho Academy, 158
Soho Square, 156, 157–158
Soho Street, 157
Somer, William, 135
Somerset, Earl of, 82
Song of Singapore, 106
Sorcerer, The (Gilbert & Sullivan), 68
Sound of Music, The, 163
South Africa House, 52, 55
South Bank, 15, 70
South Bank Centre, 236
South Kensington tube station, 213
South Pacific, 213
South Square, 24, 27
Southampton Buildings, 31, 42, 43
Southampton House, 40, 43
Southampton, Earl of, 41, 42
Southhampton Street, 223
Southwark, 4, 58
Southwark Bridge, 10
Southwark Bridge Road, 16
Southwark Cathedral
  churchyard, 5
  Harvard Chapel, 7
  Shakespeare Memorial Window/Monument, 7, 21–22
  view of, 6, 16

Southwark station, 15
Southwark Street, 17
Spacey, Kevin, 230
Spanish Ambassador, 28
Spanish Tragedy, The (Kyd), 92
Spectator (Addison & Steele), 181
Speed, John, 144
Spencer, Gabriel, 32, 135
Spitalfields Market, 124, 131
Sponging house, 40, 50
Sprague, W.G.R., 196, 204
Spring Gardens, 53
Squire of Alsatia, The (Shadwell), 87
St. Albans, 138, 146
St. Albans, Duke of, 116
St. Andrew, 24, 31
St. Andrew's Hill, 35, 36
St. Ann's Blackfriars, 24, 38
St. Ann's Soho, 160
St. Benet, 138, 152
St. Botolph Aldgate, 124, 129
St. Botolph without Bishopsgate, 124, 130
St. Bride, 76, 90
St. Bride Foundation Institute, 89
St. Clement Danes, 74, 76, 77, 78
St. Clement's Eastcheap, 77
St. Clement's Lane, 48
St. Denis, Michel, 231
St. Dunstan-in-the-West, 76, 84–85
St. Etheldreda, 24, 28, 29
St. George the Martyr, 2, 18
St. Giles Square, 143
St. Giles Without Cripplegate, 7, 139, 143
St. James Church, 96, 100
St. James Hall, 99
St. James House, 108, 112–113
St. James Palace, 108, 111
St. James Square, 108, 115
St. James Street, 109, 111
St. James Theatre, 112–115
St. John's Ladbroke Grove, 178, 180
St. Lawrence Jewry, 138, 148
St. Leonard Shoreditch, 124, 131, 134–135
St. Magnus the Martyr, 2, 3
St. Margaret's Westminster, 237
St. Margaret, Lothbury, 138, 150

St. Martin's Court, 195
St. Martin's Theatre, 190, 203
St. Martin's Within Ludgate, 24, 34, 76, 85, 92
St. Martin-in-the-Fields, 52, 54–55, 58, 78, 192
St. Mary Abbot's Church, 178, 185–186
St. Mary Aldermanbury, 138, 146–147
St. Mary Aldermary, 151
St. Mary Overie. See Southwark
St. Mary-le-Bow, 138, 148
St. Mary-le-Strand, 52, 71, 76, 78
St. Nicholas Cole Abbey, 138, 151–152
St. Olave's Hart Street, 124, 127–128
St. Paul's Cathedral
  churchyard, 94
  exploration of, 93, 138
  Old, 11, 14, 24
  reconstruction of, 14, 35
  view of, 85, 152
St. Paul's Covent Garden, 190, 212, 219–221
St. Paul's tube station, 76, 94, 138, 145
St. Sepulchre Without Newgate, 24, 25, 31, 32
St. Stephen Wallbrook, 138, 150–151
Stanford's Travel Books, 190, 193
Staple Inn, 24, 28, 29, 40, 41, 42
Stationers' Hall, 76, 92–93
Statues, theatre, 200
Steele, Richard, 181
Stephens, Robert, 166
Stepping Out, 198
Stews, 11. *See also* Prostitution
Stoll, Oswald, 197
Stones in his Pockets (Jones), 199
Stony Street, 9
Strand Palace, 52, 69
Strand Theatre, 73, 199
Strand tube station, 201
Strand, The, 55, 58, 59, 61, 65, 77
Strange Interlude (O'Neill), 198
Stratford Ontario Theatre, 44
Stratford-Upon-Avon, 7, 32, 34
Stratton Street, 105
Strawberry festival, 28
Streete, Peter, 141

Strife (Galsworthy), 63–64
Suffolk Place, 122
Suffolk Street, 122
Sullivan, Arthur, 52, 56, 57, 200. *See also*
  Gilbert and Sullivan
Sunset Boulevard, 66
Surrey Street, 77
Sutherland, Jonathan, 114, 127, 130, 144, 150, 162, 196, 211, 222
Swan Song (Chekhov), 99
Sweet Nell of Old Drury, 55

Tabard Inn, 19
Tabard Street, 18
Talbot Yard, 2, 19
Taming of the Shrew, The (Shakespeare), 209
Tarleton, Richard, 34, 135
Taste of Honey, A (Delaney), 196
Tate Britain Gallery, 116, 241
Tate Modern Art Gallery, 2, 3, 12, 14
Tate, Nahum, 18
Tavistock Street, 210
Taylor, Hannah, 194
Taylor, John, 202
Television, 161
Temple Bar, 45, 76, 79
Temple Church, 76, 81, 83
Temple of Mithras, 138, 151
Temple Place, 77
Temple tube station, 77
Terriss, William "Breezy Bill"
  death of, 66
  ghost of, 222, 224
  home of, 64
Terry, Ellen, 71, 183, 200, 201, 209, 221
Terry, Kate, 183
Thackeray, William, 178, 186
Thames River, 3, 10, 11, 14
Theatre Ephemera and Books, 197
Theatre History Studies, Vol. XII, 1992 (Burkhardt), 27
Theatre Museum, 69, 190, 207, 212, 223–224
Theatre Royal (Kaufman & Ferber), 168
Theatre Royal Covent Garden. *See* Royal Opera House
Theatre Royal Drury Lane, 70, 211–212, 217
Theatre Royal Haymarket, 169
Theatre, The, 4, 16, 37, 86–87, 132–133

Theatres of London (Mander & Mitchenson), 55, 63, 65, 159, 160, 197
Theatrical Feast, A (Sharland), 67, 221, 222, 229
Theatrical London (Berry), 118
This Wooden "O": Shakespeare's Globe Reborn (Day), 11
Thomas More Highwalk, 145
Thomas Neal's shopping arcade, 207
Thomas, Brandon, 160
Thomas, Dylan, 167
Thorndike, Sybil, 114, 231
Threadneedle Street, 150
Three Grayhounds Pub, 161
Three Sisters, 165
Three Tall Women (Albee), 196
Threepenny Opera, The (Brecht & Weill), 32
Thunder Rock, 167
Tickets, half-price. *See* Half-price ticket booth
Time Out magazine, 173
Tis Pity She's a Whore (Ford), 153
Tivoli Cinema, 65
Tivoli Theatre of Varieties, 65
TKTS. *See* Half-price ticket booth
Tom Thumb (Fielding), 82
Tom's Coffee House, 215
Tooks Court, 50
Topsy Turvy (Leigh), 69
Torch Song Trilogy, 195
Tottenham Court tube station, 156, 157
Tower Bridge, 4, 5
Tower Court, 204
Tower Hill Road, 125
Tower Hill Scaffold, 126
Tower Hill tube station, 124, 125
Tower of London, 20, 60, 124, 125, 126
Toy Theatre movement, 223
Trafalgar Square, 52, 53, 61, 78
Trafalgar Square Theare. *See* Duke of York's Theatre
Travelers Club, 108, 116
Travers, Ben, 74
Trehearne, John, 6
Trial by Jury (Gilbert & Sullivan), 159
Trinity Square, 126
Trinity Square Gardens, 124, 125

Triple Tree, The: Newgate, Tyburn, and Old Bailey (Rumbelow), 33
Tudor Street, 87, 88
Turner, J.M.W., 180
Tussaud, Madame, 70
Twelfth Night (Shakespeare), 12, 68, 81, 152, 212
Twinings, 79
Two Gentlemen of Verona (Shakespeare), 11
Two Noble Kinsmen (Shakespeare), 7
Two Shakespearean Actors (Nelson), 160
Tyburn Gallows, 32
Tynan, Kenneth, 72, 210

Udall, Nicholas, 237, 238
Uncommercial Traveller, The (Dickens), 127
Unicorn Theatre for Children, 192
United Services Club. *See* Institute of Directors
Upper Circle Bar, 121
Upper Phillimore Gardens, 182
Upper St. Martin's Lane, 192, 203
Upper Thames Street, 36

Vagina Monologues (Ensler), 192
Vanbrugh, John, 118, 151
Vanity Fair (Thackeray), 186
Vaudeville Theatre, 52, 66
Vaudeville, American, 59
Vedrenne/Grandville-Barker partnership, 68
Venice Preserv'd (Otway), 78
Venus and Adonis (Shakespeare), 43, 93
Vere Street Theatre, 40, 48
Verity, Thomas, 98
Verne, Jules, 174
Vestries, Eliza, 60, 72, 217
Victoria and Albert Museum, 54, 241
Victoria Embankment, 58, 88
Victoria Hall, 228
Victoria Theatre, 228-230. *See also* Old Vic Company
Victorian engineering, 31
Victorian flat block, 178, 183
Victorian Monument, 61
Victorian theatre, 59, 105, 119, 200
Victorian Tudor New Hall/Library, 46

Vigo Street, 101
Villiers Street, 56, 58, 59, 61
Villiers Theatre, 58
Vinopolis, 10
Virgin Queen. *See* Elizabeth I

Waiting for Godot (Beckett), 99, 192
Wallbrook, The, 150
Waldorf Hotel, Meridien, 73–74
Wales, Prince of, 35, 68, 222
Wales, Princess of, 68
Walker's Court, 169
Wallside, 145
Walpole, Horace, 80
Walpole, Robert, 111, 120
Wanamaker, Sam
  Globe Theatre reconstruction by, 7, 11
  memorial to, 6, 7
War of the Roses, 82
Wardour Street, 164
Wardrobe Place, 24, 35
Warner Brothers. *See* Daly's Theatre
Water Gate of York House, 52, 57
Waterloo Bridge, 67, 70, 233
Waterloo Place, 116
Waterloo tube station, 226, 227, 233, 236
Watling Street, 151
Watson, Thomas, 133
Watts, G.F., 201
Webb, John, 48
Webber Street, 230
Webber, Andrew Lloyd, 60, 120, 162
Webster, John, 32, 130, 132, 145
Weill, Kurt, 32
Weiss, Peter, 162
Welles, Orson, 77–78, 109
Wellington Street, 70
Wesley Chapel, 138, 140
Wesley, John, 140, 145
West End, 49, 58, 60, 74, 97
West End Theatres, Society of, 114
West Point chapel, 29
West Street, 203
Westminster, 8, 38, 55, 61, 114
Westminster Abbey, 226, 237–238
Westminster Bridge, 237
Westminster School, 226, 238
Westminster tube station, 226, 238
Westminster, City of, 8, 55, 61, 114

While Shepherds Watched Their Flocks by Night (Tate), 18
White Hart Inn, 20
White Hart Yard, 2, 20
White Lion Hill, 153
White's, 108, 109–110
Whitecross Street, 141
Whitefriar's Monastery, 86
Whitefriars precinct, 87
Whitefriars Theatre, 85, 86–87
Whitehall, 53, 61
Whittington, Dick, 148
Whose Life Is It Anyway? (Clark), 69
Wibbly Wobbly Bridge. *See* Millennium Footbridge
Widower's Houses (Shaw), 159
Wig and Pen Club, 79
Wild Duck, The (Ibsen), 160
Wilde Memorial, 52
Wilde, Oscar
  home of, 65
  memorial to, 52, 114, 122, 200, 238
  social life of, 69, 100, 105
  statue of, 61
  works of, 102, 114, 122
Wilder, Thornton, 121
Wilkins, William, 54
Will's Coffee House, 215
William III, 49, 80
Williams, Emlyn, 72, 210
Williams, Harcourt, 229
Williams, Tennessee, 121
Wilson, Jean, 38, 142
Wilson, Sandy, 59
Winchester Geese. *See* Prostitution, 11
Winchester Palace
  Clink Prison for, 9–10
  excavation of, 2, 8–9
  liberty area of, 8, 11
Winchester Square, 2, 8
Winchester Walk, 8
Winchester, Bishop of, 58
Windmill Theatre, 156, 168–169
Wine Office Court, 91
Winslow Boy, The (Rattigan), 168
Winter's Tale, The (Shakespeare), 11, 68
Wireless Telegraph Company, 71
Wittich, John, 67
Woffington, Peg, 215
Wolf Parlour Club, 67
Wolfit, Donald, 85
Wood Street, 148
Wood, Tom, 202
Woodhouse and Son, Ltd., A., 49

Wordsworth, William, 237
World Theatre Season, 74
World War I, 28, 63
World War II
  Allied headquarters during, 115
  damage during, 8, 27, 31, 35, 48, 63, 65, 77, 81, 90, 127, 146, 160, 181, 213, 229
  National Gallery during, 54, 77
  reconstruction after, 100, 143, 146
Worship Street, 131, 132
Worthing, John, 167
Wren Spire, 34
Wren, Christopher
  buildings by, 80
  churches by, 3, 14, 31–32, 36, 77, 93, 126–127, 146, 150, 151
  Great Fire memorial, 3
  reconstruction by, 35, 90–91, 152
  spires by, 34, 100, 148
  St. Paul's Cathedral by, 11–12, 93, 139
  theatres by, 48, 88, 212
  tomb of, 93
Wriothesley, Henry. *See* Southampton, Earl of
Wyatt, Benjamin, 213
Wycherley, William, 92, 215, 221
Wyndham's Theatre, 190, 194, 195–196
Wyndham, Charles, 99, 194

Ye Olde Cheshire Cheese, 76, 91
Yeats, William Butler, 82
York House, 58
York House Water Gate, 61
York, Archbishop of, 58
York, Duke of, 82, 108, 116, 121
You Can Never Tell (Shaw), 160
Young Street, 186
Young Vic Theatre, 226, 230–231